THE BRIEF
AGAINST
OBAMA

THE BRIEF AGAINST OBAMA

*The Rise, Fall & Epic Fail
of the Hope & Change Presidency*

HUGH HEWITT

**CENTER
STREET**

New York   Boston   Nashville

Center Street
Hachette Book Group
237 Park Avenue
New York, NY 10017

www.centerstreet.com

Printed in the United States of America

RRD-C

First Edition: June 2012
10 9 8 7 6 5 4 3 2 1

Center Street is a division of Hachette Book Group, Inc.
The Center Street name and logo are trademarks of Hachette Book Group,
Inc.

The Hachette Speakers Bureau provides a wide range of authors for speaking events. To find out more, go to www.hachettespeakersbureau.com or
call (866) 376-6591.

The publisher is not responsible for websites (or their content) that are not
owned by the publisher.

ISBN: 9781455516308

LCCN: 2012936720

For Elisabeth Lucy,
and all of her future siblings and cousins

Contents

Contents

Introduction

From "Hope and Change" to Epic Fail

America, this is our moment. This is our time. Our time to turn the page on the policies of the past. Our time to bring new energy and new ideas to the challenges we face. Our time to offer a new direction for the country we love.

The journey will be difficult. The road will be long. I face this challenge with profound humility, and knowledge of my own limitations. But I also face it with limitless faith in the capacity of the American people. Because if we are willing to work for it, and fight for it, and believe in it, then I am absolutely certain that generations from now, we will be able to look back and tell our children that this was the moment when we began to provide care for the sick and good jobs to the jobless; this was the moment when the rise of the oceans began to slow and our planet began to heal; this was the moment when we ended a war and secured our nation and restored our image as the last, best hope on earth. This was the moment—this was the time—when we came together to remake this great nation so that it may always reflect our very best selves and our highest ideals. Thank you, God bless you, and may God bless the United States of America.

—Senator Barack Obama, June 3, 2008,
upon securing the support necessary to receive
the Democratic nomination for president.[1]

"If you make a promise in your opening statement," Gary told me, "you had better have kept it or the jury will hear about it in closing argument."

Gary is Gary Wolensky, one of the country's most accomplished trial lawyers, specializing in the defense of products claims made against the manufacturers of automobiles and motorcycles, medical devices and pharmaceuticals, sporting goods and consumer products, as well as claims made against the providers of services such as large amusement parks and other venues where Americans are severely injured and sometimes, sadly, killed.

Gary is also my law partner, so I know how hard he works to win, and how patient is his accumulation of facts via discovery and the interrogation of experts and witnesses, victims and defendants. He loves to go to trial when lesser hearts want to settle, and he is forever urging clients who know they have done no wrong to press on to a jury.

Gary loves juries. He believes that nowhere in the world is there a better model than the American civil justice system. He loves the jury selection process and the variety of potential jurors who do their civic duty day in and day out.

"Facts matter to juries," Gary is fond of saying. "Juries are by and large fair. If you promise to show them facts that exonerate your client and you do show them those facts, you have a great chance of winning. It is that simple. The idea of a fair trial has been drilled into every juror over a lifetime of media, and the judge hammers home the already deeply embedded idea of 'doing one's duty' by the Republic.

"If you have the facts, you win. If plaintiff's counsel has the facts, he wins. If either of you overpromise, the one who fails to deliver will lose, provided his opposing counsel makes sure the jurors know they have been cheated.

"You can't hope to cheat a jury. Jurors are too smart. *What you promise, you have to deliver.*"[2]

The emphasis is mine. I am much more of a critic of the

American trial-by-tort system than Gary, especially on the subject of how its malpractice and products-liability plaintiffs' bar and class-action craziness are crippling many of the professions and raising the costs of everything we make and sell and every service we provide in America, but I do defer to him on how juries work and how jurors think, and I agree with him on the obvious importance of keeping the promises you make, and of never trying to trick a jury.

Voters are jurors of a unique sort.

They don't have to serve, and they can choose to watch as much or as little of the presentation of the facts as they desire.

Voters come in all shapes, colors, and income levels. They cannot be disqualified except in rare circumstances, usually involving recounts in closely contested and important races such as Florida's vote in the 2000 presidential election, the 2006 Minnesota contest for the United States Senate seat held by Norman Coleman but wrestled away by Al Franken, and the 2008 Alaska Senate contest which saw incumbent Lisa Murkowski use a write-in campaign to defeat Tea Party favorite Joe Miller.

Most elections aren't close, and that is a very good thing because if it's not close, the Democrats can't cheat—which happens to have been the title of my 2004 *New York Times* bestseller on the presidential race of that year.

Two years later I wrote *Painting the Map Red*. On the first page I predicted electoral disaster for the GOP, a gloomy assessment that prompted the wonderful Stephen Colbert to tear out the offending page on air and castigate me for defeatism. But not even Colbertic enthusiasm could save the Republicans that year because of the facts.

One year after that, in 2007, I returned with a book on Mitt Romney, the likely GOP nominee in 2012 who also had sought the job in 2008. I argued in that book that John McCain should not be the nominee—the Arizona senator and war hero was a great American, but a terrible senator and a lousy Republican.

These were the facts about McCain. They could not be changed. They weren't, and he lost.

Each of these three books, somewhat prescient in their predictions, assessed elections in an era where the facts that existed were facts about how Republicans had been doing in office. Republicans, from President George W. Bush to Vice President Dick Cheney, to Secretaries Colin Powell and Condoleezza Rice at State, Donald Rumsfeld and Robert Gates at Defense, Denny Hastert as Speaker, and both Trent Lott and Bill Frist as Senate Majority Leader, had made promises about which facts could be collected and assessed. Senator McCain made promises of his own, including the readiness of Sarah Palin to be president and the utility of suspending his campaign during the financial crisis of that awful fall in 2008.

The crushing defeats delivered the Republicans in 2006 and 2008 meant the biggest jury of them all had ruled conclusively on the promises they all made. Promises they hadn't kept.

President Obama began making promises in wintry Iowa in 2007. The biggest of them all was the promise of "Hope and Change."

The most absurd of all his promises was that the moment of the election would be the moment that "the seas ceased their rise."

The most important of all his promises was that he would revive a moribund economy and keep the rate of unemployment below 8 percent.

This last promise has been in breach since February 2008, and has remained there for more than thirty months, each month of unemployment above 8 percent being a fact about a promise broken.[3]

Many books have already been written about President Obama and about his record.

Some, like Jonathan Alter's *The Promise*, have mounted a vigorous defense of the president's plans and actions.

Others, like Stanley Kurtz's *Radical-in-Chief* and Dinesh

D'Sousa's *The Roots of Obama's Rage*, have been investigations into the president's deeply embedded Alinskyite ideology
and psychological makeup. Still others, like David Freddoso's
Gangster Government, are full-throated policy critiques of various aspects of the most radical president in American history.
This is a book about facts. A book about facts written by a
long-time lawyer and law professor as well as a broadcast journalist with more than twenty years' experience in television, radio,
and columns.

My experience lawyering has been gained before elites—
administrative agencies and appeals courts, not juries.

My teaching experience has been a decade and a half as
a professor of law at Chapman University School of Law in
Orange, California, during its years of rocketing reputation
among the bar and popularity among applicants. Making cases
before elites and federal judges, to fellow commissioners on various boards, or to faculty colleagues across the wide ideological
spectrum is not remotely like making cases to juries about who
is responsible for injury or death.

Making a case to find for a defendant that he or she ought
not to pay for the victim's loss is a hard hill to climb when
sympathy tends to want to empty a deep pocket just to help the
victim. Only facts can turn back such emotion-driven pressures.

And a plaintiff's lawyer seeking a jury award against a popular or even beloved public figure is going to have to marshal
the facts that leave a fair jury no choice.

Here's my opening argument.

The facts of President Obama's first three-plus years in
office are so awful as to compel any fair-minded voter to vote
for the Republican nominee.

Whether Governor Romney or someone else, the Republican
nominee will enter the showdown with the president armed with
three central arguments and many secondary ones. The "Big
Three": (1) Obamacare was a disaster, one which is growing
worse in its consequences; (2) unemployment is much too high

and the official numbers don't even capture the real level of unemployment; and (3) the 2009 "stimulus" that was supposed to fund the "shovel ready" infrastructure that produced the "summer of recovery" was a huge bust.

The fourth big argument is that President Obama has seriously weakened our national security by harming our friends abroad and empowering our enemies while stripping our defenses.

The fifth is that he has relentlessly abused the powers of the presidency in a single-minded assault on the powers of the other branches, the states' governments, and the citizens.

The brief against Obama goes much deeper than these "Big Three" broken promises, and the fourth and fifth arguments.

There are scores and scores of broken promises and fraudulent forecasts, dozens of dodges and hundreds of disastrous innovations. It has been a reign of incompetency not before seen in the country—ever.

President Obama is not just a failed president, but the most spectacularly failed president of modern times.

On top of this incompetency—I refer on my radio show to the shorthand "o-i-i-o-h-h," or "o-double-i-o-double-h," as code for "Obama is in over his head"—is the president's immense arrogance and sense of entitlement, an overweening, overpreening, over-the-top partisanship that simply does not restrain itself ever.

The president is never gracious. Not toward his current congressional opponents. Not to his critics in the media. And certainly not to former president Bush.

He is, however, extremely solicitous of our worst enemies, doing nothing to encourage Iranian resistance when the fanatical mullahs and the Iranian Revolutionary Guard stole the presidential election there in 2009.

He waited for months to call for Syria's butcher Bashar Assad to depart, even as the butcher murdered thousands of innocent citizens.

He "led from behind" in Libya and produced a six-month bloodbath when bold and decisive action could have removed Muammar Qaddafi in days at the outset of the crisis. The chaos that followed the dictator's fall led to the looting of massive weapons depots, and reports of missing shoulder-fired missiles and even chemical weapons are alarming.

He has cut and run from Iraq and is in the process of doing so in Afghanistan, announcing to the Taliban they need wait only a year or two at most to reclaim de facto control of the country, and "apologizing" to Afghans after the worst of their number had assassinated men sent to help them secure their freedom

President Obama's small gestures have combined to send a message of American eclipse and American confusion over its role in the world.

He returned the bust of Winston Churchill that had been in the Oval Office to the British government. He did not want the last century's greatest leader, the man who saved the West and was himself half American, to represent the alliance at the forefront of the new war to defend civilization.

President Obama bowed to the Saudi king and Japanese emperor, while courting Iran's fascists and bashing Israel's democratic leadership.

When Benjamin Netanyahu visited the White House as the freely elected head of the government of our strongest, most reliable ally in the world, the president upbraided the prime minister and left him to cool his heels in a basement conference room as an overbearing, pompous schoolroom tyrant might an unyielding student. Israel, throughout the Obama years, has been made the scapegoat for Palestinian terror and intransigence even as rockets fall by the hundreds on southern Israel and terrorists slip across the Egyptian desert from Gaza to murder innocent Jews heading to a holiday at the beach.

In 2006, the last year that the Republicans controlled the Congress, the budget deficit was $269 billion.[4] In George W.

Bush's last year in office—Democrats had controlled the Congress and thus spending for a mere two years—the deficit was $466 billion.[5] In 2009 the deficit was $1.4 trillion.[6] In 2010 the deficit was $1.3 trillion.[7] In 2011 it was $1.5 trillion.[8] In 2012 it is estimated to be $1.1 trillion.[9]

The defense budget in 2007—again, the last year of GOP control of the Congress—was $660 billion.[10] In 2011 it is $779 billion, is being cut to $735 billion in 2012, and is scheduled for a disastrous "sequestration" cut the following year, which would slash the Department of Defense budget to $662 billion.[11]

The president has appointed two hard-left justices to the United States Supreme Court, Sonia Sotomayor and Elena Kagan. If he receives one more appointment, he could shift the Court far to the left for a generation at least.

The president directed his Department of Justice not to defend the Defense of Marriage Act, a unilateral and radical act of imperial presidential power that is unprecedented when a federal statute has not been called into question by even a single appeals court.

The president appointed "czar" after unaccountable "czar" whose radical views and policies could be shielded from congressional oversight.

The president used the "recess appointment" authority in the Constitution to make controversial appointments when the Congress was not in recess. On January 4, 2012, the president appointed Richard Cordray to lead the new Consumer Financial Protection Bureau and three members of the National Labor Relations Board.

Two weeks after this assault on the authority of the United States Senate to confirm such appointees, the president launched an attack on the Roman Catholic Church, allowing his Department of Health and Human Services to mandate that every Catholic college and university in the land, every Catholic elementary school and high school, and every Catholic hospital and social service agency be obliged to pay for health insurance that provided contraception, sterilization, and "morning after" pills.

The president's Department of Justice authorized the sale of thousands of lethal weapons to the Mexican drug cartels, weapons which have largely gone missing except for the few we know have killed an American law enforcement official and many Mexican authorities. Now Attorney General Eric Holder is engaged in brazen stonewalling of the "Fast-and-Furious" investigation led by Congressman Darrell Issa; and senior officials in Arizona and Washington, D.C., have resigned, taken the Fifth, or both.

The president's EPA, frustrated by the refusal of even an overwhelmingly Democratic Congress led by Nancy Pelosi and Harry Reid to pass cap-and-tax, have decided to proceed without statutory authority to impose such regulations on a struggling economy.

The president's Department of the Interior botched the handling of the BP oil spill in the Gulf of Mexico, with a clueless and unfocused president making erratic statements and refusing Gulf governors the help they needed, followed by an illegal permitorium that cost the country oil and jobs when it needed both.

His appointees at the United States Fish and Wildlife Service and the Consumer Products Safety Commission have greatly empowered the enemies of both economic growth in the environmental movement and mass-tort plaintiffs' bar by incredibly obtuse rule makings such as that which cut off water (and destroyed tens of thousands of jobs) in California's otherwise fertile Central Valley and which stranded billions' worth of excellent product because of absurd lead limits in children's products—like within the tailpipes of off-road vehicles created and designed specifically to enhance the safety of children using ORVs.

Incredibly, the president encouraged the crooked Chris Dodd and the highly partisan and economically illiterate Barney Frank to rewrite the banking rules of the country, and the consequences have been catastrophic for lending and especially for the home lending and refinance markets, which typically lead American recovery from recession.

Then there are the soft factors that are still based in facts—the beer summit, the "I won" moment, the attack on Paul Ryan, the constant attacks on Bush, the staged meetings on health care where the president talked endlessly and listened to no advice from the GOP followed by the staged meetings on the debt ceiling where the president talked endlessly and listened to no advice from the Republicans, and of course the endless tidal waves of speeches, speeches, speeches and of press conferences that are really just buffets of speeches.

Other cringe-worthy moments include the "57 states," the "corpse-man," the honoring of the wrong Medal of Honor recipient—verbal gaffes that accumulate unnoticed by the president's legion of acolytes in the Beltway-Manhattan media elite but that are watched and tallied by our enemies and competitors abroad as they compile their picture of a feckless, vain, and befuddled fellow who has somehow risen to an office he simply was not prepared for and has no genuine sense of how to conduct.

Promoted far above his core competencies of looking good and acting the part of an intellectual, the president has failed, but his ego refuses to admit what most of the country knows: he needs to leave. He is the Peter Principle president, our first modern "Epic Fail" president. We cannot afford and perhaps could not survive another four years of his tenure.

Thus this book, written months before the GOP nominee was formally selected and made available to assist every citizen concerned with firing the president. Because it is not just the GOP nominee's job to defeat the president. It is the job of every American with a concern for the future of the country to equip themselves to make the case for voting President Obama into retirement.

The book is organized to make available to you the facts of the president's first three years in office. It is a miserable record, but one that needs memorizing and repetition, publicity, and endless pounding into the public's consciousness.

Send new high school graduates and college graduates copies for their graduation presents. Place copies with your most talented and energetic debate partners and suggest your book club, small group, or Tea Party club read the book together.

This is a season for facts, not attack ads or the politics of personal destruction.

Facts are stubborn things, President Reagan liked to quote John Adams as saying. Arm yourself and your allies with these stubborn things.

I
DOMESTIC POLICY FAILURES

Chapter 1

The Nightmare of Obamacare

What we do is set up a plan that allows anybody to get health care that is as good as the health care I have as a member of Congress. We will subsidize those who can't afford it. People won't be able to be excluded for preexisting conditions so that anybody who's self-employed, anybody who doesn't have health insurance or is underinsured can join this plan. Now, we also work to lower costs for those who already have health insurance, and so we expect to provide about $2,500 of relief per family for their premiums. That's the kind of cost reduction that I think is going to be so important to make sure that the plan is sustainable.

Here's the concern. If you haven't made it affordable, how are you going to enforce a mandate? I mean, if a mandate was the solution, we can try that to solve homelessness by mandating everybody to buy a house. The reason they don't buy a house is they don't have the money. And so, our focus has been on reducing costs, making it available. I am confident if people have a chance to buy high-quality health care that is affordable, they will do so. That's what our plan does and nobody disputes that.

—Candidate Barack Obama, Super Tuesday, 2008[1]

If you look at the package that we've presented—and there's some stray cats and dogs that got in there that we were eliminating, we were in the process of eliminating. For example, we said from the start that it was going to be important for us to

be consistent in saying to people if you can have your—if you want to keep the health insurance you got, you can keep it, that you're not going to have anybody getting in between you and your doctor in your decision making. And I think that some of the provisions that got snuck in might have violated that pledge.
                    —President Obama at a House Republican
                          Caucus retreat, March 2010[2]

I know that there are millions of Americans who are content with their health care coverage—they like their plan and they value their relationship with their doctor. And that means that no matter how we reform health care, we will keep this promise: if you like your doctor, you will be able to keep your doctor. Period. If you like your health-care plan, you will be able to keep your health-care plan. Period. No one will take it away. No matter what. My view is that health-care reform should be guided by a simple principle: fix what's broken and build on what works.
              —President Obama speaking to the American Medical
                          Association, June 15, 2009[3]

Obamacare is a public policy cancer. It is that simple.

It is a metastasizing disease that is destroying employment and health care at the same time, pushing the United States to an era of scarcity and rationing in health care, toward vast public bureaucracies, and unresponsive hospitals and clinics.

And it is doing so at great—indeed vast—expense.

It is doing so at the expense of our first freedom—the freedom of religion contained in the first two clauses of the First Amendment, now tossed aside by President Obama and his Department of Health and Human Services with a demand on every Catholic college and university, elementary and secondary school, hospital or social service agency, to provide Obamacare-molded health insurance that must include payment for sterilization and "morning after" pills, which are abhorrent to the Roman Catholic conscience.

Obamacare should never have been jammed down the country's throat. Especially after two gubernatorial elections in 2009 in New Jersey and Virginia and a special United States Senate election in 2010 in Massachusetts, all three of which sent unmistakable signals that the American people were saying no to this legislative monstrosity.

In November 2009, Governor Chris Christie was elected in the Garden State and Governor Bob McDonnell in the Commonwealth on platforms opposed to the then-pending Obamacare proposals. Their opposition to many features of the legislation has continued, even as details about its provisions and their effects have become clear.

Here's what Christie has said about Obamacare:

> As a governor what I'm most concerned about is getting us some more flexibility in Medicaid. It's really kind of drowning the states....I mean, our Medicaid program is $1.4 billion in deficit this year and because of Obamacare we can't change the level of benefit that we offer because of the mandates they've put on us. And, I think, you know, if we're going to pay for 50 percent of it, we should have some control over it, and the way this administration's done it is they want to control all of it.[4]

Here's what McDonnell has said:

> Turning over the best doctors, the best hospitals, the best pharmaceutical research and development system to the federal government for a co-op or a public option is [an idea] I don't hear Virginians very excited about.[5]

In a speech responding to Obama's 2010 State of the Union address, McDonnell said:

> It was Thomas Jefferson who called for "a wise and frugal government, which shall leave men free to regulate their

own pursuits of industry, and shall not take from the mouth of labor the bread it has earned." He was right. Today, the federal government is simply trying to do too much....In recent months the American people have made clear that they want government leaders to listen and then act on the issues most important to them. We want results, not rhetoric; we want cooperation, not partisanship. There is much common ground. All Americans agree that we need a health-care system that is affordable, accessible, and high-quality. But most Americans do not want to turn over the best health-care system in the world to the federal government....[The GOP's solutions] aren't thousand-page bills that no one has fully read, after being crafted behind closed doors with special interests.[6]

A couple of months after saying those words, McDonnell signed the Virginia Health Care Freedom Act, prohibiting implementation of health-care legislation that includes an individual mandate in Virginia. At the signing, McDonnell said: "We all agree that we must expand access to quality health care and reduce costs for all Virginians. However, that should not be accomplished through an unprecedented federal mandate on individuals that we believe violates the U.S. Constitution.... The Act was passed with bipartisan support, in sharp contrast to the...partisan vote that enacted the federal health-care bill on Sunday night."[7]

Senator Scott Brown and his pick-up truck barnstormed Massachusetts and defeated the Democrat designated to take the "Kennedy seat" almost solely on his arguments that Obamacare was a nightmare and his election would be the referendum to stop it.

Here's one example of Brown's campaign rhetoric from early 2009:

Massachusetts wants real reform, and not this trillion-dollar Obama health care bill being forced on the

American people.... It is not in the interest of our state or country—and as your senator, I will insist we start over. I will work in the Senate to reform health care in the right way, the honest way.... We can do better, and as the 41st senator I'll make sure of it."[8]

Christie won by a goodly margin in a blue state: 49 percent to 44 percent.[9]

McDonnell won by a far larger margin in a state President Obama had carried just a year earlier. McDonnell's margin of victory was 17.4 percent.[10] Obama had beaten McCain in the Commonwealth by 52.7 to 46.4 percent just the year before.[11]

And Scott Brown defeated Martha Coakley in deep blue Massachusetts, even after a personal intervention and visit by President Obama, by the margin of 52 percent to 47 percent.[12]

There was no mistaking the message of Americans who were voting in the fall and winter of 2009, and not merely protesting: the Tea Party movement that began on CNBC with Rick Santelli answering Joe Kernan's question on February 19, 2009, had grown larger and stronger with each passing week. Grassroots leaders like Mark Meckler and Jennie Beth Martin and their TeaPartyPatriots.org website spearheaded popular demonstrations against the massive power grab on health care, but it wasn't until actual voting began to occur in statewide races that the real views of significant majorities of Americans came into undeniable, unmistakable clarity.

The first sin of Obamacare is that it was passed over the outspoken, often expressed, and impossible to miss message from the American people to stop.

This arrogance, this indifference to genuine public opinion, has been the defining mark of this radical president. The sad confluence of events—the war, the exhaustion of the country, the financial panic, the relentless boosterism of the MSM for Obama, and of course the lousy campaign of John McCain— all worked to put a hard-left president in the White House, and after spending nearly a trillion dollars on his friends and allies, he turned to the legislative program that would forever change the face of America by pushing it inexorably into neo-European-socialism lite: the control of American health care.

The bill itself—unread by everyone, as Nancy Pelosi famously pointed out when she said, "We have to pass the bill before you can find out what's in it"—was an incoherent mess of promises and half-baked commissions and regulatory zeal.[13]

The public does not need much persuasion on this case, or on the urgent need for repeal. But five points bear repeating.

First, nothing of this order of magnitude has ever before been jammed through on a purely party-line basis and in the teeth of widespread opposition. The decisions to go to war in Afghanistan and Iraq—twice—were very divisive questions, but ultimately the votes empowering those three invasions passed with bipartisan support, as did the Civil Rights Act (Southern Democrats leading the die-hard opposition), and all the tax reform and tax cut bills of the '80s, '90s, and the past decade.

This country simply does not force vast changes unless at least some of the opposition party can be brought to the side of change. This tradition—unwritten but real—has worked to preserve the republic and civic space.

President Obama has trashed this tradition.

Second, the law is unconstitutional in the eyes of many scholars and many judges. Some judges have upheld the law, but the question is now before the Supreme Court, and there will be at least some of the justices who say it is unconstitutional, and possibly a majority.

This deep flaw was known, debated, and ignored by a radical president unconcerned with breaching the Constitution's outer limit of power. A prudent president would have seen the opposition and sensed how far he was pushing government's authority, and pulled back for fear of crossing over to the place where the Constitution forbids the government to go—but not Obama. He simply didn't care.

Third, it was passed on false premises with transparently impossible-to-keep claims. This became an admission even by the Obamians in October 2011, when the president's team at Health and Human Services admitted they could not possibly comply with the subset of provisions within Obamacare known as "The CLASS Act."

The Community Living Assistance Standards and Supports (CLASS) Act is the component of Obamacare designed to provide long-term care. As legislated, it was a guaranteed-issue, voluntary program that was supposed to pay its enrollees approximately $50 a day for care, after the individual paid premiums for five years.[14]

Health and Human Services (HHS) was tasked with implementation of the CLASS Act, along with the other provisions of Obamacare. The law required that CLASS not be implemented unless it would remain financially self-sustaining for seventy-five years, without requiring additional taxpayer money to support it.[15]

At the beginning of December 2010, President Obama's deficit commission, co-chaired by Senator Alan Simpson and Erskine Bowles,[16] released its report, which indicated "federal health care spending represents our single largest fiscal challenge over the long-run."[17] The commission recommended that the CLASS Act be either reformed or repealed because "it is viewed by many experts as financially unsound....Absent reform, the program is therefore likely to require large general revenue transfers or else collapse under its own weight."[18]

In February 2011, HHS Secretary Kathleen Sebelius assuaged concerns about the financial stability of the program in a speech to the Kaiser Family Foundation: "It's important to remember that the law already provides plenty of flexibility to make sure CLASS is successful. And today, I can tell you that we are committed to using that authority to make sure this program meets people's needs while remaining fiscally sound."[19]

Reports circulated in September that HHS was closing the

CLASS office, but the administration maintained that they were continuing to pursue implementation, just with a smaller staff.[20]

Then, in October 2011, HHS announced that after nineteen months of research, it had determined the program could not be implemented in a way that met Congress's sustainability requirements, and was therefore dissolving the initiative.[21] Actuarial models showed that premiums for enrollees could have gone as high as $3,000 a month for $50 a day in benefits[22]—a far cry from the $60 to $100 a month premiums discussed while the bill was making its way through Congress.[23]

Fourth, the immediate consequences of the law are dire. The cost of health care continues to skyrocket even as employers drop hundreds of thousands from their coverage.

A survey published by the Kaiser Family Foundation on July 28, 2011, indicated that 59 percent of Americans with private health insurance said their health insurance premiums were already increasing. Half of those surveyed said their co-pays and deductibles had risen as well.[24]

Some health insurers reported plans to increase rates because of the new legislation as early as September 2010.[25]

Policy experts have noted that Obamacare's reliance on community rating and guaranteed issue provisions means that premiums for young adults will increase disproportionately.[26] Several studies predict that premiums for young adults will increase anywhere from 17 percent (about $500 on average) to 30 percent.[27]

Maine passed popular health-care reforms of a similar nature (with guaranteed issue and community rating provisions) in 2003, making it one of the examples of what to expect under Obamacare.[28] They now have more uninsured citizens than they did in 2003,[29] and those that have insurance are paying an average of 36 percent more in premiums than the rest of the country despite significantly higher deductibles and taxpayer subsidies to the tune of $183 million,[30] both of which keep costs down.[31]

In July 2011, the Congressional Budget Office estimated that approximately 7 percent of employers currently providing health insurance to their employees would drop employee health benefits because of Obamacare.[32] However, another study released at the same time by McKinsey & Company indicate that as many as 30 percent of employers will probably or certainly stop offering insurance to their employees after 2014.[33]

Furthermore, a survey by Towers Watson released in May 2010 indicated that 86 percent of employers believed Obamacare would increase the cost of their health benefits. The most interesting part of this survey is that 88 percent of the employers interviewed indicated that they planned to pass the cost of this increase to their employees, and 74 percent indicated they would consider reducing the health benefit programs they offered to employees.[34]

Verizon, a company that prides itself on being "a great place to work",[35] has already made attempts to pass on some of the increased cost to their employees.[36] Other companies are considering similar measures, and some basic number crunching makes clear that large companies can actually turn a reasonable profit by dropping all employer-sponsored insurance plans and paying federal fines.[37]

Fifth, as noted above, President Obama authorized his Department of Health and Human Services to open an assault on every Catholic institution in the country not covered by a narrow "exemption," which will oblige every Catholic college and university—yes, Boston College and Notre Dame and Georgetown and all the rest—plus every Catholic elementary and high school and every Catholic hospital and arm of Catholic Charities to pay for sterilization and the "morning after" pill. This massive breach of faith with Roman Catholics and assault on the First Amendment stunned observers in and outside of the

Roman Catholic Church, and has triggered a widespread commitment to civil disobedience if the regulations are not withdrawn. "We cannot—we will not—comply with this unjust law," declared Phoenix archbishop Thomas Olmsted, and his fellow bishops echoed this sentiment across the land.

Even if the president retreats under the political threat of the nation's Catholics mobilized to defeat him, still everyone has seen behind the mask of Obamacare: it is the left's giant lever with which to move aside every other institution in the country that holds different values than it does.

Finally, the worst part of the bill is that beginning in 2012, fifteen unelected bureaucrats will in fact decide the health-care futures of all Americans.

The Independent Payment Advisory Board—IPAB, for short—will be given enormous power over American health care when it comes into existence in 2014.

In a rare bit of candor, a *New York Times* article by Duff Wilson declared on November 4, 2010, that IPAB was the "biggest cost-cutter of all."

"The Independent Payment Advisory Board," Wilson correctly continued, "would have the power to rein in Medicare payments beginning in 2015 unless Congress acted each year to achieve similar cost-cutting targets."[38]

It is a rationing board, and it will ration, unless it is repealed—unless Obamacare is repealed.

There are many, many other arguments against Obamacare and in favor of its repeal, but these are all one needs to do battle with the Obamians in the debate ahead. The public hates this bill and needs to only be reminded of the circumstances of its birth and the recklessness of this approach as well as the by now well-documented adverse consequences of its rollout, and the disaster that will fall on every American if its rollout continues.

Go back to the top of the chapter, though, and look to the

promise President Obama made—one I play frequently on my radio show.

The president promised that if you liked your doctor, you could keep him, and that if you liked your insurance, you could keep it.

Those were both bold, indeed startlingly large, lies. Every honest observer knows and will admit that hundreds of thousands of Americans have already lost either the doctors or the health insurance they had and wanted to keep.

The president lied in his core promise on Obamacare, and every explanation he offers and new promise he sends out via his friends in the MSM should be received with that knowledge in the forefront of your mind.

President Obama lied about your health care and your insurance. Why would you trust him on anything else?

Chapter 2
A Failed "Stimulus"

Only government can break the vicious cycles that are crippling our economy—where a lack of spending leads to lost jobs, which leads to even less spending; where an inability to lend and borrow stops growth and leads to even less credit.

That is why we need to act boldly and act now to reverse these cycles. That's why we need to put money in the pockets of the American people, create new jobs, and invest in our future. That's why we need to restart the flow of credit and restore the rules of the road that will ensure a crisis like this never happens again.

That work begins with this plan—a plan I am confident will save or create at least three million jobs over the next few years.

Candidate Barack Obama on his American Recovery and
Reinvestment Plan, or Stimulus Plan[1]

Most Americans know that the "American Recovery and Reinvestment Plan" is known as "the Stimulus."

The Stimulus was the first priority of Barack Obama when he was sworn in, and it was supposed to cost $767 billion, which rose to $862 billion, when the fire hose of money was finally turned off.[2]

This money was all borrowed, so even at the low, roughly 3 percent annual interest cost a year the Treasury has been able to pay on this particular borrowing over the past three years,

26

the interest cost of the Stimulus has been approximately $80 billion to date, and that cost rises every day.

Thus, we taxpayers have shelled out more than $940 billion for the Stimulus already, with billions more to come for the many years the borrowing remains unpaid.

I will review the unemployment numbers—which soared past 8 percent and had not fallen even to that exceedingly high level by March 2012—elsewhere, but the Stimulus deserves a chapter of its own.

The Stimulus was supposed to deliver millions and millions of jobs. Joe Biden declared the summer of 2010 as "the summer of recovery," in which those jobs were finally going to appear.[3] They didn't.

Even as unemployment soared and the promised jobs didn't appear, the by then ex-Speaker Nancy Pelosi was still defending the botched attempt at massive Keynesian manipulation.

"We're very, very proud of it," Pelosi declared in 2011. "It was definitely worth it.

"It created and saved jobs for our country," Pelosi continued. "People from all over the world have been very complimentary," she added, as though the judgment of Europeans or anyone else on economic issues matters to American voters.

"It proved President Obama was an innovator from day one," Pelosi concluded. "As time goes by people will be more appreciative of it."[4]

Really? Mitt Romney should hope that the president campaigns on the effectiveness of the 2009 Stimulus. If he does, the former Massachusetts governor should simply ask: "What did it accomplish?"

Or simply, "Where did it go?"

MSNBC's Jonathan Alter is a frequent and very welcome guest on my radio program. He is, along with the *Washington Post*'s E. J. Dionne and Harold Meyerson, Fox News's Juan Williams, the *New Republic*'s Jonathan Chait, and others, one of the able defenders of President Obama I ask to come on and do their best. (Other regular guests include reporters who try to keep their opinions out of the stories they write, like Politico's Mike Allen, the *Post*'s Chris Cillizza, and the *New Yorker*'s Ryan Lizza, though my audience detects in them a definite inclination to defend the president nine out of ten times.)

Jonathan Alter was my guest on September 15, 2010, and we discussed the question "Where did it go?"

> HH: I'm going to ask you, would you point me to any single project, a power plant, a nuclear power plant, a new bridge, a new college, a new campus, that the Stimulus built? What do you look at when you say here's what the Stimulus gave us, a new runway, a new anything? What did it build?
>
> JA: Well, this is, first of all, there are lots of, know, where I live in New Jersey, I just about less than a mile from my house, there's a big, poorly designed, you know, by some bureaucrat sign about the American Recovery Act, that it paid for this road construction. So there are projects all over the country that I agree with your point. I think you're absolutely right about this. One of the great failures of the Stimulus was that they did not, you know, put in money, in part because there are $300 billion in tax cuts in the Stimulus, but they did not, they have more infrastructure spending than any bill since the Highway Act of the 1950s. But as you say, not enough memorable projects. It's a lot of sewage systems, you know, ramp extensions on various highways, things that help create jobs, help communities, helped to stop the bleeding, but do not leave a permanent legacy. So I think you're absolutely right about that.
>
> HH: Jonathan, I see lots of these signs, too. I think actually they put most of the Stimulus into sign creation. But as I say, I asked Howard Dean, and I'll ask you. Can you name one particular, one bridge, one power plant, just one particular geographic GPS site that you know Stimu-

lus dollars went to, you can say this would not have happened?

JA: Well, I, you know, I live in New Jersey. Route 3. I mean, Route 3 in New Jersey. But you can go in many, many communities and find these projects. I think one of the really unfortunate things is that you know, there was money in the Stimulus that the Republicans, the moderate Republicans, for their vote, they insisted be taken out for school construction, which people would have seen it much more when they drove their kids to school, they saw that their Stimulus was building classrooms. But that was taken out by Susan Collins at the last minute. That was sponsored by Ben Chandler of Kentucky and taken out. So I agree with you, there's not enough memorable stuff. But I wish that the critics would stop, and it is a lie to say the stimulus has done nothing. That's simply a lie. And people have to quit saying that.[5]

"Not enough memorable stuff" actually means nothing worth remembering. I ask this question frequently of Democrats. Perhaps by the time the voting begins they will have come up with a list that is better than Jonathan's New Jersey Route 3.

In the fall of 2011, the *Weekly Standard*'s Jonathan Last accurately evaluated the Stimulus as the first of many Obama punts:

Instead of crafting his own bill, which put government money into projects with both economic impact and practical benefit—like, say, defense procurement—he handed the job to Nancy Pelosi and Harry Reid. The result was $787 billion for Democratic clients and "shovel-ready projects" that, Obama now says laughingly, were never really shovel-ready.[6]

Nothing was "shovel ready."[7] Nothing lasting was built.[8] No lasting jobs were created.[9]

Nothing impacted the country's downward economic spiral. What might have happened is too sad to contemplate. A trillion dollars can buy a lot of things. It could have endowed a thousand city health centers with a billion each, allowing for the construction of clinics and staffing from banked funds so that destitute people could have health care, not the promise of health insurance they will find difficult to access even as its availability cripples the American medical care delivery system.

The refurbishment of the depleted American military warehouse could have been quickly accelerated, benefiting both job and defense agendas simultaneously. The F-22 could have been built to its full production run (more on this later). The fleet could have been expanded to its full complement instead of the 283 ships now providing the full measure of our naval strength. Defense is covered elsewhere, but the president might have used the Stimulus in ways to strengthen our military and the industries and contractors that provide materials, skills, and knowledge to the military.

Instead it went... well, no one really can say for sure. It vanished into the Great Maw of the special-interest left, and no lasting sign of it can be found except signs on freeways extolling the president's leadership.

Ask your friends who are thinking about voting for the president again what they would think of a person who, having won the lottery for a trillion dollars, or even a thousand people winning a billion-dollar lottery, would have nothing lasting to show for it three years later.

Would they let that person handle their money?

Would they give them another chance to steward a budget that reached $4 trillion—every year?

Chapter 3
Doubling Down on Failure: *"Stimulus 2.0"*

I don't pretend that this plan will solve all our problems. It shouldn't be, nor will it be, the last plan of action we propose. What's guided us from the start of this crisis hasn't been the search for a silver bullet. It's been a commitment to stay at it—to be persistent—to keep trying every new idea that works, and listen to every good proposal, no matter which party comes up with it.

from President Obama's Jobs Speech to Congress,
September 9, 2011[1]

This chapter is designed to remind the reader of the patently absurd and wholly transparent attempt by President Obama last fall and winter to set up the Congress as a scapegoat for the widespread unemployment misery brought about by his own policies.

With unemployment having stuck above 9 percent for month after month, and with little hope that even with the improvements of early 2012 it would drop below 8 percent before the voting began—in February 2012 the nonpartisan Congressional Budget Office predicted a return to 9 percent plus unemployment in 2013[2]—President Obama initiated a sustained attempt to persuade the American people (1) that he had a solution for the unemployment mess, (2) that Congress could pass it quickly, and (3) that only the Republicans in Congress would oppose it.

31

The president took this idea to a much-heralded Joint Session of the Congress and proceeded to demand that the members assembled "Pass this bill!" some seventeen times in the course of an hour's appearance.[3] He emphasized the "unpartisan" nature of his bill throughout his speech: "There should be nothing controversial about this piece of legislation. Everything in here is the kind of proposal that's been supported by both Democrats and Republicans."[4]

The president once again misjudged his own (rapidly diminishing) abilities to persuade, and the speech became an instant source of ridicule.

Among the reactions:

Senator Jon Kyl of Arizona said: "President Obama, perhaps not knowing what else to do, is simply calling for more of the same, as if giving us more of the failed policies of the last two and a half years will somehow yield different results. I believe President Obama's new 'stimulus' will further delay economic recovery and continue to inflict harm on so many Americans."[5]

Senate Minority Leader Mitch McConnell said: "By all accounts, the president's so-called jobs plan is to try those very same policies again and then accuse anyone who doesn't support them this time around of being political and overly partisan, of not doing what's needed in this moment of crisis. This isn't a jobs plan. It is a reelection plan."[6]

Douglas Holtz-Eakin, a conservative economist, agreed: "It's a philosophy that is more of the same—more temporary policies of a stimulus nature on the tax and infrastructure side that are unlikely to be significant enough to move the dial. It's more political than real."[7]

The president was undeterred despite the obvious incoherence of attempting to cure an unemployment problem that had grown after a 2009 spending spree of nearly twice the amount he proposed in September 2011. The president took to the campaign trail in a variety of places and using a new, supercharged bus—whose shell was designed in Canada[8]—to carry his appeal for more spending and a bigger government from state to state.

The president also dispatched Joe Biden to the trail, but with mixed results.

In Flint, Michigan, the vice president did the Chamber of Commerce no favors by claiming that the number of murders and rapes in the city was skyrocketing even as he pledged that Stimulus 2.0 would provide the cops to keep the criminals at the city's edge.[9]

In Philly he denounced critics of the job plan's emphasis on onetime, temporary spending—and fell off a rhetorical cliff—warning his audience about robbers and rapists following in the wake of a failed stimulus.[10]

The low point of the Biden Unplugged Tour came in front of a classroom of Philly fourth graders on October 19, where he instructed the ten-year-olds on taxes and federal policy.[11]

I discussed this trio of Biden greatest hits with Mark Steyn on my radio show on October 20, 2011:

HH: I've got to jump down to Joe Biden talking to fourth graders in Philadelphia yesterday, Mark Steyn, because I think you need to hear this and comment on it. Here's the vice president yesterday in Philadelphia:

Biden: *What it's like to be a president is it's harder than being a vice president. You know why? Because I can give the president all the advice in the world, but guess what? He has to make the decision all by himself. And so these really difficult decisions he has to make, for example, one of the decisions we're trying to make now, we think that because here in this school, your school, you've had a lot of teachers who used to work here, but because there's no money for them in the city, they're not working. And so what happens is, when that occurs, each of the teachers that stays have more kids to teach. And they don't get to spend as much time with you as they did when your classes were smaller. We think the federal government in Washington, D.C., should say to the cities and states, look, we're going to give you some money so that you can hire back all those people. And the way we're going to it, we're going to ask people who have a lot of money to pay just a little bit more in taxes.*

HH: Mark Steyn, he's propagandizing fourth graders.

MS: *(laughing)* I know, I know. What is this, the start of the Biden Youth Movement?

HH: *(laughing)*

MS: Look, this is an idiotic example. The people/teacher ratio in the United States is half of what it was a century ago. And this statistic, by the way, is from an excellent book that some guy called Mark Steyn wrote, called *After America*. So you can check it up in there. It's all sourced up the wazoo. And since 1970, public school employment has increased ten times faster than public school enrollment. And I bet if you asked a lot of those fourth graders, they wouldn't be averse to actually having fewer teachers, because there's way more than there were when their parents were in school, and when their grandparents were in school.

HH: But the idea of telling them we want D.C. to give more money to your city to hire teachers, it just teaches exactly the opposite of the federal system. It is despicable.

MS: Oh, well, but there's no federalism anymore. I don't think we should even use the word. This isn't a federal government. This is a national government. This elementary school, whatever it's called, that Joe Biden was at, this is part of, one of fifteen thousand school districts in the United States of America. And I think that school district should be able to make its own decisions on what teachers it can hire, and can afford to hire. And as he said, the only correct part of that statement he said is that some teachers who used to be here aren't here anymore, and that's because there's no money to pay them. Well, there's no money to pay them in Washington, either. We're broke at the local level, we're broke at the county, we're broke at the state level, and we're broke at the federal level. And no matter how you shuffle the brokenness around, what's consistent at all levels is the brokenness of the brokenness.

HH: Well then, that means, given Joe Biden's comment in Flint, Michigan, when he made a stop there, that we're all going to be murdered. Here's Joe Biden in Flint earlier this week:

Biden: *Pat Moynihan said everyone's entitled to their own opinion, but they're not entitled to their own facts. Let's look at the facts. In 2008, when Flint had 265 sworn officers on their police force, there were 35 murders and 91 rapes in this city. In 2010, when Flint had only 144 police officers, the murder rate climbed to 65, and rapes, just to pick two categories, climbed to 229. In 2011, you now only have 125 shields. God only knows what the numbers will be this year for Flint if we don't rectify it.*

HH: And then, he took his magical mystery tour to Philadelphia, Mark Steyn, and he said this, cut number two:

Biden: *The other thing I've heard from my friends who oppose this, this whole jobs bill, and this, that this is just temporary. Well, let me tell you. It's not temporary when that 911 call comes in, and a woman's being raped, if a cop shows up in time to prevent the rape. It's not temporary to that woman. It's not temporary to the guy whose store is being held up and has a gun pointed at his head if a cop shows up and he's not killed. That's not temporary to that store owner. Give me a break. Temporary? I wish these guys who thought it's temporary, I wish they had some notion of what it's like to be on the other side of a gun, or a two-hundred-pound man standing over you, telling you to submit. Folks, it matters.*

HH: It matters, Mark Steyn, it matters.

MS: So the idea is that we've advanced, by the way. This is an advance. Harry Reid, you know, just a couple of months

ago, was saying oh, no, the Republicans are going to deci-
mate the federally subsidized Cowboy Poetry Festival. Now,
we've moved beyond that to a land where cowboy poets
are going to be raped and murdered by the thousands
because of those Republicans. So I don't know, at this rate
of ratcheting up, I don't know where the rhetoric's going to
be in a couple of months beyond this. Nobody believes any
of this stuff. Nobody believes any of this stuff.[12]

The key point—of many wonderful points made by Steyn—
is that "nobody believes any of this stuff," and that is 100 percent true.

The president doesn't believe it. The vice president doesn't
believe it. Harry Reid and his Democratic colleagues in the Senate don't believe it (and indeed many Senate Democrats didn't
want to vote yes on all, or even part, of Stimulus 2.0 because it
will ruin their already fading prospects for reelection).[13]

There was simply nothing believable about Stimulus 2.0—
so why did the president push it?

He has failed to deliver on any of his promises, and the laws
he superintended through Congress and signed have become
anchors around the neck of the American economy.

This became obvious by the summer of 2011, when he real-
ized the need for a reelection strategy that somehow took the
focus off of his many failures.

Thus the idea of demanding a Stimulus 2.0 that would not
and could not be passed, even through a Democrat-controlled
Senate, was born—useful only as a prop to a failing president,
an alleged magic policy pill that would have cured every ill if
only the GOP had swallowed it on behalf of the country.

The president has thus fallen to another low: to become a
thorough huckster, a traveling patented-medicine salesman or a
political phrenologist.

Perhaps he believed in the first stimulus, but he couldn't
have believed in the second very much, and he certainly did not

think much about its prospects for passage. But he unleashed it anyway, and got back ridicule. He turned Joe Biden loose and took the level of argument to a new low.

And then he and the rest of Team Obama got cozy with Occupy Wall Street.

President Obama's desperation led to his embrace of class warfare—an endlessly repeated demand that the wealthiest pay "a little bit more" of that vast wealth.

Such appeals to class have never played well in America, where everyone can rise—and, indeed, rise quite high quite fast—and where there has generally been a belief that the government does not have a right to your money or your property simply because you have a lot of it.

But Obama took out the tired rhetoric of the class warriors and put it in the service of his rapidly declining political fortunes. Here are just two examples from two different press conferences by the president:

> If we're going to make spending cuts—many of which we wouldn't make if we weren't facing such large budget deficits—then it's only right that we ask everyone to pay their fair share. You know, last week, Speaker of the House John Boehner gave a speech about the economy.... That option...relies entirely on cuts....It would cripple our competitiveness and our ability to win the jobs of the future. And it would also mean asking sacrifice of seniors and the middle class and the poor, while asking nothing of the wealthiest Americans and biggest corporations.[14]

And also:

> It would be nice if we could keep every tax break there is, but we've got to make some tough choices here if we want to reduce our deficit. And if we choose to keep those tax breaks for millionaires and billionaires, if we choose to keep a tax break for corporate jet owners, if we choose to

keep tax breaks for oil and gas companies that are making hundreds of billions of dollars, then that means we've got to cut some kids off from getting a college scholarship. That means we've got to stop funding certain grants for medical research. That means that food safety may be compromised. That means that Medicare has to bear a greater part of the burden. Those are the choices we have to make.

So the bottom line is this: any agreement to reduce our deficit is going to require tough decisions and balanced solutions. And before we ask our seniors to pay more for health care, before we cut our children's education, before we sacrifice our commitment to the research and innovation that will help create more jobs in the economy, I think it's only fair to ask an oil company or a corporate jet owner that has done so well to give up a tax break that no other business enjoys. I don't think that's real radical. I think the majority of Americans agree with that.[15]

This full-throated embrace by the president of the Saul Alinsky–inspired politics of envy coincided with the birth of the Occupy Wall Street movement. Others have captured the essence of this collection of college kids wanting their student loans forgiven, and professional anarchists and aging hippies out for a last lark in the park. The videos carefully compiled by Andrew Breitbart and his colleague Larry O'Connor at Breitbart.tv are an archive of absurdity, but the president's team has refused to distance itself from this small but vocal assault on the private sector and the free market.

Obama appeared on Jay Leno's *The Tonight Show* on October 25, 2011, and discussed the Occupy Wall Street movement:

Look, people are frustrated, and that frustration has expressed itself in a lot of different ways. It expressed itself in the Tea Party. It's expressing itself in Occupy Wall Street. I do think that what this—what this signals is that people in leadership, whether it's corporate leadership, leaders in the banks, leaders in Washington, everybody needs to understand that the American people feel like nobody is looking out for them right now.[16]

White House Press Secretary Jay Carney answered questions about the president's opinion of the protests in a press conference later that week:

The president has said that he understands people's frustration, he understands that those frustrations are felt very broadly by the American people—at least those frustrations that have to do with the fact that the economy isn't strong enough, the fact that unemployment is too high and the fact that Washington is dysfunctional.[17]

Vice President Joe Biden had already offered his reflections on the movement earlier that month:

Let's be honest with one another. What is the core of that protest? The core is: the bargain has been breached. The core is the American people do not think the system is fair, or on the level. That is the core is what you're seeing with Wall Street. There's a lot in common with the Tea Party. The Tea Party started, why? TARP. They thought it was unfair. The middle-class folks, these guys with the debit cards, are on their back. And [banks] are going to charge them $5 to use the cards? At minimum, [the banks] are totally tone-deaf.[18]

House Democratic Leader Nancy Pelosi joined the conversation soon thereafter, saying,

I support the message to the establishment, whether it's Wall Street or the political establishment and the rest, that change has to happen. We cannot continue in a way that is not relevant to their lives.[19]

Senate Majority Leader Harry Reid agreed, saying on the Senate floor:

> In recent days, Republicans showed new interest in the gulf between rich and poor that has motivated thousands to occupy parks across the country and make their voices heard. Apparently they believe the staggering income inequality makes a good talking point. While Democrats fight for jobs for the middle class, Republicans fight for tax breaks for the 1 percent of Americans who don't need our help.[20]

OWS wasn't a movement, but it was a moment, and one that provided another glimpse of the president's abject ambition combined with his contingent appreciation for the free market.

The president could have abandoned his failed economic policies any time after the "recovery summer," as he and his team branded the summer of 2010, failed to produce robust job growth. (The White House's press release on June 17, 2010, was titled "Administration Kicks Off 'Recovery Summer' with Groundbreakings and Events Across the Country: President Obama, Vice President Biden and Other Administration Officials to Highlight Surge in Recovery Act Infrastructure Projects This Summer.")[21]

Certainly after the shattering losses his party suffered in the fall of 2010, he could have tacked to the center, and even appeared ready to do so when he agreed with Mitch McConnell to a two-year extension of the Bush tax rates during the lame-duck Congress that followed.

But no sooner had his political bruises healed than the president was back up and pushing left, left, left—this time proposing more of the same but backed by farcical arguments and a Greek chorus of the unwashed in parks and squares across the country.

Stimulus 2.0 and Occupy Wall Street were made for each other, and the president's failed economics are deeply entrenched in both.

Chapter 4

The Biggest Spendthrift—in History

> *The problem is, is that the way Bush has done it over the last eight years is to take out a credit card from the Bank of China in the name of our children, driving up our national debt from $5 trillion for the first forty-two presidents—number forty-three added $4 trillion by his lonesome, so that we now have over $9 trillion of debt that we are going to have to pay back—$30,000 for every man, woman, and child. That's irresponsible. That's unpatriotic.*
>
> —Senator Barack Obama, campaigning for president on July 3, 2008, in Fargo, North Dakota[1]

First, just the facts:

The federal government collects an enormous amount of revenue every single year, mostly from taxes of one sort or another, but also from licenses, sale of stuff, etc.

The federal government spends an enormous amount of money every year.

When the government spends less than it takes in any given year, it runs a surplus.

When the government spends more than it takes in, it borrows the money it doesn't have from anyone willing to buy a promissory note—a bond—from the U.S. government, and the amount borrowed annually is the deficit. Those bonds are contracts to pay back the borrower all that was borrowed plus a rate of interest on the borrowed amount.

Governments, like families, strive to balance their budgets and not spend more than they take in. The key reason is that borrowing is expensive. Interest has to be paid on the money borrowed. When families can no longer pay for their living expenses and the cost of what they have borrowed in the past, they are bankrupt and are usually forced into dire circumstances.

When state governments spend more than they take in, they have to cut services or raise taxes. They don't have much choice, as they have only very limited abilities to borrow to cover shortfalls, and most state constitutions prohibit unsecured borrowing.

When the federal government spends more than it takes in, it doesn't face such restrictions; it just keeps borrowing and adds the total amount borrowed to the total national debt.

Under President Obama and his allies in Congress—Nancy Pelosi and Harry Reid—the federal government has gone on a spending and borrowing binge, and our annual deficits have skyrocketed as a result.

Let's use fifteen years of data and follow the amount of the deficit accumulated in that year by the president and Congress:

1996: $107 billion
1997: $22 billion
1998: No deficit ($69 billion surplus)
1999: No deficit ($125 billion surplus)
2000: No deficit ($236 billion surplus)
2001: No deficit ($128 billion surplus)
2002: $158 billion
2003: $377 billion
2004: $412 billion
2005: $318 billion
2006: $248 billion
2007: $161 billion

2008: $459 billion
2009: $1,413 billion ($1.4 trillion)
2010: $1,293 billion ($1.3 trillion)
2011: $1,299 billion ($1.3 trillion)[2]

The deficit for Fiscal Year 2012 is estimated to be $1,101 billion, or another $1.1 trillion in borrowed money.[3]

In the last year that Republicans controlled Congress and George W. Bush was president—Fiscal Year 2007—the budget deficit was $161 billion.[4]

In the first two years that Speaker Pelosi and Harry Reid shared control of the budget with President Bush, they pushed deficits way up. And then when President Obama combined forces with Nancy Pelosi and Harry Reid, federal spending went to the moon.

President Obama has said, "I found this deficit when I showed up. I found this national debt doubled, wrapped in a big bow waiting for me when I stepped into the Oval Office."[5] Regardless of who steps into the Oval Office in 2013, the size of the government's deficits poses a greater threat to U.S. economic stability than it did in 2008: it is vast, staggering, and deeply destructive to the nation's future.

In addition to trends in annual budget deficits, we have to look at how much the federal government has to spend every year on interest charges for the money it has borrowed over all of its existence.

First we need to know the total national debt for the past thirty years so we know how much we have borrowed that has not been paid back and thus how much interest we have to pay on it.

As of the beginning of August 2011, the total national debt was a staggering $14.587 trillion, and is growing rapidly even at current nominal interest rates.[6]

Which presidents borrowed the money? Here's a quick review of how much each of the last several presidents added to the national debt:

Ronald Reagan's First Term: $732 billion increase
Ronald Reagan's Second Term: $1.021 trillion increase
George H. W. Bush's Term: $1.493 trillion increase
Bill Clinton's First Term: $1.146 trillion increase
Bill Clinton's Second Term: $339 billion increase
George W. Bush's First Term: $1.934 trillion increase
George W. Bush's Second Term: $3.104 trillion increase[7]

President Bush presided over an eight-year expansion in the total national debt that was truly huge: almost $5 trillion.

President Obama, by comparison, added more than $4 trillion to the national debt in the first three years of his presidency, with another trillion in borrowing certain, thus borrowing more money in forty-eight months than George W. did in ninety-six months![8]

Here is a chart of the amount of interest the federal government has spent on its accumulated debt over the same timeframe:

1996: $344 billion
1997: $356 billion
1998: $364 billion
1999: $354 billion
2000: $362 billion
2001: $360 billion
2002: $333 billion
2003: $318 billion
2004: $322 billion
2005: $352 billion
2006: $406 billion
2007: $430 billion
2008: $451 billion
2009: $383 billion
2010: $414 billion
2011: $444 billion[9]

Although the cost of our borrowing has gone from only $344 billion annually to $444 billion annually over the past fifteen years—an increase of about 29 percent—this increase significantly understates the crisis we face. We are living on borrowed time since worldwide interest rates generally—and those paid on U.S. Treasuries specifically—are so low. When borrowers begin to insist on a greater return on their investment in U.S. bonds via higher interest rates, those interest rates will rise, and with them the amount of interest we have to pay on the national debt we have accumulated. Interest rates can increase very quickly.

Please understand this: If interest rates rise even a little bit, the costs to the U.S. federal government rise immediately and significantly. If interest rates spike because of worldwide or national economic conditions, the interest cost to the federal government will also spike.

If the annual interest cost is $400 billion at 3 percent, then it will be $800 billion at 6 percent—and that is an annual cost, not a onetime cost.

Financial analysts are confident that rates will rise in the coming years (in all U.S. markets, not just U.S. Treasury bonds).[10] The Fed cannot keep rates near zero forever; eventually market pressures and investor demand will force interest rates higher. The last time the gross national debt reached its current levels—the early 1980s—the interest rate for U.S. Treasuries averaged around 15 percent.[11] While economists generally do not think rates will return to those highs, "the question is not whether rates will go up, but rather by how much."[12]

This is the fiscal cliff that Barack Obama has brought us to. It will be difficult indeed for the next president to back away from it and fix the massive spending, debt, and interest cost problems we are facing.

If President Obama is reelected, it will simply be impossible to recover. His reelection guarantees a financial crisis that may make the recession seem tame in comparison.

Chapter 5

The Community Organizer Collapses Housing

It is a fair economic argument that some people make that say, you know what, just leave it alone, and if people are losing their homes, they've got to lose their homes, and if the housing market has to go down another 10 percent, just let it go down another 10 percent, and eventually it will find bottom.

I guess my job as president is to think about those families that are losing their homes not as some abstract numbers. I mean, these are real people who worked really hard for that house. We think it's very important to acknowledge that some people just bought too much house; they couldn't afford it. And it's not fair for the rest of us to have to subsidize them because of bad judgments and mistakes that they made.

On the other hand, we also think it's important to recognize that if you've got communities where you've got—every other house is foreclosed, that that's bad for the economy as a whole.

So these are all tough decisions. But the main point I want to make is, is that we are going to constantly reexamine what we're doing. We are open to new ideas that are out there, and if we think something is going to work to put people to work, then absolutely we're going to try to make it happen.

—President Obama to CNBC in a town-hall-style meeting, September 20, 2010[1]

Housing is the great engine of American prosperity and a centerpiece of the American dream.

In the last year before Nancy Pelosi and Harry Reid took control of Congress, 2006, approximately 23,869,000 homes were built in the United States.[2]

Compare that with the 7,866,000 new homes built in all of 2010,[3] or the 4,014,000 new homes built in 2011.[4] This represents approximately a 75 percent decline in the number of new houses being built in the United States.

It takes a lot of hands to raise a house. Each house not built during Obama's administration compared to the years before his presidency represents an average of 219 jobs.[5] The process begins with collaboration between the builder and the architect. Once the initial concept and plans are agreed upon, the blueprints are given to an engineer and a survey crew for certification, before making the rounds through the local government departments for permits. A lot of heavy machinery operators are required to grade the ground, laborers to dig a foundation, and cement men to pour cement; framers buy materials that are delivered to the construction site and then used to create the skeleton; roofers cover the roof, drywall men seal up the work of the electricians, plumbers, and HVAC (heat, ventilation, and air-conditioning) specialists, all of whom are superintended along the way by city inspectors; painters and trim carpenters apply the finishing touches while landscapers create the lawn and bushes that surround the new home; final interior details such as tile, cabinets, appliances, and furnishings are then purchased and installed, although only some are as new as the carpet. Finally, Realtors, listing agents, lenders, attorneys, insurance agents, utility companies, and local government get involved in the sale and maintenance of the home. Then the property tax bill arrives to pay for city services and public schools.

Thus the market proceeds, until economic conditions so undermine home values that investors will no longer provide capital to buy the land and entitle it.[6] When home values fall, people feel less wealthy because they are, often by a lot. Foreclosures add to the spiral.

There were 1,259,118 foreclosures in 2006,[7] 2.2 million in 2007,[8] 2.3 million in 2008,[9] 2.8 million in 2009,[10] and 3.8 million in 2010.[11] Financial experts anticipate the number of foreclosure-related filings in 2011 to, once again, break previous records.[12]

The average price for the sale of a new home was $303,500 in 2006, $314,000 in 2007, $289,600 in 2008, $268,200 in 2009, $271,500 in 2010, and $267,900 in 2011.[13] The current average foreclosure sales price in the United States is $175,968.[14]

This is a disaster for home owners, for the people who build new houses or sell old ones. If the number of foreclosed houses continues to increase, the oversupply of homes could cause another significant drop in home prices and halt new building projects.[15] There are approximately 517,800 Realtors in the United States.[16]

Do you recall President Obama giving a speech on the housing market? He has often spoken of foreclosures and the pain they cause the onetime owner who is obliged to abandon his or her dream, but has he ever discussed the reasons why that foreclosure happened, or the spiral down in home prices that led to the house being "upside down"?

There are approximately 10.9 million homes in America on which more is owed to the bank than would be gained even via a market sale.[17] If the owner values only economic calculation, he will walk away from the home, and the housing crisis will deepen.

The president has launched many initiatives, all of the worst sort, because they sought to save individual homeowners and not the housing market.[18]

But that's what community organizers do—focus on individuals who become clients then activists and opinion leaders, and who then mobilize voters—a political organization built on misery and resentment, assembled by a political operator unconcerned about returning to a healthy housing market.

It was the wrong focus, and the consequences are clear.

Chapter 6
Swelling the Rolls of the Unemployed

[The pledge to keep unemployment under 8% percent came] via a Jan. 9, 2009, report called "The Job Impact of the American Recovery and Reinvestment Plan" from Christina Romer, chairwoman of the president's Council of Economic Advisers, and Jared Bernstein, the vice president's top economic adviser.

Their report projected that the stimulus plan proposed by Obama would create 3 million to 4 million jobs by the end of 2010. The report also included a chart predicting unemployment rates with and without the stimulus. Without the stimulus (the baseline), unemployment was projected to hit about 8.5 percent in 2009 and then continue rising to a peak of about 9 percent in 2010. With the stimulus, they predicted the unemployment rate would peak at just under 8 percent in 2009.

—from the *St. Petersburg Times'* Politifact.com[1]

The fact is the recovery act is working.

—Vice President Joe Biden, announcing "Recovery Summer" on June 18, 2010[2]

The facts of the country's unemployment crisis are relatively straightforward. They come from the Bureau of Labor Statistics. Here is the annual rate of unemployment for the past dozen years:[3]

2000: 4.0 percent
2001: 4.7 percent
2002: 5.8 percent
2003: 6.0 percent
2004: 5.5 percent
2005: 5.1 percent
2006: 4.6 percent
2007: 4.6 percent
2008: 5.8 percent
2009: 9.3 percent
2010: 9.6 percent
2011: 8.95 percent[4]

Bill Clinton bequeathed a low unemployment rate to George W. Bush, who spent years after the attack on America and economic crisis of those days grinding the rate down until the panic of the fall of 2008 brought it sharply higher.

Nothing matters more to a nation's sense of well-being than the unemployment rate. When it is low, or even somewhat high but falling, the country gathers economic momentum and begins to grow at the sort of rate associated with George W. Bush's middle years, Ronald Reagan's last six years, and the aftermath of the JFK tax cut.

Gross Domestic Product ("GDP") is defined by the Bureau of Economic Analysis, which keeps the statistics, as "the output of goods and services produced by labor and property located in the United States."[5]

It is a measure of our national wealth expansion (or contraction).

Here is the annual percentage change in GDP growth for the same dozen years as the unemployment statistics above.

Positive change means the economy was growing by that percentage rate:[6]

2000: 4.1 percent
2001: 1.1 percent
2002: 1.8 percent
2003: 2.5 percent
2004: 3.5 percent
2005: 3.1 percent
2006: 2.7 percent
2007: 1.9 percent
2008: −0.3 percent
2009: −3.5 percent
2010: 3.0 percent
2011: 1.7 percent[7]

The economy grew every year of George W. Bush's presidency, but the Panic of 2008 left the economy in a recession, and negative growth occurred in 2009. The standard business cycle brought recovery back to the country in 2010 with a solid if not spectacular 4.2 percent growth rate.

Then the "recovery" stalled. In 2011 the economy fell to near zero growth in some quarters, and it felt like the recession had returned.

"Confidence among U.S. consumers plunged in August to the lowest level since May 1980, adding to concern that weak employment gains and volatility in the stock market will prompt households to retrench," reported Bloomberg News's Jillian Berman on August 12, 2011.

"The Thomson Reuters/University of Michigan preliminary index of consumer sentiment slumped to 54.9 from 63.7 the prior month," she continued.[8]

The three years of President Obama's tenure have been disastrous for the economic well-being of the United States.

There was no "Recovery Summer" in 2010, and the "recovery" we experienced in the entire year was short-lived and without staying power—not able to effectively dent national unemployment or restore consumer confidence.

These are just the facts, and the president and his defenders routinely break out the violins and play sad songs about the desperate circumstances they inherited.

Those circumstances were desperate, but the massive American economy recovered, *and then slumped again*—all on President Obama's watch. As Michael Boskin says in the *Wall Street Journal*, "The president constantly reminds us that he was dealt a difficult hand. But the evidence is overwhelming that he played it poorly."[9]

We saw in the previous chapter that by the administration's own measurement and predictions the Stimulus failed to produce jobs. It may have juiced GDP for a very short period of time, but this false positive of growth could not be sustained.

On November 4, 2011, another disappointing jobs report was received, and though the national unemployment rate ticked down by 0.1 percent, it remained at 9 percent.

At the *New York Times*, reporter Richard Stevenson's assessment of that round of news could not be starker. "Early Economic Projections Could Haunt Obama in 2012" was the headline, and the reality of the vast gap between what was promised as Obama began his presidency and what he had wrought through three long years of failed policies was blunt:

Ten days prior to Mr. Obama's taking the oath of office in January 2009, his economic team released a report outlining the estimated benefits of the $775 billion stimulus plan he was seeking. The projections were quite specific. The stimulus legislation passed just a few weeks later at about the size the White House had sought. Had all gone as promised by the report, the unemployment rate right

now would have been around 6.5 percent, heading down
to around 6 percent by the end of this year and a little over
5 percent at the end of next year.

The Federal Reserve has already projected that the
unemployment rate will be at least 8.5 percent at the end of
next year, meaning the next presidential term would start
with a higher rate than the 7.3 percent Mr. Obama inherited when he took office.

To the White House's intense frustration, the chart
showing the early 2009 projections has become the centerpiece of the closing Republican argument against Mr.
Obama's re-election and against the economic policies his
party stands for.[10]

Stevenson presents a very accurate summation of the politics of the situation, but of course it isn't the politics that ought
to matter to reporters, editors, or anyone observing what the
president has wrought.

The gap between what was promised and what has been
delivered, even if it improves marginally between now and
November, is a huge tally of real sorrow and real lost years
for millions of Americans who have not only been unemployed throughout the Obama tenure, but whose savings have
been exhausted, homes lost, families stressed and sometimes
shattered.

President Obama is simply clueless about how to respond
to chronic sluggish growth and the possibility of extended,
chronic unemployment at levels above 8 percent or even higher.
Even if the economy struggles back to and maintains 3 percent
growth in the first half of 2012, it won't be enough to bring
down the devastating unemployment figures. The steps necessary for long-term growth—permanent cuts in corporate and
individual tax rates coupled with a massive deregulation of job
creators—are simply not in the president's inventory of options
because they run against his deeply ingrained big government/

big spending ideology, and the ideology of Nancy Pelosi, Harry Reid, and most of the Democrats on the Hill.

They cannot bring themselves to look at this data—a vast gap between what they thought would happen and what did in fact happen—and conclude that everything they have proposed has failed and that all of their plans have turned to ash in their mouths.

Why anyone would vote for them and expect anything different from a continuation of what these charts show is hard to understand. Remember the old cliché about the definition of insanity: repeating the same actions but expecting a different result.

What Democrats, including President Obama, have always believed in is government spending. In the next chapter we look at those figures. If federal government spending could trigger economic growth or solve unemployment, it would have done so by now.

Never before have we spent such sums. Never have we so endangered our long-term fiscal health in such a fashion. A second Obama term—another four years of this profligacy—will destroy the credit of the United States and the prospect of a return to robust growth for as many years as anyone can imagine.

And the unemployment rate could easily exceed its highest measures and exceed even its prolonged run at unprecedented levels in a second Obama term.

The president says, of course, that this won't be the case. He presents rosier scenarios. He has experts to back him up.

He has studies, reports, and, of course, promises.

And we have, quite literally, heard and read them all before.

Chapter 7

Soaring Gas Prices and Green Energy Scams

The truth is, there's no silver bullet that can bring down gas prices right away. But there are a few things we can do. This includes safe and responsible production of oil at home, which we are pursuing. We need to invest in clean, renewable energy.... That's the key to helping families at the pump and reducing our dependence on foreign oil. We need to harness the potential I've seen at promising start-ups and innovative clean energy companies across America. That's how we'll not only reduce the deficit, but also lower our dependence on foreign oil, grow the economy, and leave for our children a safer planet. And that's what our mission has to be.

—President Obama in his weekly address,
April 23, 2011[1]

This is our generation's Sputnik moment. Two years ago, I said that we needed to reach a level of research and development we haven't seen since the height of the Space Race. In a few weeks, I will be sending a budget to Congress that helps us meet that goal. We'll invest in biomedical research, information technology, and especially clean energy technology—an investment that will strengthen our security, protect our planet, and create countless new jobs for our people.

—President Obama's 2011 State of the Union address[2]

First, just the facts.

The U.S. Energy Information Administration (EIA) reports that on average, retail motor gas prices in the United States were $1.89 per gallon when President Obama was inaugurated.[3] That is only $0.38 more per gallon than when President Bush was inaugurated.[4]

By February 2011, average gas prices had increased 68 percent, to $3.18 per gallon.[5] By May 2011, the national average topped $4 per gallon, remaining just under the record levels set during the housing market crisis.[6]

The president responded to concerns in April 2010 with a summary of his energy policy, which will form a rough outline for this chapter.

On April 23, 2011 (when the EIA reported that gas prices were nearing $3.93 per gallon at the pump),[7] the president addressed energy concerns in his weekly address:

> With gas prices at $4 a gallon....It's just another burden when things were already pretty tough.
>
> Now, whenever gas prices shoot up, like clockwork, you see politicians racing to the cameras, waving three-point plans for two-dollar gas. The truth is, there's no silver bullet that can bring down gas prices right away.
>
> But there are a few things we can do. This includes safe and responsible production of oil at home, which we are pursuing.
>
> We need to invest in clean, renewable energy....That's the key to helping families at the pump and reducing our dependence on foreign oil. We need to harness the potential I've seen at promising start-ups and innovative clean energy companies across America.
>
> That's how we'll not only reduce the deficit, but also lower our dependence on foreign oil, grow the economy, and leave for our children a safer planet. And that's what our mission has to be.[8]

First, let's focus on the president's opening point: "There are a few things we can do. This includes safe and responsible production of oil at home, which we are pursuing."

President Obama made his first newsworthy decision about domestic oil policy in late March 2010. He announced that he was lifting a ban on offshore drilling and exploration off the Atlantic seaboard.[9]

Then, on April 20, 2010, an explosion and fire on BP's Deepwater Horizon drilling rig killed eleven workers.[10] Obama waited nine days to make his first public mention of the incident.[11] Ten days later, White House senior adviser David Axelrod told *Good Morning America* that the administration would not allow new drilling until the cause of the accident was known.[12]

As part of the state's cleanup efforts, Louisiana requested permission to build dredge barriers and construct berms on May 11; partial permission was granted on May 29. Full permission was finally granted on June 2, along with the announcement of a civil and criminal investigation of BP from the Department of Justice.[13]

The Oil Pollution Act of 1990 indicates that "the president is ultimately responsible for leading the oil spill clean-up."[14] Obama's rhetoric underscores his leadership role in containment and relief efforts:

> Just after the rig sank, I assembled a team of our nation's best scientists and engineers to tackle this challenge.[15]

However, all reports from the affected areas cited confusion and delays:

> From the beginning, the effort has been bedeviled by a lack of preparation, organization, urgency and clear lines of authority among federal, state and local officials, as well as BP. As a result, officials and experts say, the damage to the

coast line and wildlife has been worse than it might have been.[16]

The United States was slow[17] to accept foreign aid: "Four weeks after the nation's worse environmental disaster, the Obama administration saw no need to accept offers of state-of-the-art skimmers, miles of boom or technical assistance from nations around the globe with experience fighting oil spills."[18]

On May 27, 2010, the secretary of the interior, Ken Salazar, announced a six-month extension of the moratorium on new deepwater oil drilling permits, on the advice of seven experts.[19] However, the seven experts actually disagreed:

[A] blanket moratorium...is not the answer. It will not measurably reduce risk further and it will have a lasting impact on the nation's economy which may be greater than that of the oil spill.... The Secretary [of the Interior]... should not be free to use our names to justify his political decisions.[20]

Bob Bea, an engineering professor at UC Berkeley and one of the seven, wrote in a separate letter, "Word from [the Department of the Interior] was [the moratorium] was a [White House] request."[21]

A federal district judge blocked the administration's moratorium in a ruling released on June 22, 2010. Judge Martin Feldman cited the mischaracterization of the experts' advice, poor logic ("if some drilling equipment parts are flawed, is it rational to say all are?"), and the effects of the moratorium: "The effect on employment, jobs, loss of domestic energy supplies caused by the moratorium as the plaintiffs (and other suppliers, and the rigs themselves) lose business, and the movement of the rigs to other sites around the world will clearly ripple through the economy and this region."[22]

White House Press Secretary Robert Gibbs said the

administration would appeal the ruling.[23] The Fifth Circuit denied the appeal by upholding the injunction.[24]

The administration kept trying. They issued a new, slightly modified moratorium on July 12, 2010.[25] Ken Salazar announced that he was lifting this new moratorium on October 12, 2010, but noted that offshore rigs would not be able to resume drilling until the companies could confirm that they had met new safety, spill response, and containment requirements. He could not confirm when the administration would begin approving drilling permits.[26]

Then, in December, the administration reversed its March decision, reinstating the ban on opening currently undeveloped coastal areas to exploration and energy development. The announcement included additional delays for pending applications, like Shell's proposal to drill in Alaska's Beaufort Sea.[27]

The president of the American Petroleum Institute expressed the concern felt by many:

> I'm surprised and disappointed by this decision, which will stifle investment and clearly stop the creation of tens of thousands of jobs. This really compounds the problem with the existing de facto moratorium in the gulf. Eventually the oil and gas pipeline for production for the country will slow to a trickle.[28]

The de facto moratorium he refers to was the permit approval process instituted by Ken Salazar and the Department of the Interior (DOI). Before any of the rigs in the Gulf or any new projects could begin producing oil, the administration had to inspect and give the rig a permit to operate. Despite officially lifting the contentious moratorium on deepwater drilling operations earlier in October, the Department of the Interior refused to issue permits until "the oil industry...persuaded [Ken Salazar]"[29] that the industry could conduct a "safe ocean program."[30]

By the end of February 2011, when average gas prices were at $3.44 a gallon,[31] only a handful[32] of the 103 applications for permits[33] were approved. Representatives of the oil industry cited confusion about the new process as a deterrent to applications.[34]

By the time Ken Salazar finally began approving permits in March 2011,[35] the DOI had been held in contempt of court[36] and ordered to begin either denying or approving applications for permits.[37] By that time, however, a number of rigs had moved out of the Gulf to work in other areas.[38] At the time of this writing, the number of permits approved per month is still lower than the historical average.[39]

Ironically, oil companies and their employees (or potential employees) are not the only ones who lost money in this process. In January 2011, one estimate suggested that the federal government was losing $3.7 million in royalties on oil sales, from the Gulf alone, every day (the government also makes money selling leases for exploration and collecting rent on developed resources).[40] IHS Global Insight, an economic forecasting firm, estimated that total government revenue from the Gulf oil industry (to local, state, and federal governments) in 2009 was $19 billion.[41] The Gulf supplies approximately 30 percent of the United States' domestic oil production.[42]

In addition to limiting oil production in the Gulf, the administration has pushed for new, tighter regulations on "greenhouse gas emissions' from power plants and oil refineries...in an attempt to curb global warming."[43] The White House has also been hesitant to pursue plans to develop other sources of domestic oil production, plans like the Keystone XL[44] pipeline from Canada,[45] which the president astonishingly vetoed in early 2012, and further development of resources on federal land.[46] In the meantime, the DOI has been "implement[ing] a smart permitting process that is efficient, thorough, and unburdened by needless red tape" for wind farms on the East Coast.[47]

While many forces affect market prices and a single factor

can rarely be called *the* cause of changes in the market, significant movements in price require significant motivation. Why did the national average for gas prices rise above $4 per gallon in 2008? It was largely a result of the worldwide economic uncertainty and turmoil which drove oil to a price of close to $150 per barrel.

Why did the national average for gas prices rise above $4 per gallon after the administration's "recovery summer"? Well, the administration's domestic energy policies—which simultaneously restricted immediate domestic oil production, limited oil exploration that would eventually increase domestic supply, increased legislation on much of our existing energy sector, and has slowed initiatives that would increase domestic supply from sources other than offshore drilling (such as the Keystone XL pipeline and development on federal land), thereby increasing our dependence upon imports of foreign oil—certainly contributed substantively. Even if the average consumer has not been paying attention to these policies, the energy sector and its investors certainly have been.

At this writing, national gas prices average well above $4 a gallon,[48] still well over a dollar higher than they were when Obama stepped into office, despite Obama's decision in June 2011 to temporarily increase domestic oil supply by authorizing the "largest ever release of oil from the nation's Strategic Petroleum Reserve."[49] In contrast, gas prices rose only $0.31 on average during Bush's first term.[50] When gas prices were nearing their all-time high, during the turmoil of the economic crisis in his second term, Bush encouraged increased domestic exploration and production, in the hope that it would lower prices.[51] The numbers are compelling: the average retail cost of motor gasoline dropped by 9 percent (when adjusted for inflation) over the duration of Bush's two terms—only a $0.38 increase.[52] By contrast, Obama's domestic energy policies are not helping "families at the pump."[53]

Let's turn to Obama's promised "investments" in "clean, renewable energy," investments he underscored in his April 23, 2011, radio address:

That's the key to helping families at the pump and reducing our dependence on foreign oil.... We need to harness the potential I've seen at promising start-ups and innovative clean energy companies across America.[54]

Like Solyndra.

The green energy industry has received lots of investment in the past decade. According to data gathered by Cleantech Group, venture capital has invested approximately $42 billion in a variety of green technology opportunities since the beginning of 2008.[55] In addition to venture capital companies, green energy technology has received major contributions from other sources: state retirement funds (such as CalPERS[56] and Cal-STRS,[57] which have invested over $600 million); successful technology companies (such as Google, which has invested $75 million);[58] fossil fuel companies (Chevron has invested nearly $200 million);[59] and private individuals and angel investors, many of whom are connected to successful technology, energy, or venture capital firms (Bill Gates has committed at least $84 million and Jon Doerr, who invested in Google and Amazon, has invested $100 million).[60]

Several countries in the Middle East are investing billions in renewable energy sources as well: "To hedge their positions, then, an increasingly sophisticated generation of largely Western-educated leaders in the Middle East are seizing on green business opportunities, by seeding research in faraway nations."[61] The article I cited specifically mentions several grants totaling $15.25 billion.

Despite all the funding and support given to the American green energy industry over the past decade, it has failed to grow at anything like anticipated levels.[62] In some key areas, it has shrunk.[63] New investment in the industry has shrunk as well.[64] It fell 30 percent nationally in the third quarter of 2011 alone, and 61 percent in California in the same time frame.[65]

This is bad news for the sector because it has already

spent about half of the money given to it in Obama's Stimulus.[66] At that rate, it will quickly burn through the rest of its investments.

Industry insiders have admitted that without incentives like cap-and-trade legislation, the industry will not grow quickly in the near future: "Having a market mechanism that helps drive these new technologies would have made a significant difference. Without that the industry muddles along."[67]

To be clear, this means that so far, even with the significant investments just described, the industry is still struggling to compete in the market. It certainly has not turned into the economic boom some anticipated. Immediate growth at the levels envisioned by political proponents of the industry[68] would require legislation to force the market to implement current green energy technology and products.[69]

Most profit being made is in selling shares, rather than through the creation of marketable products.[70] And most companies do not make it that far.[71] As Des King, the president of Chevron Technology Ventures (the division of Chevron U.S.A. Inc. that identifies, evaluates, and demonstrates emerging technologies) has said, clean power—from solar to biofuels—remains uncompetitive and unprofitable.[72]

Recently policy experts suggest that the smart way to invest in the industry is to take a long view and support research and development.[73] Don't bank on companies,[74] but seek to lower the technological barriers to clean energy products, enabling the production of more efficient, competitive, and scalable products in the future—ones that can actually succeed in the market without direct government intervention. But, even with this strategy, payout is uncertain—sometime in the distant future.

Diana Farrell and Thomas Kalil of the president's National Economic Council wrote a summary of the president's Strategy for American Innovation.[75] In their commentary, they identified "three critical roles for the federal government" in "establish[ing] the foundation for sustainable growth and the creation of quality jobs."[76] The first is investments in research and infrastructure; the second is using policy and legislation to "create the right environment for private-sector investment and competitive markets"; and third, "the government should serve as a catalyst for breakthroughs related to national priorities such as clean energy, health care, and other grand challenges of the 21st century."[77]

Solyndra provides a good example of this third "critical role" for the government. I don't choose it because of its emergence as a bankrupt example of the president's "crony capitalism," but because Obama and his administration repeatedly chose Solyndra as an example of his economic and green energy policies at work; and, apparently he does not regret it.[78]

Solyndra was founded in 2005 on the premise that light-weight, high-efficiency, thin-film solar panels would effectively compete against the traditional silicon-based flat panels. An initial round of private investment totaling $78 million got the company up and running in 2006.[79]

President Bush's Energy Policy Act of 2005 authorized the Department of Energy (DOE) to help "support innovative clean energy technologies that are typically unable to obtain conventional private financing due to high technology risks."[80]

Solyndra submitted a loan request in 2006 to finance a new manufacturing plant in Fremont, California. It took some time for the DOE to process their request, but when it was finally reviewed by the Office of Management and Budget (OMB) in January 2009, it was remanded back to the Department of Energy for further review and modification.[81]

When the American Recovery and Reinvestment Act of 2009, or Obama's stimulus plan, was passed in early 2009, the Department of Energy had not yet approved its first loan. The stimulus bill doubled the budget for the DOE's loan program and set a deadline for spending the money: September 30, 2011. The focus of the loan program became "more on creating jobs than creating energy,"[82] and those jobs had to be created fast.

The White House then took an interest in Solyndra's application. George Kaiser, a major investor in Solyndra and, incidentally, a major donor to Obama's campaign, visited the White House several times to discuss "information on...energy policy."[83]

In March 2009 the DOE conditionally approved Solyndra's revised loan application and forwarded it to the OMB for their consent. From the time the revised application was approved, e-mails between various people representing the White House's interests and the OMB passed continually until Solyndra's loan application was funded in the amount of $535 million on September 2, 2009.

The e-mails indicate that decision makers at the OMB felt pressured to make a funding decision by White House representatives, who were concerned primarily about the political value offered by the loan announcement.

A memo from the White House dated August 11, 2009, reads: "As the closing of the Solyndra deal nears, we want to think about the potential announcement value in this. We know that the conditional agreement was already announced in March. That said, the VP will be in California in early September, and wants to see if it's worth doing something here."[84]

An e-mail between staff at the DOE sent on August 20, 2009, indicates that earlier concerns about Solyndra's solvency still were not resolved: "How can we advance a project that hasn't funded working capital requirements...? This is a serious issue we need to resolve as a credit matter. It simply won't stand up to review by oversight bodies."[85]

An e-mail from an assistant of Rahm Emanuel, then chief of staff to President Obama, to White House staffers instructed them to schedule the loan announcement by Biden: "It's the same day unemployment numbers come out, and we want to use this as an example where the Recovery Act is helping create new high tech jobs."[86]

On August 31, a White House staffer e-mailed the DOE

expressing concern that the press might catch wind of Biden's schedule before the loan was actually finalized: "Our concern on the press end is that this leaks out before the OMB portion is cooked. If there is any way to accelerate, would give a lot of peace of mind/flexibility on that front. The final step will be the loan closing, which will happen on Thursday regardless."[87]

The same day an e-mail was sent from OMB staff to Biden's staff articulating the effects of the pressure the OMB and DOE felt from the White House on the scheduling issue: "We have ended up in the situation of having to do rushed approvals on a couple of occasions (and we are worried about Solyndra at the end of the week). We would prefer to have sufficient time to do our due diligence reviews and have the approval set the date for the announcement rather than the other way around."[88]

The loan was finalized on September 2, 2009.[89] On September 4, 2009, Vice President Biden joined Secretary of Energy Stephen Chu in Fremont via satellite to announce the $535 million loan guarantee at the groundbreaking ceremony for Solyndra's new plant.[90] Biden's comments on the occasion were, as usual, "prophetic":

> Part of our plan is to make sure that…we are creating jobs of the future, like the ones you are creating. Jobs you can raise a family on…jobs that will serve as a foundation for a stronger American economy. Which is why it is so important we invest in Solyndra….Not just to get us through today, but to power our way to a much brighter tomorrow.[91]

Biden's speechwriters had been working overtime to find just the right draw from history.

"There was a nineteenth-century Scottish author and political reformer named Samuel Smiles," the vice president continued. "He once said…'Hope is like the sun, which as you journey toward it, casts the shadow of our burdens behind us.' Well that is exactly, exactly what we are doing here today."[92]

The key, of course, was all the jobs Solyndra was going to create.

"These jobs are going to be permanent jobs," Joe Biden promised. "These are the jobs that won't be exported. These are the jobs that are going to define the twenty-first century and the jobs that are going to allow America to compete and to lead like we did in the twentieth century."[93]

In late 2009 Solyndra raised another $219 million from private investors,[94] despite continued worries about its long-term solvency.[95] Before the end of the year, Solyndra filed an application for another loan from the DOE, for $469 million. The second loan was given an initial green light by the DOE.[96]

Despite plenty of advice to the contrary,[97] President Obama visited the Solyndra plant on May 25, 2010. In his speech, he touted Solyndra as a harbinger of American prosperity.

"You're demonstrating that the promise of clean energy isn't just an article of faith—not anymore," the president declared. "It's happening right now. The future is here."

And that future looked great: "We're poised," the president said, "to lead our competitors in the development of new technologies and products and businesses. And we are poised to generate countless new jobs, good-paying middle-class jobs, right here in the United States of America."[98]

But despite the president's cheery assessment, worries about Solyndra's viability continued. An e-mail from an unnamed OMB staffer was sent on January 31, 2011, advising that someone warn Energy Secretary Stephen Chu of the implications of Solyndra's financial turmoil:

Given the PR and policy attention Solyndra has received since 2009, the optics of a Solyndra default will be bad whenever it occurs. While the company may avoid default with a restructuring, there is a good chance it will not. If Solyndra defaults down the road, the optics will arguably be worse later than they would today. At that point, additional funds have been put at risk, recoveries may be lower, and questions will be asked as to why the Administration made a bad investment not just once…but twice… In addition, the timing will likely coincide with the 2012 campaign season heating up, whereas a default today could be put in the context of (and perhaps even get some credit for) fiscal discipline/good government because the Administration would be limiting further taxpayer exposure letting bad projects go.[99]

As late as May 2011 Solyndra's executives were reassuring White House aides of the company's success: "Things are going well. [Solyndra has] good market momentum, the factory is ramping up and our plan puts us at cash positive later this year. Hopefully, we'll have a great story to tell toward the end of the year."[100]

Contrary to expectations, obtaining government loans actually made it harder for Solyndra to raise additional private capital. Private investors saw correctly that in the event of bankruptcy, the government loan would be repaid before their investments—a risk they were hesitant to make in an already risky industry.

Thus, the Department of Energy agreed to subordinate the government's (and thus the taxpayers') primary position in the event of Solyndra's bankruptcy.[101] This is "an unorthodox move that may have violated the law."[102] George Kaiser put in another $75 million, but it did not stop the inevitable from happening.[103]

Solyndra filed for bankruptcy on September 6, 2011.[104] Two days later, the FBI raided Solyndra's offices,[105] possibly looking for evidence of accounting fraud.[106]

Concerns about "crony capitalism" have also continued to rise.[107] Brian Harrison, the chief executive of Solyndra, and Wilbur G. Stover, its senior vice president and chief financial officer, pled the Fifth Amendment in a hearing of the House

Oversight and Investigations Subcommittee of the House Energy and Commerce Committee.[108] Solyndra's senior executives continued this behavior into their own bankruptcy proceedings, refusing to "identify the company's customers or talk about its contracts...because 'the topic would likely be the subject of investigation and possible litigation.'"[109]

More recently, in October 2011, Jonathan Silver, the director of the DOE's loan office, resigned.[110]

As more information comes out, it is clear that relevant parties knew the high risk of investing in Solyndra from day one.[111] Some critics have made convincing arguments that Solyndra was not just high-risk but was bound to fail without significant changes to market conditions.[112] Solyndra's bankruptcy has stirred conversations about the appropriateness of governmental loan programs for start-ups.[113]

The *Washington Post* provided this bit of background:

In late 2009, Brad Jones of Redpoint Ventures warned Larry Summers, director of the National Economic Council, that the Energy Department didn't seem "well-equipped to decide which companies should get the money and how much." He noted that Solyndra, which his company was backing, had received its loan despite having no profits and revenue of less than $100 million. "While that is good for us, I can't imagine it's a good way for the government to use taxpayer money," Jones wrote. Summers agreed: "I relate well to your view that gov is a crappy vc [venture capitalist] and if u were closer to it you'd feel more strongly," then added: "What should we do?"[114]

Steven Hayward voiced his agreement with Summers in the *Weekly Standard*:

How far we've come since 1979, when there was a serious national debate about whether it was appropriate for the government to provide a mere $1.5 billion loan guarantee to Chrysler—a legacy company with more plausible prospects for profitability than Solyndra. Opponents argued then that once the government starts backstopping individual businesses, it will undermine the discipline of the marketplace and create a moral hazard. Now we're bailing out auto companies directly and handing out billions in loan guarantees like Halloween candy to shaky *startups*, with scarcely any debate. Looks like the Chrysler loan critics had a point.[115]

The president, by the way, has no regrets over the investment in Solyndra.[116]

While Solyndra is the only recipient of a DOE federal loan to declare bankruptcy, many of the department's loans—many of them to other "green energy" companies—did not have even the benefit of a long approval process.

"The Energy Department, under fire over its management of a program that offers loan guarantees to clean-technology companies, has been finalizing additional multimillion-dollar guarantees in the program at a rate of more than one a week since the beginning of August," the *Washington Post* reported in September 2011. "It now has just two weeks left to commit the program's remaining $9.3 billion."[117]

What new wasteful horrors will emerge from the Department of Energy's spending spree will take years to figure out, but Solyndra is the one-word summary of the president's competence as a venture capitalist, and a one-word summary of why the voters should want to revoke his ability to "invest" their hard-earned money with his friends and associates.

Chapter 8

The "Dodd-Frank" Head-Fake: Inmates Keep the Asylum

This reform will help foster innovation, not hamper it. It is designed to make sure that everybody follows the same set of rules, so that firms compete on price and quality, not on tricks and not on traps.

It demands accountability and responsibility from everyone. It provides certainty to everybody, from bankers to farmers to business owners to consumers. And unless your business model depends on cutting corners or bilking your customers, you've got nothing to fear from reform.

—President Obama's remarks upon
signing the Dodd-Frank Act, July 21, 2010[1]

One of the least-reported fiascos of the Obama years is the passage of the Dodd-Frank bill—or, officially, the Dodd-Frank Wall Street Reform and Consumer Protection Act—which was signed into law on July 21, 2010.

Two months after the law passed, Matthew G. Lamoreaux, senior editor of the *Journal of Accountancy*, took to the pages of his magazine to give a brief overview of what the bill purported to do. Mr. Lamoreaux wrote that the new law established a "Financial Stability Oversight Council" and a "Bureau of Consumer Financial Protection," while also carving out a "SOX 404(b) Exemption" and adding powers to the Public Company Accounting Oversight Board, changing the duties of "registered investment advisers," "advisers to private funds," and "listing exchanges" when it came to executive pay.[2]

Makes a lot of sense, doesn't it?

The new law by Barney Frank and Chris Dodd was touted as the most far-reaching financial reform since those that followed the Great Depression.[3] The *Journal of Accountancy* can be forgiven if it didn't really give you a sense of what the law actually does, which is gum up the wheels of finance at every level, greatly exacerbating the credit crunch that plagues the economy, and unleashing a new horde of bureaucrats on the private sector.

Barney Frank, of course, couldn't get elected outside of his hyper-left district in Massachusetts—except for a few other bastions of way-outside-the-mainstream hyper-left districts such as Nancy Pelosi's in San Francisco. He's a smart, hyperpartisan radical who by dint of seniority and the anti-GOP waves of 2006 and 2008 found himself in charge of the overhaul of American banking, the worst matchup imaginable for the economy: a left-wing ideologue free to impose his fractured and distorted view of markets and lending on the people he perceived as enemies.

Chris Dodd, the law's coauthor, couldn't get elected anywhere in 2008, period. In his thirty years as senator from Connecticut, Dodd came to personify all that was wrong with D.C. and the culture of crony capitalism. This "master legislator" had to flee what should have been a certain defeat at the polls to remain a few steps ahead of the investigators poking into the sweetheart deals he got from his friend, former Countrywide CEO Angelo Mozilo.[4]

The "nexus between Mr. Dodd's public duties and Countrywide's interests is a serious matter involving the Senator's personal ethics and accountability to taxpayers who will be paying for Fannie's bad loans for years to come," the *Wall Street Journal* wrote on February 3, 2009. "If, as Mr. Dodd claims, he has nothing to hide, then why is he still hiding it?"[5]

We never got a full explanation about that particular bit of sleaze. Frank and Dodd also never explained their consistent protection of Fannie Mae and Freddie Mac through the years when the Bush administration urged reform. Rather than addressing concerns about the time bomb of subprime lending excess fueled by the "government sponsored enterprises," they maintained the status quo that eventually blew up the American markets.[6]

Then, instead of confessing their role when the bomb went off, the country was treated to a giant head-fake: the perpetrators of the big con brazenly pointed their fingers at Wall Street and proposed an incredibly complex reform law—a law that still leaves Fannie and Freddie untouched despite promises from the White House.[7] The "reform" distracted the Beltway media from the participation of Democratic Party elites in the Fannie and Freddie meltdown.

So, what has Dodd-Frank done? On the anniversary of the law's enactment, former House Speaker Newt Gingrich provided a summary of the law's devastating impact on the American economy. The key excerpts:

[Dodd-Frank] codified "too-big-to-fail" by allowing the government to guarantee "systemically important" banks, created the Consumer Financial Protection Bureau (headed by a single regulator and given sweeping, unchecked authority), and imposed hundreds of new regulations which make compliance very costly for small community banks.

Dodd-Frank plunged these banks and the small businesses that depend on them into even greater uncertainty, authorizing bureaucrats to write the details of over 300 new rules and inviting them to study over 100 more. The House Financial Services Committee reported this month that even a year later just 21 of these rules have been written; 62 percent have yet even to be proposed.[8]

The former Speaker was simply giving voice to what tens of thousands of community bankers, small businessmen, and would-be home refinancers would gladly testify to: credit is in short supply *even though* interest rates are low. A major part of the problem is Dodd-Frank.

Newt went even further in a Republican presidential debate in Manchester, New Hampshire, on October 11, 2011.

"If you want to put people in jail, you ought to start with Barney Frank and Chris Dodd," he told the national audience, giving voice to the widespread anger at the shattered credit markets.

Newt touched a chord there: the fact that those responsible for the first collapse—because of their obstinate refusal to tackle the problem of the GSEs (Government-Sponsored Entities) when George W. Bush had proposed to do so throughout his presidency—had been allowed to craft nine hundred pages of cover-up legislation and still keep their jobs as if nothing had happened on their watch.[9]

President Obama was of course an accomplice to this charade, and to this day touts Dodd-Frank as an achievement of his administration. Like Obamacare, Dodd-Frank needs repealing and replacing—its vast workforce of government bureaucrats should be sent back to the real world, and the oversight of the banking system returned to competent, experienced, and stable hands, not the zealots who are looking for enemies of the people behind every loan.[10]

On the day he signed Dodd-Frank into law, President Obama was exultant:

> For years, our financial sector was governed by antiquated and poorly enforced rules that allowed some to game the system and take risks that endangered the entire economy. Soon after taking office, I proposed a set of reforms to empower consumers and investors, to bring the shadowy deals that caused this crisis into the light of day, and to put

a stop to taxpayer bailouts once and for all. Today, thanks to a lot of people in this room, those reforms will become the law of the land.

"This reform will help foster innovation, not hamper it," he continued. "It is designed to make sure that everybody follows the same set of rules, so that firms compete on price and quality, not on tricks and not on traps. It demands accountability and responsibility from everyone.

"It provides certainty to everybody, from bankers to farmers to business owners to consumers," the president concluded. "And unless your business model depends on cutting corners or bilking your customers, you've got nothing to fear from reform."[11]

Obama has consistently blocked efforts to change or reform Dodd-Frank during his term, and has struck out at the commonsense objections to the law.[12]

"There is an army of lobbyists and lawyers right now working to water down the protections and the reforms that we passed," he has warned.

"They've got allies in Congress who are trying to undo the progress that we've made," he argued. "We're not going to let that happen.

"I will fight any efforts to repeal or undermine the important changes that we passed," he pledged. "And we are going to stand up for this bureau and make sure it is doing the right thing for middle-class families all across the country."[13]

Thus does the president stand on the side of continuing the credit crunch, preferring the political solace of cheap rhetoric against bankers to the real—indeed, enormous—benefits of increased liquidity.

When the GOP regains control of the Senate, it will have to join with the House GOP to tackle the housing finance issues, and it will almost certainly have to do some excavation about what really happened in 2008. They will have to establish a real record of the Panic of 2008 as a marker for future generations.[14]

Their first order of business, however, will be to encourage capital to begin its renewing and rebuilding via repealing the dead hand of the Dodd-Frank Act.

Chapter 9

The "Fast and Furious" Debacle and Cover-Up

Well, first of all, I did not authorize it. Eric Holder, the attorney general, did not authorize it.... There may be a situation here in which a serious mistake was made. If that's the case, then we'll find out and we'll hold somebody accountable.

—President Obama in an interview with Univision's Jorge Ramos in March 2011[1]

As you know, my attorney general has made clear that he certainly would not have ordered gun running to be able to pass through into Mexico. The investigation is still pending. I'm not going to comment on a current investigation. I've made very clear my views that that would not be an appropriate step by the ATF, and we've got to find out how that happened. As soon as the investigation is completed, I think appropriate actions will be taken.

—President Obama at a White House press conference, June 29, 2011[2]

First, the facts.

Operation Fast and Furious began in the fall of 2009 and continued until early 2011. "In this operation...the federal government purposefully allowed known or suspected gun smugglers to purchase guns at federally licensed firearms dealers in Arizona. The government did not seek to abort these gun purchases, intercept the smugglers after the purchases, or recover the guns they had purchased."[3]

According to a briefing paper published January 8, 2010, by the Bureau of Alcohol, Tobacco, Firearms and Explosives (ATF) Phoenix Field Division:

> The ultimate goal is to secure [REDACTED] to identify and prosecute all co-conspirators of the DTO [Drug Trafficking Organization] to include the 20 individual straw purchasers, the facilitators of the distribution cell centered here in Phoenix, the transportation cells taking firearms South, and ultimately to develop and provide prosecutable information to our Mexican law enforcement counterparts for actions.[4]

The Obama administration had approved selling guns to Mexican drug cartels in the hope of tracing those guns to the big dealers of weapons and the big dealers of drugs. It was a huge and risky scheme that had tragic consequences and is now the subject of a massive government cover-up that has reached deep into the Department of Justice and perhaps the White House.

On December 14, 2010, U.S. Border Patrol Agent Brian Terry was murdered in Rio Rico, Arizona, by suspected drug-smuggling operatives with two weapons that a known straw purchaser had purchased in January 2010 as a part of Operation Fast and Furious.[5]

The ATF and the DOJ had long ago lost control of the weapons they shopped to the cartels, and now one of those weapons had killed an American law enforcement agent.

When Congresswoman Gabrielle Giffords was shot while meeting with her constituents in Tucson, Arizona, on January 8, 2011, the ATF Phoenix Field Division's agents were concerned that she had been shot with a Fast and Furious weapon: "There was a sense like every other time, even with Ms. Giffords' shooting, there was a state of panic, like, oh, God, let's hope this is not a weapon from that case."[6]

When arrests resulting from the operation were finally made, around January 19, 2011, only twenty straw purchasers were arrested—the same number of straw purchasers the January 8, 2010, ATF briefing paper indicated were known to law enforcement before Operation Fast and Furious began.[7]

In the approximately fourteen months of operation, Fast and Furious attempted to track over 2,500 gun sales to suspected straw buyers.[8]

On February 15, 2011, Immigration and Customs Enforcement agent Jaime Zapata was killed and agent Victor Avila was wounded in Mexico. The Associated Press reported that the weapon used "was shipped through Laredo with the possible knowledge of the ATF," suggesting that this weapon was also a part of the operation.[9]

Janice K. Brewer, governor of Arizona, released a statement about Operation Fast and Furious on June 15, 2011. "I am outraged by findings in a new Congressional report that alleges federal agents were instructed to stand aside and do nothing as up to 2,000 weapons were illegally purchased in Arizona and resold," the governor declared. "In many cases, the end result appears to have been the arming of violent drug cartels south of the border. If the allegations contained in this Congressional report are accurate, then Operation Fast and Furious endangered the lives of innocent people on both sides of the border.

"The people of Arizona deserve answers from the Department of Justice and ATF as to how this could have been sanctioned, let alone encouraged," the governor concluded. "We may never know how many weapons illegally sold as part of this operation later turned up at a crime scene."[10]

Answers have not been not forthcoming from the Obama Department of Justice.

On July 5, 2011, Representative Darrell Issa, chairman of the House's Committee on Oversight & Government Reform, and

Senator Charles E. Grassley, from the Senate's Committee on the Judiciary, sent a letter to Eric Holder, the attorney general of the U.S. Department of Justice, about Acting ATF Director Kenneth Melson's interview on Fast and Furious the day before.

The letter asserted that Mr. Melson "claimed that ATF's senior leadership would have preferred to be more cooperative with our inquiry much earlier in the process.

"However," the letter continued, "he said that Justice Department officials directed them not to respond and took full control of replying to briefing and document requests from Congress. The result is that Congress only got the parts of the story that the Department wanted us to hear." The Issa-Grassley letter continued:

> If his account is accurate, then ATF leadership appears to have been effectively muzzled while the DOJ sent over false denials and buried its head in the sand. That approach distorted the truth and obstructed our investigation. The Department's inability or unwillingness to be more forthcoming served to conceal critical information that we are now learning about the involvement of other agencies, including the DEA and the FBI.[11]

The letter also claims that "the evidence we have gathered raises the disturbing possibility that the Justice Department not only allowed criminals to smuggle weapons but that taxpayer dollars from other agencies may have financed those engaging in such activities."[12]

Several congressional leaders leading the investigation of Fast and Furious have expressed frustration with the Department of Justice's "stonewall[ing]" tactics.

In a press interview, Rep. Issa said:

> We try. We send communications including subpoenas [to the Justice Department]. This is one of those situations in which they haven't admitted that they let guns walk even

though there's no credible way to say they not only let them walk, they let them run.... [But cooperation from the Department of Justice has been] closer to zero percent.[13]

In a letter to the Department of Justice, House Judiciary Committee Chairman Lamar Smith wrote:

I would be remiss if I did not express my growing concern with the [Justice] Department's handling of the Fast and Furious investigation.... Following his election in 2008, President Obama promised to usher in a new era of openness and transparency. Despite this promise, the Justice Department has been less than cooperative with this Committee's requests.

Chairman Smith sent a letter to the Justice Department on March 9, 2011, requesting six items of information related to Operation Fast and Furious. Five of those questions were unanswered by the time of his second letter, sent May 3, 2011.[14]

In addition to not answering letters, the Department of Justice is not complying with congressional subpoenas. In an interview with me, Rep. Darrell Issa spelled out just how unprecedented the Department of Justice's behavior has been:

"Well Hugh," he said, "usually, what happens is once we go to the almost unprecedented requirement of issuing a subpoena, or it's been written and we're asking where to have the marshals deliver it, then we get this 'Oh, we'll give you something.'" Issa continued:

And normally, you say okay, fine, we've gotten through this. The problem is, and this is what I think your listeners need to know, Hugh, is when we get discovery, repeatedly it looks like a black cow eating a licorice at midnight. They redact everything. We get whole pages that say nothing, and you look and say wait a second here, this is not a

Freedom of Information request, this is not somebody who says can we post it on a website. This is the only Congressional committee that is primarily formed for the purpose of oversight and investigations. And they act as though we're only allowed to see what's already on a website.[15]

The Department of Justice isn't just stonewalling requests for information. Their attempts to influence the testimonies given to congressional inquiries[16] suggest something more pernicious—an active cover-up.[17]

In an interview, Rep. Darrell Issa noted that the operation has to be approved at top levels of the Department of Justice because it "was a joint exercise. It required funding and coordination from virtually all of law enforcement."[18]

One of Congress's concerns about Operation Fast and Furious is a lack of communication between partner bureaus within the Department of Justice. Congressional investigators have found evidence that the Drug Enforcement Administration and the FBI had information that might have ended Operation Fast and Furious as many as ten months earlier, if it had been shared with ATF.[19]

When asked whether he thought the Department of Justice was attempting to cover something up, Issa responded, "Ultimately when you delay and deter us getting to the facts it's a cover-up.

"It's one that can be remedied," he continued, "but so far we see no willingness by Attorney General Holder to tell his people to cooperate, just the opposite, we're still being stonewalled."

We think there is protection of people at the top," he concluded.[20]

Just how far up approval for the operation went is unclear. Despite all the media attention, documents demonstrating—contrary to prior official statements—that details of the operation were known to the White House,[21] and despite the congressional investigations and occasional references to Watergate in the media, senior administration officials have remained very quiet about the whole affair.

Attorney General Holder was asked about the operation on May 3, 2011. "Under questioning from Issa, Holder said he was not sure of the exact date he first heard of the operation, but said it was 'probably...over the last few weeks,'" CNSNews reported. "Holder also could not say who authorized the operation."[22]

Department of Justice memos have been released, however, about Operation Fast and Furious that are addressed to Holder dated as early as July 2010.[23]

Under questioning from the Homeland Security and Government Affairs Committee, Secretary of Homeland Security Janet Napolitano[24] gave a response similar to Holder's,[25] although her personal and professional connections to ATF and former U.S. attorney Dennis Burke makes her claim of ignorance as to the origin of the operation seem suspicious as well.[26]

On March 22, 2011, President Obama was asked about Fast and Furious on Univision, a Spanish-language network:

> Well, first of all, I did not authorize it. Eric Holder, the attorney general, did not authorize it....There may be a situation here in which a serious mistake was made. If that's the case, then we'll find out and we'll hold somebody accountable.[27]

He made a similar comment on June 29, 2011, in response to a reporter's question:

> As you know, my attorney general has made clear he certainly would not have ordered gun running to pass through into Mexico. The [inspector general's] investigation is still pending, and I'm not going to comment on a pending investigation....As soon as the investigation is complete appropriate action will be taken.[28]

Rep. Darrell Issa noted in response that

President Obama's remarks today on Operation Fast and Furious [had no]...sign of urgency to provide answers or explain why no one at the Justice Department has accepted responsibility for authorizing an illegal gunwalking operation....The American people expect more from the President.[29]

Contrary to the administration's statements, statements from lower-level ATF agents confirm that they were ordered to effectively let the guns walk.

In his report to the House Committee on Oversight & Government Reform, Special Agent John Dodson said that "[o]ver the course of the next 10 months that I was involved in this operation,...rather than conduct any enforcement actions, we took notes, we recorded observations, we tracked movements of these individuals for a short time after their purchases, but nothing more.

"I can recall," Dodson continued, "for example, watching one suspect receive a bag filled with cash from a third party then proceed to a gun dealer and purchase weapons with that cash and deliver them to this same unknown third party.

"Although my instincts made me want to intervene and interdict these weapons, my supervisors directed me and my colleagues not to make any stop or arrest, but rather, to keep the straw purchaser under surveillance while allowing the guns to walk," Dodson continued. "Surveillance operations like this were the rule, not the exception...[and] [a]llowing loads of weapons that we knew to be destined for criminals—this was the plan."[30]

Despite reluctance to follow the new Fast and Furious policy from at least one gun-store owner[31] and lower-level ATF personnel[32]—opposition among ATF agents was vociferous enough (including a screaming match over police radio)[33] that a supervisor wrote an e-mail to address the "schism" among the agents[34]—suspected traffickers purchased over 2,500 firearms throughout the operation,[35] most of which are still missing.[36]

Gun-store owners were instructed to comply with the Fast and Furious policy, even when, according to Agent Dodson, "a 22-year-old girl walks in and dumps $10,000 on...AK-47s in a day, when she is driving a beat up car that doesn't have enough metal to hold hubcaps on it."[37]

The increased sales of Fast and Furious weapons coincided with an upswing of Mexican drug violence. According to a report in the *Richmond Times-Dispatch*:

> In an e-mail dated April 2, 2010, the group's supervisor reported that in the month of March "our subjects" had purchased 359 firearms and that 958 people were killed in Mexico in drug violence. It was the bloodiest month since 2005 and included 11 policemen in the state of Sinaloa.[38]

The same e-mail reported that some supervisors viewed the increased violence as a sign that their policy was a success:

> An increase of crimes and deaths in Mexico caused an increase in the recovery of weapons at crime scenes. When these weapons traced back through to the Suspect Gun Database to weapons that were walked under Fast and Furious, supervisors in Phoenix were giddy at the success of their operation.... "The 'sentiment' from higher-ups," according to one agent's testimony, was 'if you are going to make an omelet, you need to scramble some eggs.'"[39]

On August 30, 2011, the Department of Justice announced that Acting Director Kenneth Melson was being transferred from ATF to another post with the Department.[40]

Other officials associated with Operation Fast and Furious either have resigned (U.S. Attorney for Arizona Dennis Burke)[41] or have been reassigned (Assistant U.S. Attorney in Phoenix Emory Hurley and ATF Phoenix special agents Bill Newell, George Gillett, and Jim Needles).[42]

Appearing on my show on February 1, 2012, Congressman Issa assured the audience that the investigation would go on until all the facts were known and all those responsible named.

"Remember," he told me, "more people have died in Mexico by far than north of the border," and many of those killings were done with weapons "supplied by 'Fast and Furious.'"[43]

Unlike most Beltway cover-ups that involve sex, money, or power, this one involves murder—indeed, multiple murders—so the stakes are much much higher than the average D.C. embarrassment, and thus the tenacity of the cover-up is even more pronounced than normal.

This is President Obama's Department of Justice. He broke DOJ. He owns it.

Chapter 10

The President's Attacks on Catholics, Congress, and the Constitution

Under the rule, women will still have access to free preventive care that includes contraceptive services—no matter where they work. So that core principle remains. But if a woman's employer is a charity or a hospital that has a religious objection to providing contraceptive services as part of their health plan, the health plan—not the charity—will be required to reach out and offer the woman contraceptive care free of charge, without co-pays and without hassles.

—President Obama, announcing "compromise" on HHS Regulations, Friday, February 9, 2012

When Congress refuses to act and as a result hurts our economy and puts people at risk, I have an obligation as president to do what I can without them. I will not stand by while a minority in the Senate puts party ideology ahead of the people they were elected to serve.

—President Obama, announcing recess appointments to the National Labor Relations Board and the Consumer Financial Protection Bureau on January 4, 2012, when the Senate was not in recess

I can't comment on where DOMA is going to go, I can only say what I believe, and that is that DOMA doesn't make sense, it's unfair, I don't think it meets the demands of our constitution.

—President Obama, in response to questions at a Latino news outlet roundtable on September 28, 2011[1]

Early in 2012 the president slipped even more of the Constitution's bonds that limit the powers of the presidency, first by making recess appointments to key jobs without the Senate voting on the nominees and while the Senate was in formal session. This was a vast expansion of the understanding of the president's powers under the Constitution's clause regulating recess appointments.

Then on January 20, 2012, the president approved a sweeping regulation from the Department of Health and Human Services requiring all employers except for a very narrow category limited essentially to actual houses of worship to provide "morning after" pills, sterilization, and birth control to all employees.

The dismay over the first expansion of power was limited to constitutional scholars, political scientists, senators concerned with the historic balance of power between the executive and legislative branches, and to the businesses and individuals likely to be regulated by the president's illegitimate appointees.

The second action, as well as its subsequent pseudo-revision announced on Friday, February 9, as a "compromise" by the president after a storm of protest had broken over him and his re-election campaign, was a far more wide-ranging abuse of power, a direct attack on the Roman Catholic Church and on the "Free Exercise" clause of the Constitution.

The regulations and their subsequent revision fooled no one among the Roman Catholic hierarchy or indeed among constitutional scholars, and certainly not among Mass-attending Catholics.

"[N]o similarly aggressive attack on religious freedom in our country has occurred in recent memory," wrote Philadelphia Archbishop Charles Chaput in the *Philadelphia Inquirer* two days after the president unilaterally announced his absurd, indeed preposterous "compromise," which still left Roman Catholic institutions paying for "morning after" pills, sterilzation, and contraception.

Whether the president persists in pushing his anti-Catholic agenda for political purposes, or whether the Supreme Court relieves him of this error by striking down the entire malignant mess that is Obamacare, the record of the president's abuse of his authority—his unilateralism in a system of checks and balances, his studied indifference to the rights of people of faith, his disdain for the Senate's role—will be a key issue in the fall election.

And no issue illustrates that contempt for the constitutional traditions and the Constitution's express limits on executive power so much as his record on the issue of the Defense of Marriage Act.

As a candidate, Barack Obama made his beliefs about marriage clear on a number of occasions. In the debate hosted by Pastor Rick Warren on August 16, 2008, Obama answered a direct question about the marriage debate in the United States.

"I believe that marriage is the union between a man and a women. Now for me as a Christian it is also a sacred union," then senator Obama ,said on that occasion. "You know, God's in the mix."

"No," he said in response to a question from Warren, "I would not [support a constitutional amendment with that definition]… because historically we have not defined marriage in our Constitution, it's been a matter of state law; that's been our tradition.

"Now, let's break it down," he continued just four years ago. "The reason that people think that there needs to be a constitutional amendment, some people believe, is because of the concern about same-sex marriage.

"I'm not somebody that promotes same-sex marriage, but I

do believe in civil unions," Obama assured voters. "I do believe that for gay partners to want to visit each other in the hospital, for the state to say 'that's all right,' I don't think in any way inhibits my core beliefs about what marriage is. I think my faith is strong enough and my marriage is strong enough that I can afford those rights to others even if I have a different perspective or view."[2]

In official statements as a candidate Obama commonly made a distinction between the use of the word *marriage* and the rights and responsibilities socially and legally associated with marriage. But he also consistently maintained the rights of states to decide this question—in favor of civil unions—for themselves.

Obama answered a relevant questionnaire from the Human Rights Campaign in this way:

I believe civil unions should include the same legal rights that accompany a marriage license. I support the notion that all people—gay or straight—deserve the same rights and responsibilities to assist their loved ones in times of emergency, deserve equal health insurance and other employment benefits currently extended to traditional married couples, and deserve the same property rights as anyone else.

However, I do not support gay marriage. Marriage has religious and social connotations, and I consider marriage to be between a man and a woman. If I was President, however, I would oppose any effort to stifle a state's ability to decide this question on its own. Whether it was a Constitutional amendment banning gay marriage or a bill like the Defense of Marriage Act, I would oppose such efforts. I think the President should do all he or she can to advance strong families. Whatever the make-up of the family, it is the President's role to provide policies and leadership that enable the family to thrive.[3]

Obama also made clear, in an open letter to the LGBT community, that he would advocate for "equality for gay and lesbian couples" as president:

> As your President, I will use the bully pulpit to urge states to treat same-sex couples with full equality in their family and adoption laws. I personally believe that civil unions represent the best way to secure that equal treatment. But I also believe that the federal government should not stand in the way of states that want to decide on their own how best to pursue equality for gay and lesbian couples—whether that means a domestic partnership, a civil union, or a civil marriage.[4]

The Defense of Marriage Act was signed into law by Bill Clinton on September 21, 1996. Its key provisions are:

Section 2. Powers reserved to the states

No State, territory, or possession of the United States, or Indian tribe, shall be required to give effect to any public act, record, or judicial proceeding of any other State, territory, possession, or tribe respecting a relationship between persons of the same sex that is treated as a marriage under the laws of such other State, territory, possession, or tribe, or a right or claim arising from such relationship.

Section 3. Definition of marriage

In determining the meaning of any Act of Congress, or of any ruling, regulation, or interpretation of the various administrative bureaus and agencies of the United States, the word "marriage" means only a legal union between one man and one woman as husband and wife, and the word "spouse" refers only to a person of the opposite sex who is a husband or a wife.[5]

On February 23, 2011, Attorney General Eric Holder wrote Speaker John Boehner to announce the president's decision to no longer defend the Defense of Marriage Act as a constitutional exercise of power by the legislative and executive branch.

"After careful consideration, including review of a recommendation from me, the President of the United States has made the determination that Section 3 of the Defense of Marriage Act ("DOMA"), 1 U.S.C. § 7, as applied to same-sex couples who are legally married under state law, violates the equal protection component of the Fifth Amendment," Holder wrote. "Pursuant to 28 U.S.C. § 530D, I am writing to advise you of the Executive Branch's determination and to inform you of the steps the Department will take in two pending DOMA cases to implement that determination.

"While the Department has previously defended DOMA against legal challenges involving legally married same-sex couples, recent lawsuits that challenge the constitutionality of DOMA Section 3 have caused the President and the Department to conduct a new examination of the defense of this provision," continued Holder. "In particular, in November 2010, plaintiffs filed two new lawsuits challenging the constitutionality of Section 3 of DOMA in jurisdictions without precedent on whether sexual-orientation classifications are subject to rational basis review or whether they must satisfy some form of heightened scrutiny."

Holder named those challenges, which are neither unique nor had they reached the level of appellate review.

The cases named were *Windsor v. United States*, No. 1:10-cv-8435 (S.D.N.Y.); and *Pedersen v. OPM*, No. 3:10-cv-1750 (D. Conn.).

"Previously, the Administration has defended Section 3 in jurisdictions where circuit courts have already held that classifications based on sexual orientation are subject to rational basis review, and it has advanced arguments to defend DOMA

Section 3 under the binding standard that has applied in those cases," Holder continued.

"These new lawsuits, by contrast, will require the Department to take an affirmative position on the level of scrutiny that should be applied to DOMA Section 3 in a circuit without binding precedent on the issue," he went on. "As described more fully below, *the President and I* have concluded that classifications based on sexual orientation warrant heightened scrutiny and that, as applied to same-sex couples legally married under state law, Section 3 of DOMA is unconstitutional."[6]

I have added the emphasis so the reader understands that the president who said "I do not support gay marriage" in 2008 unilaterally withdrew the federal government's opposition to same-sex marriage less than three years later despite no change in law, and no Supreme Court or federal circuit court review. The president and his attorney general just decided it was time to overrule unilaterally the statutory framework of the United States, including the Defense of Marriage Act.

Although the Holder letter goes on at great length to explain why the president and Eric Holder believe DOMA is unconstitutional, it should be noted that no appeals court in the entire country had reached that decision when the letter was sent.

A Massachusetts district court—one judge—had so ruled twice before the president's announcement,[7] but nothing in the way of an important decision had arrived that could have led the president and the attorney general to such a unilateral and radical action.

And it *was* unilateral and radical. Hans von Spakovsky, a senior legal fellow at the Heritage Foundation, indicates why:

> While the President has a duty to interpret the Constitution through his decisions to enforce statutes, it is the well-established policy of the Justice Department to defend a federal statute unless no reasonable argument may be made in its defense, or unless the statute would infringe on some

core presidential constitutional authority.... Applying this policy, the Executive Branch has traditionally defended federal statutes vigorously even in cases where it had strong constitutional doubts, and where it had strong policy reservations.[8]

Seth Waxman, solicitor general for the second Clinton administration, also articulated this principle in an essay for a Georgetown Law journal:

> The Solicitor General generally defends a law whenever professionally respectable arguments can be made in support of its constitutionality.... Vigorously defending congressional legislation serves the institutional interests and constitutional judgments of all three branches.... It reflects an important premise in our constitutional system—that when Congress passes a law and the President signs it, their actions reflect a shared judgment about the constitutionality of the statute.... [The attorney general and solicitor general] do not attempt to reach [their] own best view of a statute's constitutionality; rather, they try to craft a defense of the law in a manner that can best explain the basis on which the political branches' presumed constitutional judgment must have been predicated.[9]

Congress had of course passed the law, and so the Speaker of the House reacted quickly to the unilateralism of the executive branch. House Speaker John Boehner declared on March 4, 2011, that he would organize a legal defense of DOMA:

> I will convene a meeting of the Bipartisan Legal Advisory Group for the purpose of initiating action by the House to defend this law of the United States, which was enacted by a bipartisan vote in Congress and signed by President Bill Clinton. It is regrettable that the Obama Administration has opened this divisive issue at a time when Americans want

their leaders to focus on jobs and the challenges facing our economy. The constitutionality of this law should be determined by the courts—not by the president unilaterally—and this action by the House will ensure the matter is addressed in a manner consistent with our Constitution.[10]

This was an appropriate and full-throated response from the Speaker, acting as a representative of a coequal branch of the federal government against the president's usurpation of the right to nullify a duly passed constitutional statute, signed into law by his predecessor Bill Clinton.

That is what Obama and Holder did: nullification of a valid law by executive decree and without the benefit of judicial review.

These three instances of aggressive, unilateral, and very radical actions by the president in just eighteen months should alert every voter to how the president will interpret his power and authority if he is reelected and won't have to worry about reelection again. He recognizes few limits on his power, and he has been rejecting traditional limits on a regular basis as the clock winds down on his term in office.

Voters are forewarned. This is not a president who respects the Constitution as it is written but rather believes it to be a starting point for his authority, not a limiting set of binding rules.

II

FOREIGN POLICY FAILURES

Chapter 11

Standing By As Iranians Die: Or, Learning to Love the Mullahs and Their Bomb

The Iranian government must understand that the world is watching. We mourn each and every innocent life that is lost. We call on the Iranian government to stop all violent and unjust action against its own people. The universal rights to assembly and free speech must be respected, and the United States stands with all who seek to exercise those rights. Martin Luther King once said, "The arc of the moral universe is long, but it bends toward justice." I believe that. The international community believes that. And right now, we are bearing witness to the Iranian people's belief in that truth, and we will continue to bear witness.

—from President Obama's public statement, released June 20, 2009[1]

On June 12, 2009, the Islamic Republic of Iran appeared to conduct an election for its president.

The incumbent was the fanatic Mahmoud Ahmadinejad, who first came to power in the election of 2005.

Though not the Supreme Leader of the theocratic state—that is Ayatollah Ali Khamenei, who assumed that post in 1989 after the death of Ayatollah Ruhollah Khomeini—Ahmadinejad has been extending his power with the cooperation of the hard-core Revolutionary Guards for many years, developing a state within a state. Ahmadinejad is a malevolent force, a hater of Israel who often speaks of destroying it, as well as a religious fanatic with visions of a restored caliphate and the return of the "Hidden Imam," whose appearance can be rushed along by the creation of chaotic conditions in the world.

Ahmadinejad is a dangerous fanatic in a position of great power: the leader of a fascist state equipped with a powerful and technologically advanced military force on the brink of securing nuclear weapons and already possessed of potent long-range missile capabilities.[2]

Thus, when the election of 2009 provided an opportunity for an allegedly reformist candidate to compete with Ahmadinejad, the West watched closely and hoped that the regime might allow the people of Iran to select a leader to take them away from the brink of confrontation.

When the "results" were announced,[3] the world laughed at the brazenness of the theft.[4] Ahmadinejad was reported by Iranian authorities to have received 62 percent of the vote and his leading opponent, Mir-Hossein Mousavi, only 34 percent.[5]

Demonstrations and riots broke out almost immediately in the streets of Iran and around the country "of a size and intensity unprecedented since the Iranian Revolution."[6] The Iranian government responded by banning unauthorized public gatherings, restricting the activities of foreign and domestic journalists, disrupting cell phone networks, limiting access to some websites, mass arrests, and sometimes violence directed at protesters.[7] Despite the government's intransigence, protests continued steadily for two months, when Mahmoud Ahmadinejad was sworn into office in early August. The election has continued to be a source of civil discontent and has motivated occasional protests in the region ever since.[8]

Many in the West condemned the election fraud and the violence. Karim Sadjapour, an analyst at the Carnegie Endow-

ment for International Peace, said, "I don't think anyone anticipated this level of fraudulence.

"This was a selection, not an election," he added. "At least
authoritarian regimes like Syria and Egypt have no democratic
pretences. In retrospect it appears this entire campaign was a
show: [Supreme Leader] Ayatollah [Ali] Khamenei wasn't ever
going to let Ahmadinejad lose."[9]

Mark Fitzpatrick, senior fellow for non-proliferation at the
International Institute for Strategic Studies in London, said,
"I'm surprised at the regime's audacity in declaring such a large
margin for Ahmadinejad, given that in the run-up, the momentum seemed to be in the other direction.

"The hardliners in the regime seem to have exercised all
their levers of power to keep Ahmadinejad in place," Fitzpatrick continued. "Undoubtedly, one of the key reasons was their
concern about losing control of the country through policies
such as willingness to engage with the United States."[10]

Elliot Abrams, a former Bush administration official now
with the Council on Foreign Relations, commented that "at this
point one has to wonder about vote fraud," and "the two-to-one
margin for Ahmadinejad may well appear to millions of Iranians as bizarre and unlikely, and meant to avoid a run-off he
might lose.

"If that's what millions of voters think, especially young
voters in this very young country," Abrams concluded with
a very accurate forecast of events that rapidly unfolded, "there
could well be large demonstrations. And the legitimacy not
only of an Ahmadinejad second term, but of the whole regime,
would be in question in the eyes of many Iranians."[11]

"I'm in disbelief that this could be the case," said Trita Parsi,
president of the National Iranian American Council. "It's one
thing if Ahmadinejad had won the first round with 51 or 55
percent. But this number...just sounds tremendously strange
in a way that doesn't add up....It is difficult to feel comfortable
that this occurred without any cheating."[12]

Leaders from around the world condemned the fraud.

French president Nicolas Sarkozy said, "The extent of the fraud is proportional to the violent reaction.... It is a tragedy, but it is not negative to have a real opinion movement that tries to break its chains."[13]

The United Kingdom's prime minister, Gordon Brown, said, "We are with others, including the whole of the European Union unanimously today, in condemning the use of violence, in condemning media suppression.... [It] is for Iran now to show the world that the elections have been fair...that the repression and the brutality that we have seen in these last few days is not something that is going to be repeated.... We want Iran to be part of the international community and not to be isolated. But it is for Iran to prove...that they can respect these basic rights."[14]

The German chancellor, Angela Merkel, said, "Germany stands by the people in Iran who want to exercise their right to freedom of expression and freedom of assembly."[15]

The German foreign minister, Frank-Walter Steinmeier, said, "The actions of the Iranian security forces are completely unacceptable."[16]

In stark contrast, President Obama did and said next to nothing.[17]

His first reference to the election and the protests was in response to a reporter's question on Monday, June 15, 2009:

> Obviously all of us have been watching the news from Iran. And I want to start off by being very clear that it is up to Iranians to make decisions about who Iran's leaders will be; that we respect Iranian sovereignty and want to avoid the United States being the issue inside Iran.... [Our national security interests] are core interests not just to the United States but I think to a peaceful world in general. We will continue to pursue a tough, direct dialogue between our two countries, and we'll see where it takes us.... I want

them to know that we in the United States do not want to make any decisions for the Iranians, but we do believe that the Iranian people and their voices should be heard and respected.[18]

In an interview on June 16, Obama downplayed the importance of the election in terms of the United States' foreign policy: "It's important to understand that although there is some ferment taking place in Iran, that the difference between Ahmadinejad and Mousavi in terms of their actual policies may not be as great as has been advertised."[19]

President Obama released another soft-footed response on June 20:

"The Iranian government must understand that the world is watching," the president noted. "We mourn each and every innocent life that is lost." He then added this ringing demand: "We call on the Iranian government to stop all violent and unjust action against its own people. The universal rights to assembly and free speech must be respected, and the United States stands with all who seek to exercise those rights.

"As I said in Cairo, suppressing ideas never succeeds in making them go away," he continued, referencing himself as though that would impress the killer mullahs. "The Iranian people will ultimately judge the actions of their own government. If the Iranian government seeks the respect of the international community, it must respect the dignity of its own people and govern through consent, not coercion."

The president then quoted an American hero, but not necessarily one the Mullahs would find persuasive:

Martin Luther King once said, "The arc of the moral universe is long, but it bends toward justice." I believe that. The international community believes that. And right now, we are bearing witness to the Iranian people's belief in that truth, and we will continue to bear witness.[20]

That "long arc" did little for the dead in the streets of Iran.

As time and the protests went on, Obama's rhetoric escalated slightly, but retained its passivity. One example:

> The United States and the international community have been appalled and outraged by the threats, the beatings, and imprisonments of the last few days. I strongly condemn these unjust actions, and I join with the American people in mourning each and every innocent life that is lost.
>
> I've made it clear that the United States respects the sovereignty of the Islamic Republic of Iran, and is not interfering with Iran's affairs. But we must also bear witness to the courage and the dignity of the Iranian people, and to a remarkable opening within Iranian society....If the Iranian government seeks the respect of the international community, it must respect those rights and heed the will of its own people. It must govern through consent and not coercion. That's what Iran's own people are calling for, and the Iranian people will ultimately judge the actions of their own government.[21]

Obama's rhetoric during the election aftermath is consistent with his administration's[22] policy. He has continued[23] to emphasize diplomacy and talks with the Iranians,[24] without preconditions or, initially, serious international pressure through sanctions,[25] although Iran's refusal to come to the negotiating table has recently forced the administration into a slightly more aggressive stance.[26]

At the time of the stolen election, Obama's near silence in the face of a genuine opportunity to support crucially needed change in Iran drew enormous criticism:

Sen. Lindsey Graham said, "The president of the United States is supposed to lead the free world, not follow it. [Obama is being] timid and passive."[27]

Charles Krauthammer concluded that "Obama misses the point with [his] Iran response."[28]

Paul Wolfowitz wrote:

Iranians are protesting not just election fraud but also the growing abuses of the Iranian people by a dictatorial regime. Now is not the time for the president to dig in to a neutral posture. It is time to change course.[29]

Sen. John McCain responded to Obama's comment about the negligible difference between Ahmadinejad and Mousavi by saying:

To say there's not a bit of difference between the two candidates is beside the point. The Iranian people, obviously, think there's some difference, or tens or hundreds of thousands of them wouldn't be in the streets.[30]

But Obama did nothing and said little,[31] and the brutality of the regime crushed the opposition.

It was an enormous strategic error—a missed opportunity—and the sort of failure that historians will rank with the failure to oppose Hitler's reoccupation of the Rhine in 1936.

I wanted to stress how the president was understood to be passive at the time the uprising occurred and was crushed because the president and his supporters will try to argue in the aftermath of the Arab Spring that many are blaming him for a failure to act when the upheavals in the Middle East hadn't yet begun.

Subsequent chapters lay out the chronology of Obama's incompetence in the context of Egypt, Libya, and Syria, but the president's first and greatest failure was here: when he stood by as the mullahs and the Revolutionary Guard mowed down Iran's self-created democratic resistance.

Writing in the *Wall Street Journal* on October 23, 2009,

months after the crackdown, Douglas Feith and Bari Weiss detailed how Team Obama has systematically defunded the expatriate voices of the Iranian people:

> The *Boston Globe* reported this month that the Connecticut-based Iran Human Rights Documentation Center recently lost its State Department funding. The Center—a nonpartisan group that documents Iran's human-rights abuses—had received $3 million over the past five years. It will shut down in May, said Executive Director Renee Redman, unless private donors save it.
>
> Less widely known is that Freedom House, the nonpartisan watchdog group founded in 1941, also lost State Department funding. It applied in April for significant funds to support initiatives including *Gozaar*, its Farsi-English online journal of democracy and human rights, and was turned down in July. Since 2006, Freedom House had received over $2 million from the U.S. and European governments for Iran-related efforts. "We might have to close *Gozaar* if we run out of money," deputy executive director Thomas O. Melia told us this week.
>
> Then there's the International Republican Institute (IRI), which for several years received State Department support to train Iranian reformers and connect them to like-minded activists in Europe and elsewhere. IRI's recent application for funds was denied, an IRI official told us last week.[32]

Team Obama is in appeasement mode vis-à-vis Iran, and it has been from the first day of the president's term. On March 21, 2009, the White House released a video on the occasion of the Persian New Year (Nowruz) that was understood as an olive branch to the mullahs in Tehran, one with the gentlest push on nuclear weapons and silence on the regime's horrific human rights record and its repeated threats of genocide directed at Israel.[33]

The first major foreign policy speech of the president's tenure was delivered in a predominantly Muslim country, Turkey, and aimed at the theofascist rulers of Iran. Obama repeated the thesis of his Nowruz video in his speech to the Turkish Parliament on April 6, 2009. The key paragraph:

Now, I have made it clear to the people and leaders of the Islamic Republic of Iran that the United States seeks engagement based on mutual interest and mutual respect. We want Iran to play its rightful role in the community of nations. Iran is a great civilization. We want them to engage in the economic and political integration that brings prosperity and security. But Iran's leaders must choose whether they will try to build a weapon or build a better future for their people.[34]

The understatement is overwhelming, and of course the Iranians read this as weakness, and responded with contempt.

In response to the speech, Ahmadinejad's press adviser Aliakbar Javanfekr said that "minor changes [in foreign policy] will not end the differences."[35]

Reuters had a more complete quotation:

We welcome the interest of the American government to settle differences. The American government should realise its previous mistakes and make an effort to amend them in order to put aside differences.

The Obama administration so far has just talked. By words and talking the...problems between Iran and America can not be solved.

Nowruz (the Iranian New Year which falls on Friday) is a sign of fundamental development in nature and Obama should learn from this to make fundamental changes in his policy towards Iran.

Supporting Israel is not a friendly gesture and the new year is an opportunity for the United States to change this policy.

By fundamentally changing its behaviour America can offer us a friendly hand. So far what we have received have been unfriendly fists. Unlimited sanctions which still continue and have been renewed by the United States are wrong and need to be reviewed.

The Iranian nation has shown that it can forget hasty behavior but we are awaiting practical steps by the United States.[36]

"Iran's supreme leader Ayatollah Ali Khamenei," CNN reported, "said...he sees no change in U.S. policy toward Iran despite the U.S. promise of a 'new beginning.' Khamenei said a change in rhetoric is not enough, and Washington must practice what it preaches.... He also promised that Iran will change its policy if the United States does so as well."[37]

In particular, Khamenei "implied that the U.S. was behind Sunni terrorism against the regime in Iranian Baluchistan... complained about continued U.S. support for...the Mojahedin-e Khalq...in Iraq...complained that the U.S. continued to accuse Iran of sponsoring terrorism...complained that the U.S. continues to accuse Iran of trying to build a nuclear bomb...complained of continued U.S. economic sanctions and boycotts...[and] complained of U.S. support for Israel."[38]

Iranian officials could not be more dismissive of the president's attempts to appease them.

The *Los Angeles Times* reported on quasi-official responses from within Iran. The president is "attempt[ing] to repackage rather than reformulate U.S. policies: 'They say, "Do not be carried away. Do not be fooled by this man, Obama,"'" said Sadegh Zidakalam, a political scientist at Tehran University, characterizing the position of officials suspicious of Washington. 'He is as harsh and he is as dangerous and is as much against Iran as George Bush.... Obama is disguising his policy against Iran.'"[39]

If all that Iran's leaders and apologists had done was mock

the president,[40] still that would have been injury enough. But it is clear that the mullahs and Ahmadinejad took away from the president's repeated appeals for a deal contempt for the weakness they perceived, a contempt that has manifested itself in an utter indifference to the various blandishments Obama has tried since.[41]

Meanwhile the election came, and the election went, with only bodies and full prisons to show for the president's vaunted "engagement" with the regime.

The opportunity came, and the opportunity passed, to stand with the people of Iran and force change upon the regime.

The chance to speak out for freedom and human rights was there, and now it is gone until again the Iranian people summon the courage to stand up to the clubs and guns of the Iranian Revolutionary Guard and the fanaticism of Ahmadinejad.

We have to hope that the next moment comes before Iran's nuclear weapons are operational, and that there is a strong friend of freedom in the White House, not an appeaser looking for an invitation to visit Iran and deal.

Chapter 12

Abandoning Israel to Its Fate

That truth—that each side has legitimate aspirations—is what makes peace so hard. And the deadlock will only be broken when each side learns to stand in each other's shoes.
—from President Obama's speech to the United Nations, September 21, 2011[1]

I'm still around. Let me know if anything changes.
—President Obama on taking a sudden leave of a White House meeting with Israeli prime minister Benjamin Netanyahu on May 25, 2010[2]

When Israeli prime minister Netanyahu came to the White House on May 25, 2010, he was not respectfully, much less warmly, received by President Obama.

Here's the account of that meeting from Great Britain's *Telegraph*:

Sending a clear message of his displeasure, Mr. Obama treated his guest to a series of slights. Photographs of the meeting were forbidden and an Israeli request to issue a joint-statement once it was over were turned down.

"There is no humiliation exercise that the Americans did not try on the prime minister and his entourage," Israel's *Maarov* newspaper reported. "Bibi received in the

White House the treatment reserved for the president of Equatorial Guinea."

The biggest slight came when the president abruptly rose and ended a meeting with the Israeli prime minister, saying that he had to go to dinner with his family.

"As he left," the *Telegraph* concluded, "Mr Netanyahu was told to consider the error of his ways. 'I'm still around,' Mr Obama is quoted by Israel's *Yediot Ahronot* newspaper as having said. 'Let me know if there is anything new.'"[3]

During a press conference on September 10, 2010, President Obama continued to wage his public and private campaign against expanding West Bank settlements, urging that Israel not build new settlements in the West Bank:

President Abbas and Prime Minister Netanyahu...came with a sense of purpose and seriousness and cordiality that frankly exceeded a lot of people's expectations. What they said was that they were serious about negotiating, they affirmed the goal of creating two states living side by side in peace and security....We are actively participating in that process....It is a risk worth taking because the alternative is a status quo that is unsustainable....[4]

A major bone of contention during the course of this month is going to be the potential lapse of the settlement moratorium....What I've said to the prime minister, is that given so far the talks are moving forward in a constructive way, it makes sense to extend that moratorium so long as the talks are moving in a constructive way....And if you can get that agreement then you can start constructing anything that the people of Israel see fit, in undisputed areas.[5]

The president's top adviser was not so civil in his public remarks about Israel's settlements. "What happened there was an affront," David Axelrod declared. "It was an insult, but that's not the most important thing."

The so-called important thing to Axelrod? "What it did was it made more difficult a very difficult process." Israel's security was not the "difficult" thing. Israel's compliance was.

"We've just gotten proximity, so-called proximity talks going between the Palestinians and the Israelis," Axelrod concluded, "and this seemed calculated to undermine that, and that was—that was distressing to everyone who is promoting the idea of peace—and security in the region."[6]

Less than a year later the president upped his hostility towards the Jewish state even more via a stunning bit of rhetoric.

On May 22, 2011, President Obama gave a speech on the Middle East in which he declared that the United States believes that "the borders of Israel and Palestine should be based on the 1967 lines with mutually agreed swaps, so that secure and recognized borders are established for both states."[7]

The 1967 lines are called "the suicide lines" because they are not defensible, nor have they been the jumping-off point for negotiations on a two-state solution in the past forty-five years.[8]

But for President Obama they are the magic words that convey utter contempt for Israeli security and for the moral dimension of the conflict.

The result of this undisguised hostility has been a steady erosion of the once overwhelming support for President Obama among American Jews. The American Jewish Committee did its annual survey of Jewish American public opinion in 2011 and reported this startling finding:

For the first time during Obama's presidency, disapproval among Jewish voters exceeded approval of his performance. Jewish approval of Obama's handling of his job as president declined to 45 percent, with another 48 percent disapproving and 7 percent undecided, according to the survey, conducted from September 6 to 21, 2011. In the last annual AJC survey, a year ago, 51 percent approved, and 44 percent disapproved.[9]

President Obama arrived in the White House with many people suspicious of his views on Israel given his longtime friendship with high-profile Palestinian activists, radical activists generally, and the Reverend Jeremiah Wright specifically.

Of particular concern was the president's friendship with Rashid Khalidi, a longtime friend of the president whose farewell dinner in Chicago featured then Illinois state senator Obama and other notables like Weatherman radical turned Obama pal William Ayers. The *Los Angeles Times* reported on the dinner on April 10, 2008, in a story by Peter Wallsten that began:

It was a celebration of Palestinian culture—a night of music, dancing and a dash of politics. Local Arab Americans [in Chicago] were bidding farewell to Rashid Khalidi, an internationally known scholar, critic of Israel and advocate for Palestinian rights, who was leaving town for a job in New York.

Wallsten's report continued:

A special tribute came from Khalidi's friend and frequent dinner companion, the young state Sen. Barack Obama. Speaking to the crowd, Obama reminisced about meals prepared by Khalidi's wife, Mona, and conversations that had challenged his thinking. His many talks with the Khalidis, Obama said, had been "consistent reminders to me of my own blind spots and my own biases.... It's for that reason that I'm hoping that, for many years to come, we continue that conversation—a conversation that is necessary not just around Mona and Rashid's dinner table," but around "this entire world."[10]

Khalidi is indeed a vociferous critic of Israel, and eyebrows rose with concern when the *Los Angeles Times* refused to release a videotape it admits to having of the dinner and the then-state-senator-now-president's remarks. What had the president and other speakers said to make the video of his remarks too hot for his pals at the *Times* to post the video, despite the enormous avalanche of viewers it would attract to the paper's struggling website?

We may never know what is on the tape, but we do have a record of the president's actions toward Israel. Very few people try to suggest that Obama's policies are an extension of President Bush's robust support for Israel, which followed the unbroken posture of American presidents toward Israel since at least the 1967 war. (Some argue that Ike was no great supporter of Israel during the Suez crisis of 1956, but even if the worst assessments of the American president's attitude toward Israel during that crisis are true—and there are other accounts which argue for Ike's steady support of the Jewish state—even then the situation changed in the wars of 1967 and 1973. It has certainly changed since the rise of radical Islamist threats to Israel's very existence from Hamas to the south in Gaza, and Hezbollah to the north in Lebanon, and of course from Syria as well as Iran.)

Israeli leaders have done their best to downplay the obvious onset of winter in the U.S.-Israel relationship, and no official negative word will pass the lips of the prime minister or Israel's ambassador to the United States, Michael Oren. They and others work to build buttresses around the crumbling support at the White House, especially in Congress.

Supporters of Israel in the United States have to bluntly assess and act upon the president's early and naked hostility to Israel, and not his election season posturing.

Voters have to ask themselves how the president will act toward the only deeply rooted, stable democracy in the region, and they must ask with particular urgency whether the president would be a 100 percent reliable ally of the Jewish state in a hot war with real missiles and real Hezbollah/Hamas/Syrian/Iranian bullets firing.

The president should not have acted as though he was a Chicago ward boss and Netanyahu a favor-seeking supplicant—that is not how a president acts toward the democratically elected prime minister of our most reliable ally.

The president must stop demanding a unilateral sacrifice concerning West Bank construction from Israel, which is not warranted given the facts on the ground and the realities of any genuine two-state solution.

The president must repudiate the 1967 borders as a starting point from which "mutually agreed swaps" should proceed.

And, crucially, the president must renounce the language of moral equivalence to Israel when talking about terrorist organizations like Hamas, which refuse to even recognize Israel's right to exist. His fantasy of reforming Hamas cripples would-be peace makers on the Palestinian side while simultaneously casting Israel in the most unflattering of lights—the equal partner of a bloodthirsty, nihilist terrorist organization.

Chapter 13

Hollowing Out the American Military

As Commander-in-Chief, I will always do whatever it takes to keep the American people safe, to defend this nation. And that's why this bill provides for the best military in the history of the world. It reaffirms our commitment to our brave men and women in uniform and our wounded warriors. But I have always rejected the notion that we have to waste billions of dollars of taxpayer money to keep this nation secure. In fact, I think that wasting these dollars makes us less secure. And that's why we have passed a defense bill that eliminates some of the waste and inefficiency in our defense process—reforms that will better protect our nation, better protect our troops, and save taxpayers tens of billions of dollars.

—from President Obama's remarks at his signing of the National Defense Authorization Act, October 2009[1]

Total Department of Defense spending in fiscal year 2001 was $414 billion.[2] That was the year war came to America.

Ten years later, President Obama initially proposed a fiscal year 2011 budget of $708 billion. (This number includes all Department of Defense spending, including the costs of the Iraq and Afghanistan deployments.)[3]

This is what national security was supposed to cost—$708 billion out of a gross domestic product of approximately $15.2

trillion. Less than 5 percent of what the nation produces goes to defending it, its people, its international interests, and the futures of our children and generations beyond.

But the ink wasn't dry on the president's own budget proposal before he began to cut it. In a wide-ranging speech on April 13, 2011, the president said that we must "find additional savings... in defense. And we can do that while still keeping ourselves safe."

The president noted that "over the past two years Secretary Gates has courageously taken on wasteful spending, saving $400 billion in current and future [defense] spending."

"I believe we can do that again," he said, and in those seven words signaled that Secretary Gates, and all of the Pentagon officials that had worked so hard to assist in the deficit crisis, had fallen for a giant presidential head-fake.[4]

Secretary Gates and his team had scoured the military for savings, slashed programs and weapon systems, and had cut to the bone. Now, though, the president would be seeking more and deeper cuts.

In the budget the president sent to Congress on February 14, 2012, he requested another huge slash in spending, with a total of $614 billion put forward as adequate to the needs of the nation's security. The president proposed cutting at least 72,000 soldiers, 20,000 Marines, and tens of thousands of Air Force and Navy personnel. Fifteen billion dollars was deleted from the proposed spending on America's next generation of aircraft, the F-35—only two years after the cancellation of production of the F-22 was announced because of the imminent arrival of these new F-35s in numbers sufficient to maintain America's air superiority.[5]

The budget battle over defense rages on the Hill as this book goes to press, but there should be no confusion whatsoever about the president's plans and what would happen to the American military if he were to win a second term.

Heritage Foundation analyst Baker Spring detailed the

consequences of the president's proposed radical cuts in defense spending, and put them in the context of the decade-long pressure on the Department of Defense budget:

> In his February statement on his FY 2012 budget submission, the President recognized the need to exempt national security spending, including the narrower category of defense spending, from a freeze on other discretionary spending accounts. Even then, the President's five-year defense budget proposal from February falls far short of what is required to sustain U.S. security commitments around the world. In fact, securing U.S. vital interests would require some $500 billion in additional spending for the "core" defense program, which excludes funding for the conduct of the wars in Afghanistan and Iraq, in the years covering FY 2012–FY 2016. The additional cuts proposed by the President on April 13 would put the core defense program almost $650 billion in the hole over the same period.[6]

This analysis is just the tip of the reaction of national security professionals to the president's meat-ax approach to defense spending. A second Heritage Foundation expert, Mackenzie Eaglen, writes:

> In April [2011], President Obama denounced his own 2012 budget request sitting on Capitol Hill and called for $400 billion in security cuts over the next decade. One of the first consequences of $400–$500 billion in military cuts would be to slice soldiers and Marines from the force and return the Army and Marine Corps to their 1990s levels. These personnel levels would allow the nation to sustain only one protracted operation overseas, but they would be insufficient to conduct two simultaneous ground efforts. This would eliminate the Pentagon's longstanding two-war force planning construct through the back door. Most worrisome, this size force would immediately reduce options

available to the commander in chief if a crisis arises while American forces are already committed elsewhere....

These cuts would also see the cancellation of what is left of the Pentagon's meager modernization plans for future military equipment. Some of the many pending long-term projects crucial to winning future conflicts— as well as deterrence, which saves money—such as a new bomber, next-generation stealth helicopter, new nuclear submarine, and various space, satellite, and missile defense capabilities could become victims of this plan.

Not only would this effectively turn the nuclear triad into a diad or worse, but it could essentially leave submarines as the only realistic long-range strike platform to confront the growing threat of anti-access and area-denial capabilities. Since submarines face long trips back to port after firing their missiles, the sortie generation rate of a long-range strike force consisting almost exclusively of submarines would be extremely low. In this kind of scenario, the United States could easily be "locked out" of the vital Asian littorals.[7]

Read the full analyses of both Spring and Eaglen to get a full picture of what nonpartisan experts on defense spending and military preparedness are saying. They and almost all other credentialed analysts are appalled at the proposed Obama cuts to the nation's military budget and thus to its national security.

This isn't a talking point or a debate strategy. The president has already embarked on a hollowing out of the American military via a bleed-it-dry series of budget cuts that will fundamentally impair America's ability to play its historic role in the world and its national security.

In the first week of January 2012, President Obama appeared at the Pentagon to announce the results of a "strategic reassessment," but it was anything but strategic. As noted above, the plans laid out by the president and his team call for the slashing of at least 72,000 soldiers from the Army and 20,000 Marines, plus deep cuts in platform acquisition and logistical support. More and deeper cuts loom under his tenure, as planes, missiles, and ships are sacrificed to stave off cutting into the domestic spending that fuels his coalition of constituencies.

If he is reelected, the consequent damage to America's security profile will be at least as great as the greatest period of isolationist build-down in the country's history, which followed our victory in World War I, and which contributed mightily to the Western world's march to a second global conflagration.

Peace through strength is expensive. But it is cheaper to maintain defenses than to rebuild them, and even that cost is far, far superior to the carnage that follows an intentional weakening of America's defenses via radical budget cuts, force reductions, and weapon system cancellations.

Chapter 14

"Resetting" Russia Back to Great Power Status

As we've both said before, when I came into office, the relationship between the United States and Russia had drifted—perhaps to its lowest point since the Cold War. There was too much mistrust and too little real work on issues of common concern. That did not serve the interests of either country or the world. Indeed, I firmly believe that America's most significant national security interests and priorities could be advanced most effectively through cooperation, not an adversarial relationship, with Russia.

That's why I committed to resetting the relationship between our two nations, and in President Medvedev I've found a solid and reliable partner. We listen to one another and we speak candidly.

—President Obama, after meeting with Russian president Dmitry Medvedev, June 24, 2010[1]

This is my last election. After my election, I have more flexibility.

—President Obama to President Dmitry Medvedev, March 26, 2012

I understand. I will transmit this information to Vladimir.

—President Medvedev in response

What a fiasco from the start. At least when President George W. Bush took a wrong measure of Vladimir Putin it was early in the emerging reign of Russia's newest czar, and there was hope that Putin would turn out to be a reformer, possibly even a Christian advocate of human rights and a just democratic government.

It turns out he's KGB to the core and almost certainly a leader for life. What Bush didn't know in 2001 everyone knew in 2009 when a new president arrived in Washington. That is, everyone except President Obama, who must have missed the significance of Russia's invasion of Georgia during the 2008 campaign.

Remember the giant "reset" (or, if you read the Russian translation correctly, "overcharged") button Hillary took to Moscow, adding an atmosphere of amateur foolishness[2] to a strategic blunder?

Remember that the United States abandoned our commitment to deploy missile defense in Poland and the Czech Republic at the insistence of Russia a few months later—barely giving our allies a courtesy call before announcing it publically?[3] When she heard of the sudden policy reversal, a spokeswoman at the Polish Ministry of Defense is reported to have said, "This is catastrophic for Poland."[4]

And don't forget how Russia has protected Iran in the U.N. Security Council.

In addition to maintaining economic and military ties with Iran,[5] Russia used its position on the Security Council as recently as October 2011 to minimize official reports about the Iranian nuclear program[6] despite "broadly consistent and credible" evidence suggesting that Iran is investigating military applications of nuclear technology.[7]

Earlier in 2011, only a couple weeks before Presidents Medvedev and Obama had another friendly meeting,[8] Russia used its Security Council veto to suppress a United Nations report that Iran was breaking a U.N. embargo by shipping weapons to Syria, which then passed them on to Lebanese and Palestinian militants.[9]

This chapter makes the easiest argument of all because the president's ineptitude vis-à-vis Russia is obvious and so enormous. The imperially minded Russia is back[10] and exerting pressure on its former captive states and neighbors in the hope of rebinding them again to the glory and service of Mother Russia.

And the American president has nothing to say, and says even that softly, while laying down every stick in his possession and sending shudders through every recently free nation on Russia's border.

When President Obama told President Medvedev that "[t]his is my last election" and that "[a]fter my election I have more flexibility," eyebrows everywhere were raised. Although it is hard to imagine how, President Obama clearly intends to be even more accommodating to "Vladimir" if voters give him that chance in November 2012.

Chapter 15

Abandoning Iraq and Afghanistan

In Afghanistan and Pakistan, we and many nations here are helping these governments develop the capacity to take the lead in this effort, while working to advance opportunity and security for their people.
> —from President Obama's remarks to the United Nations, September 23, 2009[1]

The goal that we seek is achievable, and can be expressed simply: No safe haven from which al Qaeda or its affiliates can launch attacks against our homeland or our allies. We won't try to make Afghanistan a perfect place. We will not police its streets or patrol its mountains indefinitely. That is the responsibility of the Afghan government, which must step up its ability to protect its people, and move from an economy shaped by war to one that can sustain a lasting peace. What we can do, and will do, is build a partnership with the Afghan people that endures—one that ensures that we will be able to continue targeting terrorists and supporting a sovereign Afghan government.
> —from President Obama's public statement on Afghanistan policy, June 22, 2011[2]

Good afternoon, everybody. As a candidate for President, I pledged to bring the war in Iraq to a responsible end—for the sake of our national security and to strengthen American leadership around the world. After taking office, I announced a new strategy that would end our combat mission in Iraq and remove all of our troops by the end of 2011.

As Commander-in-Chief, ensuring the success of this strategy has been one of my highest national security priorities. Last year, I announced the end to our combat mission in Iraq. And to date, we've removed more than 100,000 troops. Iraqis have taken full responsibility for their country's security.

A few hours ago I spoke with Iraqi Prime Minister Maliki. I reaffirmed that the United States keeps its commitments. He spoke of the determination of the Iraqi people to forge their own future. We are in full agreement about how to move forward.

So today, I can report that, as promised, the rest of our troops in Iraq will come home by the end of the year. After nearly nine years, America's war in Iraq will be over.

Over the next two months, our troops in Iraq—tens of thousands of them—will pack up their gear and board convoys for the journey home. The last American soldier[s] will cross the border out of Iraq with their heads held high, proud of their success, and knowing that the American people stand united in our support for our troops. That is how America's military efforts in Iraq will end.

But even as we mark this important milestone, we're also moving into a new phase in the relationship between the United States and Iraq. As of January 1, and in keeping with our Strategic Framework Agreement with Iraq, it will be a normal relationship between sovereign nations, an equal partnership based on mutual interests and mutual respect.

In today's conversation, Prime Minister Maliki and I agreed that a meeting of the Higher Coordinating Committee of the Strategic Framework Agreement will convene in the coming weeks. And I invited the Prime Minister to come to the White House in December, as we plan for all the important work that we have to do together. This will be a strong and enduring partnership. With our diplomats and civilian advisors in the lead, we'll help Iraqis strengthen institutions that are just, representative and accountable. We'll build new ties of trade and of commerce, culture and education that unleash the potential of the Iraqi people. We'll partner with an Iraq that contributes to regional security and peace, just as we insist that other nations respect Iraq's sovereignty.

As I told Prime Minister Maliki, we will continue discussions on how we might help Iraq train and equip its forces—again, just as we offer training and assistance to countries around the world. After all, there will be some difficult days ahead for Iraq, and the United States will continue to have an interest in an Iraq that is stable, secure and self-reliant. Just as Iraqis have persevered through war, I'm confident that they can build a future worthy of their history as a cradle of civilization.

Here at home, the coming months will be another season of homecomings. Across America, our servicemen and women will be reunited with their families. Today, I can say that our troops in Iraq will definitely be home for the holidays.

This December will be a time to reflect on all that we've been though in this war. I'll join the American people in paying tribute to the more than 1 million Americans who have served in Iraq. We'll honor our many wounded warriors and the nearly 4,500 American patriots—and their Iraqi and coalition partners—who gave their lives to this effort.

And finally, I would note that the end of war in Iraq reflects a larger transition. The tide of war is receding. The drawdown in Iraq allowed us to refocus our fight against al Qaeda and achieve major victories against its leadership—including Osama bin Laden. Now, even as we remove our last troops from Iraq, we're beginning to bring our troops home from Afghanistan, where we've begun a transition to Afghan security and leadership. When I took office, roughly 180,000 troops were deployed in both these wars. And by the end of this year that number will be cut in half, and make no mistake: it will continue to go down.

Meanwhile, yesterday marked the definitive end of the

Qaddafi regime in Libya. And there, too, our military played a critical role in shaping a situation on the ground in which the Libyan people can build their own future. Today, NATO is working to bring this successful mission to a close.

So to sum up, the United States is moving forward from a position of strength. The long war in Iraq will come to an end by the end of this year. The transition in Afghanistan is moving forward, and our troops are finally coming home. As they do, fewer deployments and more time training will help keep our military the very best in the world. And as we welcome home our newest veterans, we'll never stop working to give them and their families the care, the benefits and the opportunities that they have earned.

This includes enlisting our veterans in the greatest challenge that we now face as a nation—creating opportunity and jobs in this country. Because after a decade of war, the nation that we need to build—and the nation that we will build—is our own; an America that sees its economic strength restored just as we've restored our leadership around the globe.

> —President Obama announcing America's withdrawal
> from Iraq, October 21, 2011, ten years and
> forty days after 9/11[3]

In July 1967 Great Britain announced it would be withdrawing from every military base "East of Suez" over a period of years. That schedule for withdrawal accelerated, as did British national decline, until Margaret Thatcher came to power. She ushered in the United Kingdom's return to a more muscular and confident role in the world.

President Obama's decision to abandon Iraq—the October 21, 2011, announcement of which is reprinted above—was at least as stunning as Great Britain's in 1967, for the United States is not a second-tier world power trimming its reach to match its resources but the only global superpower, with responsibilities to maintain global security as best as it can, with a special obligation to at least quarantine the most belligerent of sinister nations.

Although President Obama and his advisers attempted to spin the collapse of the Status of Forces negotiations with Iraq as simply the execution of presidential policy, too much information was already on the public record for even the president's staunch allies in the MSM to swallow the wholly unpersuasive "up is down" and "left is right" rhetoric. For months the debate had raged within the Obama administration over the minimum number of troops the United States would have to maintain in Iraq in 2012 and future years to preserve Iraqi security and deter Iranian adventurism. The very low end of that scale was 3,000 troops, and the higher estimate was at least as high as 20,000.[4] This range did not reflect the input of the cadre of Iraq specialists who helped craft and implement the successful surge strategy that brought order and peace out of chaos in 2007.

"Many Iraqis—especially ethnic Kurds, secular intellectuals and Sunnis skittish about Shiite power—have expressed anxiety about what the country might become without an American military presence," reported the *New York Times* on the Sunday after the president's decision.[5] Indeed. What are Tehran's mullahs to conclude except that the door is open wide and their opportunity to fuse Iraq with Syria and Hezbollah in a united front of extremism has arrived? For if the United States won't even commit a force of a few thousands to help preserve what has been won at such extraordinary cost in lives and treasure, why should Iran be worried that the same country will dare to oppose any push against Israel or the Sunni states?

The president and his spin doctors in and outside of the government appear poised to try and cover a global retreat through the repetition of the names bin Laden, Awlaki, and Qaddafi—as though necessary victories in a series of battles somehow make up inevitable triumph in a war.

Governor Romney will have to challenge this absurd argument—that the United States can safely withdraw from the world and leave it to its own devices, except for occasionally patrolling some of the skies on some of the days with some of the drones at our command. The president's bland assurance that the "tide of war is receding" is a dangerous illusion and one that will lead to wars far greater in fury and cost than those of the last decade—as weakness in the face of aggressive outlaw states always does.

The president may have resigned himself to defeat next November and thus to a course of actions he deems legacy builders, but global retreat and the consequences of that retreat will be an indictment, not a legacy.

"President Obama's astonishing failure to secure an orderly transition in Iraq has unnecessarily put at risk the victories that were won through the blood and sacrifice of thousands of American men and women," Mitt Romney declared on the day of the president's announcement. "The unavoidable question is whether this decision is the result of naked political calculation or simply sheer ineptitude in negotiations with the Iraqi government.[6]

"The American people deserve to hear the recommendations that were made by our military commanders in Iraq," Romney added, in what was clearly an invitation to House Republicans generally and House Armed Services Chairman Buck McKeon specifically to hold hearings about this fiasco.[7]

Texas governor Rick Perry also blasted the decision, saying that the move was "bad public policy" and "bad tactics" that could endanger the men and women serving in Iraq today.[8]

These responses from candidates for the GOP nomination early in the process were reassuring in that they point to a Republican platform and campaign that will remain committed to America's exceptional role in the world—and especially to confronting Iran—but the president's increasing pace of retreat demands that Governor Romney focus on foreign policy and a critique of the president's policies and competence.

This is not only a debate worth having, but also one that must be won if the United States is going to avoid the spiral of ruin that gripped Great Britain after World War II. It is hard to anticipate how a new president can salvage this blunder, but that is what the Republican nominee must address because Iran will not waste any time in deciding how to capitalize on this unprecedented display of American fatigue and defeatism.

While there is reason for fatigue in our efforts in the Middle East, there is not sufficient reason for defeat:

> 4,479 U.S. troops had been killed in the war, as of this writing.
> 32,213 had been wounded.
> The war had cost the United States $806 billion.[9]

Another piece reacting to the president's announcement warned of the likely response within Iran. "Certainly tonight [Iran's] Supreme Leader Khamenei will dance a jig of celebration," commented Michael Rubin of the American Enterprise Institute (AEI), one of the nation's leading Iran watchers.[10]

Another of those watchers, and another AEI scholar, is Fred Kagan, who was one of the key architects of the surge that saved Iraq in 2007. I interviewed him on air the day of the president's announcement, and I reproduce the entire interview below to note that recognition of the president's strategic blunder was instantaneous and wide-ranging:

> HH: I turned on the television in the hotel, and saw the president of the United States announcing we were leaving Iraq. And even Fareed Zakaria had to say this is not a good thing. But to talk about, we were able to grab Fred Kagan, who is the resident scholar and director of the AEI, American Enterprise Institute, Critical Threats Project. And perhaps more than any other civilian, had to do with the architecture of the surge. Fred Kagan, welcome back to the *Hugh Hewitt Show*.
>
> FK: Thanks, Hugh.
>
> HH: What is your reaction to today's announcement?

FK: Well, I'm not surprised, because we've seen this building for some time that they were headed in this direction. And the administration has clearly not been serious about establishing a long-term relationship with Iraq from the outset. But it is incredibly disappointing, nevertheless. And honestly, I think it's really a humiliating day for American foreign policy, and will have done tremendous damage to our position in the world, not only because of the fact itself, but also because of the entire way that it's been presented.

HH: Fred Kagan, I want to start with the fact we recognize 4,400 Americans lost their lives in the campaign to liberate Iraq, and an enormous amount of treasure. And this is coming a week after Iran attempted, or at least we learned that Iran was attempting to blow up the Saudi Arabian ambassador. How does this move affect the Islamic Republic of Iran?

FK: This move is exactly what the Islamic Republic of Iran has been trying to accomplish for years. And in fact, what we have seen in recent months has been an escalation in the activities of Iranian-backed militias and Iranian proxies within Iraq, including a campaign of targeted assassinations against Iraqi officials, that had the precise purpose of pressuring Iraqi leaders not to make an agreement with us to extend the presence of our forces. So what we have just done is to give the most extreme elements within the Iranian leadership and Iranian military exactly what they have been pursuing. So in that sense, this is a great day for Iran.

HH: Does it threaten the peace in Iraq by threatening the Sunni tribes of Anbar, and of course, their Saudi-Arabian backers?

FK: The retreat of American forces from Iraq puts Iraqi stability at tremendous risk from many perspectives. We have already seen tremendous strains growing between the Sunni and Shia groups within Iraq, and that had to do in large part with the way that the formation of the government proceeded after the election in 2010, and the way that the Obama administration chose to play no meaningful role in attempting to broker an agreement, the formation of that government, that would be acceptable. But we're also seeing a rise in concern among the Kurds about tensions in the south, their own tensions with the Arabs. And questions will surely arise about the desirability of pushing again for some kind of Kurdish secession or independent Kurdistan. In other words, I think there's a real possibility that this decision can accelerate the descent of Iraq back into the kind of chaos from which it emerged.

HH: Fred Kagan, I'm talking with Fred Kagan, who is the resident scholar and director of the AEI Critical Threats Project. Anyone who read George Bush's *Decision Points*, or any of the memoirs of the war, knows that Fred Kagan was central to the crafting of the success there. And we're now analyzing what is an American retreat every bit as sinister, I think, as some of the retreats that took place in the face of rising German power in the thirties. And Fred, is that alarmist?

FK: Well, I think there's a larger pattern here of American retreatism and declinism, if you will, and a desire to turn inward in the United States and being led now, very actively, by the President. And that's extremely distressing, because the world is becoming a steadily more dangerous place. I think that it's very clear that the Iranians are moving rapidly forward toward being able to field a nuclear weapon. We've just revealed this indication of an Iranian determination to conduct attacks directly on the American homeland. But in addition to that, we have a growing threat of al Qaeda organizations in Yemen, a civil war in Somalia that's now involving other regional states, Pakistan, every part of which is a sort of a disaster that is terrifying in one way or another. A lot of very bad things going on, and a lot of things that are threats to the United States, one way or another. And if at this time in history, worried by our own internal economic concerns, we turn inward, then yes, we run a real risk of repeating the mistakes of France, Great Britain, and the United States in the end-of-war period, and turning inward just at the moment when we most need to pay attention to threats emerging elsewhere.

HH: All right, in terms of CentCom and your many contacts, I'm sure everyone will salute the Commander in Chief, and there will be no formal criticism of the decision. But what was the hoped-for result within the military as you understand it, Fred, vis-à-vis our long-term relationship with Iraq?

FK: Well, I have no direct insights into that, but I know what has been reported in the media is that General Austin, after having conducted a number of studies of this, had concluded that we needed 14,000, actually, I think he initially concluded we needed more than 20,000 troops to achieve the conditions that President Obama had articulated in his February 2009 speech announcing the strategy that included a stable, self-reliant Iraq, with...a sovereign, stable, self-reliant Iraq with a certain form of government. And he, General Austin, had, according to media reports, concluded that we needed upwards of 20,000 troops to accomplish that. I think that's right. But this goes beyond a question of generalship, because this, what the President has just announced is a fundamental change in American policy...

HH: Yes.

FK: ...in the region. And this is the thing, it's a little bit alarming that he's not even had the honesty to do that explicitly, but instead, both in his speech and in the press conference that followed by Dennis McDonough, there is an attempt to portray this decision to retreat under fire as the objective all along, that this is all that we were ever trying to do, and that this was always the strategy from the outset. And that's even more worrisome, because in fact, what the President has done is to announce the Obama doctrine. And the Obama doctrine is American retreat.

At the conclusion of our conversation, I asked Kagan to explain what our other enemies, specifically the Taliban, must have been thinking as this announcement of retreat from Iraq was made by the president:

HH: And last question, with a minute left, what did the Taliban conclude from this, Fred Kagan?

FK: I think all of our enemies will conclude from this that pressure [is] on us, and waiting us out is the way to go. And that's been the message for a long time, and it's something that we started to reverse with President Bush's decision to fight for success in Iraq, and honestly continued with President Obama's decision initially to reinforce in Afghanistan. But now, we will reinforce the narrative that we will ultimately leave. It will embolden our enemies.

Kagan's grim assessment was echoed in the *Wall Street Journal*'s lead editorial the day after the president's speech. I'm quoting all of these assessments to illustrate how precipitous the president's decision was—how wildly reckless, how hurried and so absolutely and stunningly deceptive in its rhetoric. The *Journal*'s editorial began:

Visiting the 101st Airborne Division in Mosul in 2003, we remember a brigade commander who explained his mission this way: He was fighting in Iraq so his son or grandson didn't have to do the same. The colonel, who is perhaps now a general, can't be reassured by President Obama's announcement yesterday.... The U.S. commander in Iraq, General Lloyd Austin, had requested between 15,000 and 18,000 troops, before reducing it to 10,000 under pressure. Such a U.S. presence would reassure Iraq and its neighbors of our continuing commitment to the region. It would help play the role of honest broker among Iraq's ethnic factions as it continues to build a more durable political system.

And above all it would reduce Iran's ability to meddle in Iraq, building local militias on the Hezbollah model with a goal of making its neighbor a Shiite vassal state. Iran's Quds force—the same outfit that wanted to assassinate a Saudi ambassador on U.S. soil—is the biggest winner from Mr. Obama's pullout.[11]

This clear-eyed editorial also noted Mr. Obama's intentions vis-à-vis Afghanistan, where the president has been steadily withdrawing the soldiers he sent on his mini-surge. "And make no mistake," the *Journal* quoted the president as reminding everyone. "It will continue down."[12]

"Let's hope," the *Journal*'s editorial board concluded, "that America's risky decision to leave Iraq behind in its dangerous neighborhood won't require that colonel's son to return to put down a security threat we could have prevented if we stayed longer to consolidate the peace."[13]

The great concern is not only whether we will have to return, but also whether we'll have to fight a much more disciplined and well-equipped enemy than Saddam's Republican Guard, and an enemy that is not willing to wait upon the sort of enormous build-up staged before the first and second Iraq invasions. What was won will be given back, and will have to be retaken a third time if the United States doesn't move quickly to resurrect the relationship and partnership with Iraq—an option not open to this president who sees wisdom in a global retreat even if his secretary of defense and his generals do not.

In Afghanistan the Taliban and the second generation of al

Qaeda must know that this president will soon order American troops to leave as well, even though this was the "good war" for the left. So must the radical Islamists who want to control Pakistan and its nuclear arsenal—they will not be content with just the remote and desolate border areas of the country. It is all one war, and President Obama is retreating from every front line, withdrawing as the British did in 1967—a very different era when the threats wouldn't follow you home.

President Obama promised "no safe haven" in Afghanistan, but that is what will certainly develop there as we accelerate the drawdown of our forces.

"An Iraq that is secure, stable, and self-reliant" is what the president promised on October 21, but of course he might as well have promised a unicorn with pink wings for every child in Baghdad.

This president is forfeiting victories he did not win in the service of, at best, a defeatist view of American power and, at worst, a malignant one that views America's necessary projection of force as imperialism.

America has been defeated on the battlefield before.

But President Obama is the first commander in chief to count the sacrifice of American lives so cheap as to give to our enemies the ground that our soldiers, sailors, airmen, and Marines have won at such great cost.

It is a shameful act, and he deserves defeat on this point alone, and an explicit repudiation by nonactive duty members of the American military—those who, with their brave allies, liberated Iraq from one of history's most brutal psychopaths only to see it left as bait for one of history's most fanatical theocracies.

Chapter 16
Ignoring the Border

Now, I strongly believe that we should take on, once and for all, the issue of illegal immigration. I am prepared to work with Republicans and Democrats to protect our borders, enforce our laws, and address the millions of undocumented workers who are now living in the shadows. I know that debate will be difficult and take time. But tonight, let's agree to make that effort. And let's stop expelling talented, responsible young people who can staff our research labs, start new businesses, and further enrich this nation.
—from President Obama's 2011 State of the Union address[1]

As a candidate, Obama wasn't quick to state his focus-group-tested position on the issues related to immigration, such as amnesty, the border fence, and cross-border violence.

"There are legitimate concerns on both sides of the debate," the president has said. "I have met countless Americans who are worried about the constant flow of illegal immigrants not because they are racists or xenophobes, but because they fear that this influx of low-skill workers threatens to depress wages that are already too low. They also rightfully expect their government to control our borders."[2]

During the campaign, Obama stated his support of measures to increase employers' accountability on hiring illegal workers: "I also think that we've got to be serious about employers' obligations to check to see whether somebody is here legally or not. Up until this point, we haven't had an employment verification system that was tamper-proof. As a consequence, employers have been getting off the hook when they hire undocumented workers. And typically, it's the undocumented workers that get arrested and punished when there are raids, but the employers themselves are frequently let off the hook."[3]

He even indicated support for some policies related to the border fence:

> I think that the key is to consult with local communities, whether it's on the commercial interests or the environmental stakes of creating any kind of barrier...As Senator Clinton indicated, there may be areas where it makes sense to have some fencing. But for the most part, having the border patrolled, surveillance, deploying effective technology, that's going to be the better approach.[4]

Despite these promises and despite the high-profile status of immigration discussions during the 2008 presidential election cycle and despite Obama's explicit commitments on border security, the border remains wildly unsecure, and the president's actions have focused on the social issues related to immigration policy and downplayed the security concerns the border represents.

Contrary to blanket assertions from the left, violence around the United States' southern border, and particularly in Arizona, is becoming more prevalent.

The Government Accountability Office (GAO) released a report in March 2011 assessing the success of the Department of Homeland Security's (DHS) efforts to secure the border.

It states that "deployment of imaging technology to detect stowaways or cargo," "increased staffing," and "border fencing... between the ports of entry...have resulted in some success in reducing the volume of illegal migration and increasing drug seizures." However, it continued:

weaknesses in POE [port of entry] traveler inspection procedures and infrastructure increased the potential that dangerous people and illegal goods could enter the country; and that currency and firearms could leave the country and finance drug trafficking organizations and sponsors of terrorism. [U.S. Customs and Border Protection] used a performance measure to reflect results of its overall border enforcement efforts, which showed few land border miles where they have the capability to deter or apprehend illegal activity at the immediate border.[5]

That's government-speak for "We don't control our border."

Although some improvements are slowly being implemented, the United States' border with Mexico has developed into a substantial national security risk.

Despite the forceful efforts of the Mexican government to uproot them, Mexican drug cartels are growing, absorbing every illegal but lucrative industry south of the U.S. border. They have become so powerful in recent years that they are beginning to threaten the stability and security of the Mexican government itself even as they have unleashed a horrific bloodbath on the people of Mexico.

The *Los Angeles Times* reported in 2010 that "nearly four years after President Felipe Calderon launched a military-led crackdown against drug traffickers, the cartels are smuggling more narcotics into the United States, amassing bigger fortunes and extending their dominion at home with such savagery that swaths of Mexico are now in effect without authority.

"The groups also are expanding their ambitions far beyond the drug trade, transforming themselves into broad criminal empires deeply involved in migrant smuggling, extortion, kidnapping and trafficking in contraband such as pirated DVDs," the story by Tracy Wilkinson and Ken Ellingwood continued. The lengthy report deserves to be read in full, but focus on this paragraph—it's really all you need to know:

"Since Calderon announced the offensive when he took office in December 2006, more than 28,000 people have been killed. Most of them have been traffickers, dealers and associates. But innocent civilians account for a growing portion."[6]

As alarming as reports like these are, the increasingly[7] documented[8] involvement[9] of Hezbollah in the Mexican drug cartels makes the mere threat of an increasingly lawless Mexico seem tame.

My colleague at Townhall.com, Katie Pavlich, provided a great summary of what Hezbollah on the southern border means.

"Hezbollah was created by Iran and has close ties to Syria," Pavlich wrote in 2011. "The group is also backed by Venezuelan Dictator Hugo Chavez, who has a cozy relationship with Iran.

"Intelligence shows the group started pushing its terrorism initiative into South America a decade ago but upped its efforts in 2005," she continued.

"Testimony shows Hezbollah is strategically positioning itself in order to possibly launch a response to an Iranian attack either from the U.S. or Israel on their nuclear program," Pavlich added. "Intelligence cited during the hearing also shows the group is interested in obtaining weapons of mass destruction.

"Hezbollah has also been supplying explosives training to Mexican drug cartels operating along the U.S.-Mexico border, and tunnels used in the area are near replicas of weapons-smuggling tunnels built by Hezbollah and used in Lebanon," she concluded. "Since 2006, violence in Mexico has rapidly escalated and cartels have become more ruthless. In addition, Mexican cartels are serving as a source of financing and easy entrance for the organization into the United States."[10]

The Obama administration's announcement that a joint Mexican cartel–Iranian terror plot has already been foiled adds substance to worries about these reports and urgency to policies and plans to address associated threats.[11]

That announcement was a rare bit of candor from Team Obama. When the president talks about the border, everything is just fine.

In May 2011 Obama traveled to El Paso, Texas, and gave a memorable speech about immigration reform, in which he detailed his alleged victories on the border beginning with his claim that "the Border Patrol has 20,000 agents—more than twice as many as there were in 2004. It's a buildup that began under President Bush and that we've continued.

"Then we've gone further," the president added, in fact going further and further into fantasy:

> We tripled the number of intelligence analysts working at the border. I've deployed unmanned aerial vehicles to patrol the skies from Texas to California. We have forged a partnership with Mexico to fight the transnational criminal organizations that have affected both of our countries...for the first time we're screening 100 percent of southbound rail shipments to seize guns and money going south even as we go after drugs that are coming north.... We have done above and beyond what was requested by the very Republicans who said they supported broader reform as long as we got serious about enforcement.

All of this was a windup to the president's purpose, which was to politicize the national security issue and trivialize it at the same time.

"I suspect there are still going to be some who are trying to move the goal posts on us one more time," the president said, in his classic combination of self-pity and bad humor. He continued:

"You know, they said we needed to triple the Border Patrol. Or now they're going to say we need to quadruple the Border

Patrol. Or they'll want a higher fence. Maybe they'll need a moat. Maybe they want alligators in the moat. They'll never be satisfied. And I understand that. That's politics."[12]

It's clear that Obama wanted this moment specifically to create tape for his coming campaign and to define the issue for his supporters. He was framing the campaign, not securing the border.

But given the seriousness of the threat posed by active cooperation between Mexican drug cartels and Hezbollah on a porous national border, it was very surprising that he chose to make a point about politics rather than national security or the benefits of a strong border. Had he simply been candid about the spiraling threat and our inability to keep up with it, he would have gained some credibility on the issue.

But talk of "goalposts moving" on issues of national security is utterly irresponsible. The president's domestic critics aren't moving the goalposts. Our enemies are moving not goalposts, but terrorists, drugs, and weapons.

It is also obvious that even the president's weak rhetoric is unwarranted: The *Washington Post* noted that Obama and his administration, rather than continuing to hire lots of Border Patrol agents, slowed the Bush-initiated surge to a trickle in its first year, while claiming responsibility for the heightened border security brought about by those newly hired agents.[13]

Whatever improvements may or may not have occurred during Obama's tenure, immigration legislation and enforcement efforts are failing.[14] States have tried to act to protect their people, and the president and his team have moved—against the states.

Clark S. Judge, the managing director of the White House Writers Group and a weekly contributor at HughHewitt.com, noted that "among the advantages of a federal system is that if one level of government abdicates its responsibilities, another can step in (within limits) to fill the space."[15]

This is what Arizona attempted to do with its Support Our Law Enforcement and Safe Neighborhoods Act, more commonly known as SB 1070.

I had Arizona governor Jan Brewer on my show in November 2011, and we discussed SB 1070 and the national reaction to it:

JB: Well, what it does is it enforces existing federal immigration law. And it says that it's illegal to be here in Arizona without documentation. It does not require police to inquire, only when practicable, that they are guilty, or under reasonable suspicion of another offense, to be requested, to request of them identification. And racial profiling is expressly, expressly prohibited under Senate Bill 1070. And I signed an executive order on top of Senate Bill 1070 requiring training of peace officers, specifically forbidding racial profiling. And I will tell you, Hugh, that when I watched and followed and impacted this bill as it went through the legislature, I had three criteria. And it was that it had to work, it had to be Constitutional, and it had to protect civil rights.

HH: Now in the aftermath of this controversy, you got hammered. Cardinal Roger Mahoney said, he wrote, I can't imagine Arizonans now are reverting to German Nazi and Russian Communist techniques, whereby people are required to turn one another in to the authorities, only on the suspicion of documentation, to which you wrote, are you kidding me, I thought. There was no provision in the bill for anything like that. And that was just the tip of the rhetorically absurd nightmare.

JB: Exactly. He...it was just pouring gas on the flames, you know, and always playing the Hitler card. And then from there, it just kept moving. It was just hysterical name calling, and certainly, followed up by the liberal left media, and they just continued to make cheap accusations to shut the debate down. And you know, I didn't back down. I just simply wasn't going to stop. And they just continued to be hateful, and I just continued to fight [for] Arizona and for America. And I'm not going to back down.

HH: After that explosion of wrath, there was, of course, the terrible tragedy in Tucson—Judge Roll and the other victims, the shooting of Congresswoman Giffords, who's a friend of yours.... And you thought, explain what the Tucson truce was, and what you thought had happened in terms of the political debate in and outside of Arizona?

JB: Well, actually, you know, it was such a horrible, horrible tragedy. And we thought that possibly, that civility would take place. The unfortunate thing about it, that civility was called out by the President, mind you, and then it just turned completely ugly again. We had a sheriff down there that just was a craven opportunist, that just took every opportunity that he could to name call, to make accusations, going after everybody for everything. I mean, Loughner was a madman. I mean, it had nothing to do with politics. I mean, he was a crazed madman. And they just turned it all around to Senate Bill 1070, holding everybody responsible, all the way to Sarah Palin. It's just unbelievable.

HH: Sheriff Dubnik, you detail his intervention in this, his appearance with Keith Olbermann, and his wildly inaccurate and terribly divisive comments, which of course were ultimately repudiated by everyone except the hard left.

JB: Absolutely. Absolutely. And you know, Hugh, these are the inside stories, the real story, the truth-telling stories that are never, ever reported. No one ever gets to hear that side of the story.

HH: I also like that you go inside the debate over the border, and that you detail going to the White House, the conversations you had, how you thought the so-called Tucson truce would evolve, in not into an agreement on how the border would be controlled, and to how we would talk about it. But then the President goes to El Paso, Texas, and he gives a speech in which he says this.

The President: *But even though we've answered these concerns, I've got to say, I suspect there are still going to be some who are trying to move the goal posts on us one more time. You know, they said we needed to triple the border patrol. Well now, they're going to say we need to quadruple the border patrol, or they'll want a higher fence. Maybe they'll need a moat. Maybe they'll want alligators in the moat. They'll never be satisfied. And I understand that. That's politics.*

HH: Governor Jan Brewer, on page 216 of *Scorpions for Breakfast*, you write, "Moats, alligators, politics? With these calculated remarks, Obama was dismissing our concerns as essentially groundless, more political grandstanding. He was making clear that in his view, the entire controversy about the border had been ginned up to polarize the electorate and win votes from Republicans. If anything, this was a case of classic Freudian projection, since that's precisely what he and his allies in the Congress and the press have been doing, even cynically exploiting the shootings in Tucson. Was this what Obama considered a constructive and civil debate? I'd hate to see him when he decides to be uncivil, I thought." Tough, tough, straight talk, Governor Brewer.

JB: Well, I was so disappointed, shocked and angry sitting at my desk in my office when he was on television making those statements, I could hardly believe my eyes. And I called it the way I heard it. And I am just, when I just heard that again, I cannot tell you the feeling that goes through my body.

HH: In terms of his reaction to Fast & Furious, do you think he's as cynical and manipulative about that as he has been about the border fence?

JB: You know, yes. *(laughing)* You know, I could say a lot of things, but yes, I do. And I believe that as we sit here in Arizona, trying to fight the battle, and have your federal government at the same time moving [guns] across our border, to have them come back into Arizona and to kill a very dedicated rancher whom everybody loved and adored, including immigrants, with one of those guns, and then a very noble, proud border patrol agent, Brian Terry, is just crushing. And you know, our federal government is supposed to be protecting us, and here they are, arming cartels in Mexico, to bring violence into America, is just unbelievable to me. And I truly believe that someone needs to be held accountable quickly.[16]

I quote this interview at length because it says it all, and all that is said is said by a governor of a border state, one who knows firsthand the president's epic incompetence on the issue, his indifference to the costs on the ground, and his disregard of anyone with an "R" behind their name.

President Obama has thoroughly abandoned his pledges about border security, and the clock is ticking. The incredible hit movie about SEALs, *Act of Valor*, debuted on Presidents' Day Weekend in 2012, and the plotline concerned an attempt to traffic Islamist terrorists across the U.S.-Mexican border with the help of Mexican cartels. The SEALs and Mexican special forces triumph in the film, and all the various agencies of the government have stopped such missions to date—as far as we know—but President Obama's fecklessness on border security has made us more vulnerable to such attempts and is a key reason he has to go back to Chicago in January 2013.

Chapter 17

Bowing to China

But, I remain convinced that a successful China can make our country more prosperous, not less.
—Vice President Biden, after his visit to China in 2011[1]

That's why the United States welcomes China's efforts in playing a greater role on the world stage—a role in which a growing economy is joined by growing responsibilities. And that's why President Hu and I talked about continuing to build a positive, cooperative, and comprehensive relationship between our nations.
—President Obama, in a press statement from China, 2009[2]

The Drudge Report often captures in a word, a phrase, or a picture what all the other news organizations cannot articulate. On April 12, 2010, the estimable Mr. Drudge ran a photo of President Obama bowing to the president of the People's Republic of China, Hu Jintao, at the Nuclear Security Summit being held in Washington, D.C., and captioned it "Obama Bows to Communist Leader."[3]

The left-wing agitprop site Media Matters then provided a handy catalog of reactions to the bow from around the media, and collectively labeled them another expression of "obsession with President Obama's bowing."[4] Previous bows by the American president to Saudi King Abdullah and Japanese Emperor

Akihito had indeed elicited widespread criticism of President Obama for his apparent lack of understanding of diplomatic protocol and/or America's place in the world, but the bow to China was by far the most symbolic of all those waist bends and head bobs, for China intends to be hegemonic and intends for the United States to bow to its designs, at least in the Pacific, and perhaps everywhere.

China will feature prominently in the campaign of 2012, because China is America's chief competitor in the century ahead, and a fierce and able one. To understand what has happened to U.S.-Sino relations during the Obama years, the dangers ahead, and the way forward, I will quote from three interviews I conducted in 2011. The first is with Dr. Henry Kissinger, the second with former U.S. ambassador Jon Huntsman—the former Utah governor who ran unsuccessfully for the GOP nomination but who remains a key voice on the challenges poised by China— and the third with the GOP nominee, former Massachusetts governor Mitt Romney.

This long excerpt is from my interview with Dr. Kissinger conducted on the fortieth anniversary of his secret trip to China in July 1971. The full interview is available on the web, but these are the forward-looking excerpts of a conversation with America's greatest expert on China:

HH: Are you writing [his new book *On China*] for the triumphalists [within the PRC] or the opponents of the triumphalists? Who is its audience in China you most want to read it?

HK: No, there are two slightly different purposes in writing the book. One is to explain how Chinese think about international affairs to non-Chinese. Not to explain the Chinese point of view so much as to explain the way of thinking, the different concepts of time, and the different concepts of deterrence and defense that the Chinese have. Now as far as the Chinese are concerned, what my book might do is to show them how their actions are interpreted by other countries, and therefore, to the extent that they care about what other countries think, to enable them to conduct a policy that leads to cooperation rather than confrontation, if that is the decision they have made.

HH: One of the themes that you document is that China historically has feared encirclement. But now, it looks to many of us who follow it from journalism that they are moving beyond defense to offense with their investments in drones, their cyber attacks, and a variety of very provocative moves. Is this the triumph of the triumphalists, Dr. Kissinger?

HK: Well, you have in China at least two groups—one that you call the triumphalists, and the others that don't have a clear label, whether I would say talk about partnership with the United States. At this moment, the partnership group seems to be the more preeminent one, but the other one is certainly vocal enough. So the big challenge that China has, and that to some extent we have, is this. When you have two major powers that impinge on each other all over the world, as we do, the outcome is very often conflict. But we know that a conflict between two countries of this magnitude is going to have catastrophic consequences. So can the leaders of both sides find a mechanism and a way of working together, and to avoid the catastrophe that happened in Europe, where nations went to war, and I'm talking about World War I, went to war. And if they had known what the world would look like five years later, they would never have done it. Can we avoid that? Can we avoid that outcome?

HH: You know, one of the bright...

HK: There are literally trends in China to worry about.

HH: One of the bracing things, alarming things, is at the end of *On China*, you quote a couple of their current bestsellers, one of which calls the United States an old cucumber painted green, another is PLA senior Colonel Liu Mingfu's

China Dream, that the great goal is to be number one, and that there's a marathon contest, a duel of the century underway with us. And then your essay on the Crowe Memorandum, I finished the book thinking you might be a fatalist about the inevitability of a big conflict.

HK: No, I'm saying if you just study history, if you insist that history repeats itself, then you become fatalistic. But when you think that you have an obligation to create a better world, and to learn from history, then you try to avoid the mistakes that previous generations have made. But one shouldn't kid oneself. If both sides are driven by nationalistic impulses, the tensions are going to get more and more severe, and that is what both sides have to try to avoid. It's not something that we can do unilaterally.

HH: Do you, you made the analogy of the United Kingdom–German relations in the early 20th Century as perhaps informing U.S.–People's Republic of China relations now. But do you also see China acting today as Japan did 90 and 100 years ago, and aggressively pushing out a co-prosperity sort of sphere?

HK: It's not the normal Chinese style. The normal Chinese style is to influence by osmosis rather than by conflict. If they were to behave like Japan, the outcome would be very similar as in the case of Japan. They haven't done that yet, but they have certainly been more assertive, especially in the South China Sea, than makes one comfortable.

HH: Why are they so afraid, Dr. Kissinger, of Christianity in China? Their persecution of the House Church has accelerated quite a lot in recent days and months.

HK: They are not afraid of Christianity as such. They are afraid of any organizational movement or face that asserts an independent control separate from the political structure of the state, because they think this would undermine Chinese cohesion, and because they also have had the experience of, in the 19th Century, where a religious, group of religious fanatics that called themselves Christians with a weird theology, and claimed that Jesus had come back in China, that produced a horrendous civil war. But the major concern is that for thousands of years, China has been dominated by a strong government, and has been suspicious of organized activity that is not subject to its influence.

HH: Now what would your advice be, since the mistreatment of Christians is such a flashpoint in the United States, you've got all these great chapters on how human rights agendas have often complicated the relationships between our country and theirs, what would your advice be to the Chinese hierarchy about how to handle the Evangelical movement in its midst?

HK: Well, let me say first of all, the sentence you read, the human rights agenda, is addressed at just one limited point, namely the use of American governmental sanctions, trying to oblige China to follow our human rights preferences, because that leads to confrontation. And my preference is to make those demarches without a formal challenge. I fully understand the concerns of Evangelicals who express their worries in private organizations, that they may, and produce public expressions of these concerns. That is not only a legitimate, but an important exercise of our democratic principles.

HH: So what would your advice be to the Chinese about accommodating or...

HK: Well, my advice to the Chinese would be to understand that America feels very strongly about certain principles of which respect for religion is an important one, and making their judgments, they should keep in mind that you can't just judge them by the mood of the moment, but by what the long-range perception of their country is in the United States.

HH: I'd like to go back now to Mao, Dr. Kissinger, especially to the chapters early in his reign. Did he make a great strategic error, one for the benefit of the free world, that he did not take Taiwan or assault Taiwan before the beginning of the Korean War?

HK: It probably, in retrospect, in the mind of the Chinese leaders, that is probably an argument that opponents used against him. And the ironical fact is that had he done that, he probably would not have intervened in the Korean War. One of the impulses in his mind obliged him to enter the Korea War was that having failed to liberate, in their terms, Taiwan, to permit a Communist country on its borders to be defeated on top of that would have been a double setback.

HH: You also, an aside here on American leadership, you talk about the Acheson speech in January of 1950, when Dean Acheson did not communicate well American objectives, and you say, "to the extent deterrence requires clarity about a country's intention, Acheson's speech missed the mark." Are we doing that today in failing to communicate around the world what is and what is not of great significance to us?

HK: Well, there are two levels of communicating. One is to make the other side understand how you view a challenge. The other is to draw a precise line, and this issue isn't always the same. Now actually, Acheson in 1950 was absolutely brilliant in his analogies of the situation. And he foresaw that someday, Russia and China would clash. What he failed to do is to make clear that an attack on Korea would be considered by America a threat to our security, partly because we didn't know that our military planning had been to have Korea outside our security zone. And General MacArthur had made a similar set of remarks that Acheson had made, but they made it in an abstract context. So when we faced the reality of Korea being occupied, and therefore Japan being potentially threatened, we were made to choose the strategically correct choice. But we had not communicated it well.

HH: Do you think President Obama, in his messages to the Islamic world, may be communicating a lack of clarity about what does and does not matter to America's national interest?

HK: I think he does not always bring together his idealistic version and his geostrategic necessities, and as something to our geostrategic necessities, which means you're going to defend them. And if you leave lack of clarity about that, you can wind up in a dangerous situation.[5]

A "dangerous situation" is exactly what President Obama has allowed to develop with the PRC, both as to its economic power vis-à-vis the United States and as to its growing military power. In November of 2011, I asked former governor Jon Huntsman, President Obama's first ambassador to the PRC and then a candidate for president, what had gone wrong with the U.S.-PRC relationship:

HH: How has the President's policy towards China worked or not worked in your view?

JH: Well, any relationship with China has to start with the assumption that you have a strong core at home. That's where he's fundamentally failed us on the most monumental of counts. We are weak at home, we have no leverage because our economy is broken. And when you have no leverage at home, you're not respected at the negotiating table in Beijing. So to start the discussion, the fact that we've failed in revitalizing our economy at home means that we are failing in the U.S.-China relationship. Second, I think there has been an inadequate push in terms of the values that really matter in China. I used to do it a lot as ambassador. I know that that probably rubs some people the wrong way. I had to pay a price for it in terms of not being able to get out to provinces I had hoped to visit, because I was sanctioned by the government there, and that is meeting with dissidents. That is going to church services of various kinds, and promoting religious tolerance, and human rights and internet freedom, all of the things that are going to make the U.S.-China relationship stable and successful longer term. Listen, there's enough that divides us already in the U.S.-China relationship. We're merely a transactional relationship, and have been for forty years now. In order for us to make us successful in the years to come, we must infuse a few shared values into a relationship that is only shared interest at this point, and that would be human rights, and that would be religious tolerance, and that would be political reform, and that would be the role of the internet in society, things like that.

HH: Do you believe that we are less respected by China now than when President Obama took office? And if so, why?

JH: We are less respected, I believe, because of where our economy is going. They respect economic might, because with economic might flows our ability to influence events in the world, because we have a strong core. And with a strong core, you're also able to radiate your values of liberty, democracy, human rights and free markets. We're less able to do that today.

HH: Are you concerned about the investment the PRC is making in their navy, specifically their submarine and their anti-ship capabilities, as well as the People's Republic Army?

JH: It's something that we have to watch very, very closely. So if you stop to consider that they're spending about 90 billion bucks a year on their military versus, you know, $650 billion or so that we are spending, inclusive of Afghanistan, and where most of it is going is to their maritime capabilities, which you're absolutely right. The submarine and their missile program is getting a good bulk of it as well. It is so lacking in transparency, in terms of our ability to understand where that money is going, or what it means in terms of systems that they're developing. We've got to know more about it, and we have to have more eyes on their capabilities, their developmental capacity, and what it means to the region specifically when you've got issues like the Spratly and the Paracel [Islands] in the South China Sea that in future years are going to be real hot spots when you've got four or five claimants in the region who take that region very, very seriously. But here's something, Hugh, that people need to remember as well. A very telling statistic about Chinese spending is the fact that they are spending more on domestic security, which is their ministry of state security and the ministry of public security, than they are on their ministry of defense, which tells you simply that they fear their people internally more than they do externally, which should put in perspective where they see their risk coming from.[6]

The day after Jon Huntsman appeared on my program, Mitt Romney did so, and again the subject was China:

HH: Yesterday on this program, Governor Romney, Governor Huntsman told me that China had lost respect for our country in recent years. What do you think of that? And why, if you agree with it, do you think it happened?

MR: Well, he was the ambassador there, so he's going to have to explain how that happened under his watch. I think President Obama has shown a weak hand not just in China, but around the world. And I think tyrants and nations generally respect strength. And they saw President Obama going around the world apologizing for America. They saw him continually cutting our military budget. And the results of these missteps, in my view, and our failure, by the way, to stand up to their theft of our intellectual property, and their hacking into our computers, has led them to conclude that we're a weak nation. And I don't agree with the policies of Barack Obama as they relate to China. I think they were very badly misguided, and I'm not surprised to hear from our ambassador there that China has lost respect for America. And it's something for which President Obama deserves a great deal of the blame.[7]

These three excerpts testify to four key lessons: (1) the People's Republic of China is a dangerous country with a history of sharp, sudden attacks to achieve their geopolitical goals—often made at great cost to themselves; (2) the PRC has lost respect for the United States in recent years; (3) America's "weak hand" at home and abroad contributes to this erosion of respect and thus to the temptation within China's "triumphalist" faction; and (4) these dangers and this erosion will grow worse if the "bowing" president is reelected.

These lessons are not true for just China, but also for its sinister neighbor on the Korean peninsula, the one until recently led by a ruthless and evil dictator, who quite possibly was crazy, and now by his very young son about whom nothing is known except that if the apple didn't fall far from the tree, the world is in deep trouble.

Chapter 18

Ignoring North Korea

On North Korea, our governments have maintained extra-ordinarily close cooperation, and President Lee and I are in full agreement on our common approach going forward. I reaffirmed my commitment to continue working together in the six-party process to achieve a definitive and comprehensive resolution of the nuclear issue. As a part of that effort, we will be sending Ambassador Bosworth to North Korea on December 8th to engage in direct talks with the North Koreans.

Our message is clear: If North Korea is prepared to take concrete and irreversible steps to fulfill its obligations and eliminate its nuclear weapons program, the United States will support economic assistance and help promote its full integration into the community of nations. That opportunity and respect will not come with threats—North Korea must live up to its obligations.

—President Obama speaking about North Korea during his visit to Seoul, South Korea, November 2009[1]

As all the other chapters in this Foreign Policy section of *The Brief against Obama* have demonstrated, our president's lack of real-world experience—evidenced both by his inability to relate to any America besides the political one and by his relatively short and unsubstantial résumé in national government prior to assuming this nation's top office—has had dramatically negative effects on our foreign policy.

Newt Gingrich said as much on my show in November 2011:

> HH: Do you think [Obama] has the capacity to be a successful president, Mr. Speaker?
> NG: I think that he's smart enough to be a successful president. I think he doesn't have the right experiences to be a successful president, unlike Bill Clinton, who had been governor for 12 years, and had negotiated with legislatures. I don't think Barack Obama knows the first thing about negotiating. And I think, frankly, he's a Saul Alinsky radical, and that gives him exactly the wrong answers. So what you have is a very smart guy who has exactly the wrong answers in his head.[2]

Obama's North Korean foreign policy is no exception.

As a candidate, Obama was a critic of the "Six-Party Talks" approach employed by the Bush administration. Indeed, he seemed to want to get down to one-on-one talks with the ruthless leadership of the gangster state.

In a *Meet the Press* interview in 2006, Obama specifically stated that the U.S. hadn't done enough at the negotiating table, and that military solutions to North Korea were not an option.[3]

"The point I would make, though, is that we have not explored all our options," then senator Obama declared, as though a completely inexperienced first-term senator from the Chicago machine would have a clue about the state of the Six-Party Talks. "We have not explored any kind of dialogue with either Iran or North Korea, and I think that has been a mistake," he added. "As a consequence, we have almost no leverage over them."

He made this declaration in a giant foreshadowing of the intellectual hubris and enormous vanity that would drive the key failures of his time as president.[4]

Our fault. Get it? Our fault. Or so the president thought when he was just a candidate for the presidency.

The Six-Party Talks deemed inadequate by Obama are described in the Council on Foreign Relations (CFR) Backgrounder as "aimed at ending North Korea's nuclear program though a negotiating process involving China, the United States, North and South Korea, Japan, and Russia."[5]

CFR's introduction continues, "Since the talks began in August 2003, the negotiations have been bedeviled by diplomatic standoffs among individual Six-Party member states—particular between the United States and North Korea." Shortly after Obama assumed office, "North Korea quit the talks and announced that it would reverse the ongoing disablement process...and restart its Yonbyon nuclear facilities." Since then, "the Obama administration has been pursuing talks with the other four countries in the process to bringing Pyongyang back to the negotiation table."[6]

So the president failed even to maintain much less strengthen the negotiating strategy he touted as inadequate as a candidate. That failure led to predictable behavior on the part of the gangster regime as it took the measure of our weak president and pushed its old strategy of pushing around Democratic presidents.

About the same time that North Korea stepped away from the Six-Party Talks, they tested a Taepo-dong 2 missile—a medium-range missile that violates a U.N. Security Council resolution and could potentially reach Alaska or the U.S. mainland.[7]

When the missile launched, the president responded—by turning to the United Nations.

"We will immediately consult with our allies in the region, including Japan and the Republic of Korea, and members of the U.N. Security Council to bring this matter before the Council," the Nobel laureate declared. " I urge North Korea to abide fully by the resolutions of the U.N. Security Council and to refrain from further provocative actions."[8]

A month later, in May 2009, North Korea detonated its second nuclear test. Obama responded with yet another ringing statement.

"The danger posed by North Korea's threatening activities warrants action by the international community," the president declared. "We have been and will continue working with our allies and partners in the Six-Party Talks as well as other members on the U.N. Security Council in the days ahead."[9]

Why, he must have wondered, weren't these fine fellows on the other side listening to him? He's the fellow who can stop the oceans from rising, after all.

North Korea doesn't seem to share the president's own estimate of his own abilities, and in fact appears to believe he is a cipher, a placeholder, and no threat whatsoever to their most aggressive plans and provocations.

On March 26, 2010, a South Korean warship, the *Cheonan*, exploded and sank in the Yellow Sea, killing forty-six sailors. Subsequent international investigation confirmed that the ship was attacked and sunk by a North Korean torpedo. The incident provoked significant posturing from all related parties, but no immediate military confrontations.[10] After bilateral discussions with South Korean president Lee the following month, Obama articulated the United States' response to the incident: "I expressed to President Lee once again the condolences of all Americans for the tragic *Cheonan* incident, and indicated to him that we are foursquare behind him. He has handled this issue with great judgment and restraint.

"He rightly is insisting on North Korea being held—held to account for its actions in the United [Nations] Security Council," the president continued. "There have to be consequences for such irresponsible behavior on the international stage."[11]

The Security Council did tighten sanctions,[12] and the president began issuing Executive Orders targeting North Korean trading privileges and access to financial resources.[13]

North Korea had already taken this new president's measure,

however. On November 23, 2010, they opened artillery fire on a South Korean island, killing at least two soldiers. The stated provocation: nonlethal South Korean military exercises.[14]

The administration, through the White House's press secretary, released a statement reminiscent of those quoted above: "The United States strongly condemns this attack and calls on North Korea to halt its belligerent action and to fully abide by the terms of the Armistice Agreement. The United States is firmly committed to the defense of our ally, the Republic of Korea, and to the maintenance of regional peace and stability."[15]

This "presidency-by-statement" didn't impact Kim Jong-il in the last years of his demented life, nor have the "new" sanctions impressed his son and the generals that surround him in the dawn of the new "Great Leader's" rule. North Korea continues to pursue its nuclear and missile research, while U.S. officials wander all over the near east trying to persuade the parties to come back to the table and talk.

In an interview on my show, Mitt Romney expressed the concern of many about the current administration's foreign policy:

HH: Governor...in terms of national security as an issue, does it remain resonant with the American people?

MR: Well, there's no question right now everybody is talking about the economy, and we're all concerned about the economy, want to see it get back on track. But national security will emerge from time to time as the leading issue in our nation. And so I believe that despite the fact that it's not on the front burner right now, it will be. And frankly, the failure of the Obama administration to do anything, to suggest concern about Iran announcing that they have mastered all steps necessary to enrich uranium, and the North Koreans launching a long range missile, these absence of actions on the part of the Obama administration are very troubling to people who are concerned about our foreign policy.

HH: Let's take them in order. Obviously North Korea launches a missile on the day that the President's talking about nuclear non-proliferation. It's kind of a sharp stick in the eye. What was wanting in the Obama administration's policy there?

MR: Well, the immediate course should have been to indicate that we're going to sue for very aggressive action. For instance, hold off on providing banking availability to the North Koreans, we're going to consider blockading again as we have in the past, we're going to take actions that severely depress the ability of North Korea to change goods around the world and to participate in the financial system. We've done it before, we can do it again. But instead, we go to the United Nations and ask for another vote of some kind of resolution, which of course North Korea flouts as they have in the past. We in the past have been tough on North Korea. It's time to do it again.[16]

But we don't just need tough—and consistently tough—policies and rhetoric. We need a president of whom the North Koreans are afraid or at least not contemptuous.

Obama's "reset" approach to foreign policy, his soft campaign rhetoric, and his emphasis on talking with tyrants have combined to portray to the world a self-consciously declining America interested more in cutting its losses than insuring its interests.

Military historian and classicist Victor Davis Hanson discussed the effect of presidential rhetoric on international groups on my show in 2009. VDH, as we call him, gave a longish answer, but a crucial one, one which applies not just to how the North Korean gangsters view us, but also to how bad actors the world over watch and react to occupant in the Oval Office.

"There's a question that I'm curious about, and it really

confounds the left's thinking," VDH began. "We only lost from 2003, '04, '05, we were losing 48, 52, 98, 97 people a year, less in a year in Afghanistan than we were in Iraq."

"Suddenly," he continued, "we're spiking up to 150, I think it's 158 this week [in Afghanistan].

"And the question is why, when Iraq is cooling?" he asked. "And I think a lot of it is that the Taliban and al Qaeda thought that they could not win last year, the years before, because of what we were doing in Iraq."

He then explained the consequences of Obama's transparent commitment to retreat and appeasement:

> We were killing a lot of al Qaeda people in a way we couldn't in Afghanistan, because there wasn't a sanctuary nearby. But more importantly, we were committed to staying there. And [in] the last 8 months, the radical Muslim world is seeing the left in America say we're going to get out of Afghanistan, they've seen the timetable in Iraq, they've heard that the Muslim world is not culpable for certain things, they've seen these apologies, they've seen the dismantling of the war on terror, they've seen the CIA officers threatened with investigations. And I think the message to the Taliban and al Qaeda is you know what? We are worn out, we are scattered, we lost in Iraq, we lost tens of thousands, but you know what? They're in worse shape than we are if we just press and escalate. And we've seen that in history when Dean [Acheson] said South Korea's not in the sphere of U.S. influence, North Korea invaded. When [U.S. Ambassador to Iraq] April Glaspie said [in 1990, to Saddam Hussein] "you know what, borders between Kuwait and Iraq are not our concern," Saddam did that. So when you give these signals from the White House, that whether you want to or not, or whether you intended to or not, or from the Democratic Congress that you're tired, we are just as culpable, that Bush did it, that Cheney is

an odious figure, that, those images and implications have consequences."[17]

The consequences of Obama's abundant weakness, fecklessness, indecision, and habits of apology combined with practices of retreat have sent all the wrong messages to the lunatics running North Korea. We have to pray that they don't push the weak president even further before he is replaced in 2013.

Chapter 19

Naivete and the Arab Spring

We must chart a more centered course. Like generations before, we must embrace America's singular role in the course of human events. But we must be as pragmatic as we are passionate; as strategic as we are resolute. When threatened, we must respond with force—but when that force can be targeted, we need not deploy large armies overseas.... Instead, we must rally international action, which we're doing in Libya, where we do not have a single soldier on the ground, but are supporting allies in protecting the Libyan people and giving them the chance to determine their own destiny.

In all that we do, we must remember that what sets America apart is not solely our power—it is the principles upon which our union was founded. We're a nation that brings our enemies to justice while adhering to the rule of law, and respecting the rights of all our citizens. We protect our own freedom and prosperity by extending it to others. We stand not for empire, but for self-determination. That is why we have a stake in the democratic aspirations that are now washing across the Arab world. We will support those revolutions with fidelity to our ideals, with the power of our example, and with an unwavering belief that all human beings deserve to live with freedom and dignity.

—from President Obama's public statement on Afghanistan and Middle East policy, June 22, 2011[1]

High-sounding rhetoric is President Obama's specialty. It appears at the moment it is needed to explain foreign policy failure, and serves to obscure his confusion, especially in matters of rapidly changing circumstances abroad.

Rarely has he been as confused as in the tumultuous year of 2011, and particularly with regard to the series of upheavals in Tunisia, Egypt, Yemen, Bahrain, Syria, and throughout the Middle East. We ought not to have expected resolve on his part because, as we noted earlier, the president fumbled the opportunity to stand with Iran's dissidents when the Green Revolution sprang up there in 2009. His pattern of dithering, established early in his term, has only increased, and while he has developed the ability to wait long enough to declare for the winning side, he has sown great fear about America's vision for the region as well as his personal indifference to the rise of Islamist elements in the popular uprisings.

We need to walk through some of the president's statements interlineated with the events on the ground.[2]

On December 17, 2010, Mohamed Bouazizi set himself on fire in the Tunisian city of Sidi Bouzid after a policeman confiscated the fruit and vegetables he was selling. The next day local protests began and spread "People are angry at the case of Mohamed," the *Guardian* declared, "and the deterioration of unemployment in the region."[3]

On January 7, 2011, riots broke out over food prices and unemployment in Algeria.[4] On the thirteenth, an Algerian man burned himself to death in protest, mimicking the Tunisian protest.[5]

The protests in Tunisia escalated until, on January 14, 2011, Zine al-Abidine Ben Ali, Tunisia's president, submitted to the pressure and fled to Saudi Arabia.[6]

It wasn't until the day that Zine Al-Abidine Ben Ali left office that Obama released an anemic press statement on the events in Tunisia:

I condemn and deplore the use of violence against citizens peacefully voicing their opinion in Tunisia, and I applaud the courage and dignity of the Tunisian people.... I urge all parties to maintain calm and avoid violence, and call on the Tunisian government to respect human rights, and to hold free and fair elections in the near future that reflect the true will and aspirations of the Tunisian people.[7]

On January 16, Muammar Qaddafi appeared on Libyan news to say he was "pained" by the fall of the Tunisian government, and condemned the protests that overturned the government.[8]

On January 17, an Egyptian man set himself on fire outside the parliament building to protest "against poor living standards."[9]

On January 18, Mohamed ElBaradei, an Egyptian law scholar and diplomat, warned that Egypt could follow in Tunisia's footsteps, even as a couple more citizens set themselves on fire and antigovernment activists announced plans for a "day of anger": "I still hope that change will come in an orderly way and not through the Tunisian model," ElBaradei declared. "But if you keep closing the door to peaceful change then don't be surprised if the scenes we saw in Tunisia spread across the region."[10]

On the twenty-third, protests in Yemen increased to include thousands in the capital, Sana'a, calling for the resignation of President Ali Abdullah Saleh.[11]

January 25 dawned on the largest nationwide demonstrations in Egypt in a generation. The protesters called for Mubarak's resignation as the government blocked Twitter and shut down mobile and Internet networks.[12] On the same day protests began in Lebanon—a "day of rage" organized to protest the appointment of Hezbollah-backed Najib Mikati as successor of the country's prime minister.[13]

Three days later protests began in Jordan, demanding governmental reform.[14] Protests continued to grow in Yemen and Egypt.

It wasn't until February 10 that President Obama gave his first "emphatic" statement about the United States' position on the Egyptian protests:

> The Egyptian government must put forward a credible, concrete and unequivocal path toward genuine democracy, and they have not yet seized that opportunity.... Those who have exercised their right to peaceful assembly represent the greatness of the Egyptian people, and are broadly representative of Egyptian society.[15]

The *Guardian* accurately described the way the White House responded to reports of the protests in Egypt throughout January:

> The administration has shifted from solidly supporting [Hosni] Mubarak to suggesting he should go now, only to back him at the weekend to remain in office until the autumn—a decision that secretary of state, Hillary Clinton, reversed hours later when she threw US support behind [Omar] Suleiman."[16]

This indecision is surprising given that the White House was told of potential instability in Egypt as early as mid-December 2010, and was kept up to date by intelligence officers[17]—certainly enough time to craft a foreign policy.

On February 11, Egyptian president Hosni Mubarak resigned and left Egypt. One of the protesters in Tahrir Square summarized the revolution:

> For 18 days we have withstood tear gas, rubber bullets, live ammunition, Molotov cocktails, thugs on horseback, the skepticism and fear of our loved ones, and the worst

sort of ambivalence from an international community that claims to care about democracy. But we held our ground. We did it.[18]

Protests spread over the next few days across the Middle East. Iran's Azadi Square in Tehran saw the largest number of protesters since the 2009 election, despite a government ban and tear gas.[19] Bahrain erupted in protests "asking for political reforms, right of political participation, respect for human rights, stopping of systemic discrimination against Shias."[20] Protesters marched in the capital and other major cities of Yemen again.[21]

Libya erupted in violent protests on February 16.[22] By the eighteenth, the Libyan government was aggressively enforcing a media blackout.

That same day, President Obama was reported to have urged King Hamad bin Isa Al-Khalifa of Bahrain to restrain violence against his citizens. The *Guardian* reported that two days later the Bahrainian military used live rounds against protesters, "with 50 or more said to have been injured and an unknown number killed, as the hospitals in Manama were filled with the wounded."[23] Similar incidents in Libya were reported the same day.[24]

On February 23, the president spoke to the press about the situation in Libya and finally articulated something like a foreign policy:

> The suffering and bloodshed is outrageous and it is unacceptable. So are threats and orders to shoot peaceful protesters and further punish the people of Libya. These actions violate international norms and every standard of common decency. This violence must stop. The United States also strongly supports the universal rights of the Libyan people. That includes the rights of peaceful assembly, free speech, and the ability of the Libyan people to

determine their own destiny. These are human rights. They are not negotiable. They must be respected in every country. And they cannot be denied through violence or suppression.... So let me be clear. The change that is taking place across the region is being driven by the people of the region. This change doesn't represent the work of the United States or any foreign power. It represents the aspirations of people who are seeking a better life.... And throughout this transition, the United States will continue to stand up for freedom, stand up for justice, and stand up for the dignity of all people.[25]

The president, however, did and said little as similar degrees of violence, repression, and human rights concerns became evident in Syria,[26] Yemen,[27] and Bahrain[28] in subsequent months.

That timeline and those excerpts of official statements underscore the hopelessly naive, chaotic, and incompetent approach that President Obama brought with him to the White House.

Why should we have expected anything different? He had almost no exposure to the complexities of the Arab world before he took office, and what exposure he had was decidedly radical, if his friend Rashid Khalidi is any indication of where he got his cues on Middle Eastern politics.

The president had been in the United States Senate for only four years when he won the White House: four years of missed hearings and votes, full-time campaigning, and book writing, little if anything in the form of serious study of complex foreign issues. He had been issued the sorts of briefing books the candidates for the presidency always get, but he was the definition of an armchair statesman,[29] full of opinions on how the world was supposed to work and precious little real experience on how it did work.

So here we are in 2012 with growing Islamist movements thrusting toward formal as well as informal power in Egypt, a surging Hamas and Hezbollah in Gaza and Lebanon, respectively, Yemen on the edge of chaos, and Saudi Arabia a powder keg now sailing toward the rule of a hard-line Wahhabist royal faction. Our most reliable allies in the Arab world—Jordan and Kuwait—are small states that are now no doubt as worried about sudden revolution, and the picture of Libya's future is even less clear than Egypt's. And Iran, of course, rushes to deploy a nuclear weapon along with its long-range missiles.

"We will support those revolutions with fidelity to our ideals," the president assured the world,[30] and then he has stood by as Bashir Assad murdered thousands and perhaps tens of thousands across Syria. The president did support, eventually, the uprising in Egypt, but how can he know what ideals an unknown ruling class there will embrace? Of course he can't, but he can be expected to dress up whatever result arrives as a great victory—for him and his farseeing strategic vision.

The *New Yorker*'s Ryan Lizza wrote the most important article on Obama's foreign policy. It is most famous for its borrowed description of the president's foreign policy: "leading from behind." That description came from Obama's own senior team—an effort to spruce up incoherence, indecision, and a desire to wait to see which way the wind blew before the president declared himself.[31]

I interviewed the estimable Lizza about his piece soon after it appeared:

HH: But what got me about this piece that's communicated so well is that the Secretary of State would tell you, however widely regarded you are as a reporter, Ryan, that the biggest problem in the administration is that they don't have a rule yet articulated. She's telling you this on the record. It confirms for me they really don't know what they're doing, and that the Department of State and the White House are at loggerheads with each other.

RL: Well, I think that they don't have a...look, Obama himself has said this pretty clearly in some of the TV interviews he did after the Libyan intervention. He said that this doesn't mean that there's a new doctrine being laid down about when we do and don't intervene. And you know, there's a school of foreign policy thinking that doctrines are the worst thing for a president, because once you have some doctrine, you are straightjacketed when presented with a new crisis or threat. And you know, I think there's a reluctance by Obama to sort of lay down something that everyone will call a doctrine, because you want to, frankly, as president, you want to have the flexibility to be inconsistent, right? You want to have the flexibility to do something in Libya, and maybe not in Bahrain or Saudi Arabia.

On the one hand, [the article] gets at this sort of split between Hillary and Obama. But it's a split in [the] perceptions of the two of them. In other words, they thought that Obama was on their side. This is a guy...and isn't that what we want? We want the guys in the Muslim Brotherhood to think you know what, the U.S. has a president that in some way I can relate to. I don't see that as a negative. I see that in some ways as a positive....So the Muslim Brotherhood guys and the liberals we want to succeed, were all trying to oust Mubarak together. And so where they agreed was that they thought that President Obama was more on the side of the protestors than on the side of Mubarak. And you know, I think the White House very skillfully maneuvered Obama into that sort of public position, even though behind the scenes, things were a lot more complicated with the whole [Frank] Wisner episode, as you point out.[32]

When dithering gets upgraded to clichés about doctrine, then we are in incompetence's endgame. Not since Jimmy Carter welcomed the return of the Ayatollah Khomeini to Iran and professed surprise at the nature of communism[33]—

his befuddlement that the Soviets would actually invade Afghanistan—has the United States been led by so incoherent a set of nostrums and riddles.

The next president had already been bequeathed a set of problems the equal of those left behind by Carter for President Reagan, and it will take Reaganesque resolve and confidence to tackle and turn the Middle East's tumble toward dictatorship and radical Islam. No outcome is certain, except what would happen if Obama was reelected: in that case the unhindered rise of a new group of governments run by and for the spread of violent jihad against Israel—and perhaps much farther afield— is virtually guaranteed.

Chapter 20

Gitmo and the Trials of Terrorists

On my first day in office, I prohibited—without exception or equivocation—the use of torture by the United States of America. I ordered the prison at Guantanamo Bay closed, and we are doing the hard work of forging a framework to combat extremism within the rule of law. Every nation must know: America will live its values, and we will lead by example.
—from President Obama's remarks to the United Nations,
September 2009[1]

Does this chapter even need writing, or does the title say everything about the hopeless, dangerous naivete of the president and the ideological extremists populating his Department of Justice?

The existence of the Guantanamo Bay detention facility ("Guantanamo" or "Gitmo," for shorthand purposes) for unlawful combatants captured in the war on terror and the future trials and treatment of those captured terrorists were significant issues in the 2008 presidential campaign. Candidates from both parties went on the record to indicate how they would deal with the controversial facility and its detainees.

Both McCain and Obama voiced their intention to close Guantanamo if elected.[2] Obama, however, declared not only that he would close the detainee facility, but that he would

174

"restore habeas corpus" to detainees[3] and give at least some of them them a trial in civilian courts.[4]

He followed through with his stated intentions. Or tried to, in any event. On his second day in office he signed an executive order mandating that Gitmo shut down within a year.[5] Three years later it remains open—and necessary.

The Congress—though completely controlled by Democrats for the president's first two years in office—didn't agree with his preposterous, deeply dangerous promises. In May 2009, the Senate voted 90–6 to block the funding needed to close Gitmo, effectively rendering the Executive Order moot, and making the president a promise breaker on one of his signature pledges.[6]

Obama tried another tactic in November 2009, ordering the Federal Bureau of Prisons to buy a prison in Thompson, Illinois, and move the remaining inmates from Guantanamo to the mainland facility.[7] Congress blocked this attempt as well.[8]

Finally, in a move led by Democrats, Congress eventually blocked all the funds necessary for closing the Guantanamo facility, ensuring its continued operation.[9]

In November 2010, one of the al Qaeda masterminds behind the horror of the 1998 bombings of two American embassies in Africa was acquitted by a New York City jury of more than 280 charges brought against him, and convicted of one. Ahmed Ghailani will spend at least twenty years in prison, we are assured, but he will not be executed despite his horrific crimes. This travesty is at the feet of President Obama and Attorney General Holder, and no matter how they try and spin it, the trial was handicapped by taking it out of the control of a military tribunal and bringing it to the United States, as would every such trial on American soil be handicapped.

In March 2011, Obama, calculating the political cost of more such outrages, reversed his original order—and all the promises made to all his hard-left ACLU lawyer-supporters—and allowed for the military trials at Gitmo to resume, although he indicated that he was still committed to closing the Guantanamo facility when and if he has the opportunity.[10]

Although the consistent opposition of congressional Democrats to their party's leader—the president—on an issue this popular with their base raises questions about the seriousness of the party's rhetoric about Guantanamo, the reasons Obama stated for issuing his initial order are even more curious.

At the time he signed the order he promised it would "return America to the 'moral high ground' in the war on terrorism." He elaborated, "The United States does not have to 'continue with a false choice between our safety and our ideals.'" His executive order, he said, would "restore the standards of due process and the core constitutional values that have made this country great even in the midst of war, even in dealing with terrorism." He also said, "This is me following through...on an understanding that dates back to our founding fathers, that we are willing to observe core standards of conduct not just when it's easy but when it's hard."[11]

Does reversing his order on trials, and do the actions of his allies in Congress mean that the president has abandoned our country's "core standards of conduct"? Or just that the president is a hypocrite who would accuse George W. Bush of such things and then quietly concede they are the necessities of a time of war with a ruthless, unlawful combatant?

President Obama's executive order rhetoric echoed a similar passage from his Inaugural Address:

As for our common defense, we reject as false the choice between our safety and our ideals. Our Founding Fathers, faced with perils we can scarcely imagine, drafted a charter to assure the rule of law and the rights of man, a charter expanded by the blood of generations. Those ideals still light the world, and we will not give them up for expedience's sake. Recall that earlier generations faced down fascism and communism not just with missiles and tanks, but also with sturdy alliances and enduring convictions. They understood that our power alone cannot protect us, nor does it entitle us to do as we please.[12]

So, have you seen the president admit yet that Gitmo was not a morally reprehensible "false choice," but actually the only choice among many hard ones? Of course not.

In early 2010, soon after the underwear bomber penetrated our defenses and got within Detroit's airspace only to have his killing explosives malfunction and his Miranda rights read, I interviewed Victor Davis Hanson on my show, and we discussed Obama's policies with respect to Guantanamo and his understanding of the issues at play:

HH: I want to play for you a segment of [Obama's] remarks today, Professor Hanson, because he talks about Guantanamo Bay as a causative agent for the Christmas attack, and I'll pick up on it after we hear it.

The President: *Some have suggested that the events on Christmas Day should cause us to revisit the decision to close the prison at Guantanamo Bay. So let me be clear. It was always our intent to transfer detainees to other countries only under conditions that provide assurances that our security is being protected. With respect to Yemen in particular, there's an ongoing security situation which we have been confronting for some time along with our Yemeni partner. Given the unsettled situation, I've spoken to the Attorney General, and we've agreed that we will not be transferring additional detainees back to Yemen at this time. But make no mistake. We will close Guantanamo prison, which has damaged our national security interests, and become a tremendous recruiting tool for al Qaeda. In fact, that was an explicit rationale for the formation of al Qaeda in the Arabian Peninsula.*

HH: Now Victor Hanson, this seems to me to be his argument Bush made the Christmas bomber do it, the underpants bomber, because no Gitmo, no bomber. This is absurd, and it's dangerous.

VDH: Yes, I think it's shameful, because we...nobody listens to what the grievances are of an enemy. That's like saying Hitler went into Poland because he had grievances from Versailles. Every aggressor always dreams up rationalizations, but anybody who's sober and judicious doesn't believe them. And if he doesn't think Guantanamo serves a purpose, then he should close it. There's no need to delay. But the very fact that it's been open one year under his administration, shows that it has some utility, otherwise he would have closed it. But he has this very strange, schizophrenic attitude that I'm going to trash Bush on tribunals, Guantanamo, renditions, Predator attacks, when I'm demagoguing as a candidate, but as a president, when I'm responsible for governance, I'm going to keep them open, and keep them useful. And it's not sustainable. It's going to get people very, very angry.

HH: I'm wondering, do you think he understands Wahhabism, Victor Davis Hanson?

VDH: No, I don't think he does. I think that all those issues that we discussed right after 9/11, that it was a rich or well-off, upscale Islamic terrorist profile that was our problem with Khalid Sheikh Mohammed, or bin Laden, or Mohammed Atta, he didn't get at all. He thought it was because of poverty, and then we get Major Hassan, and Mutallab, who just confirm the profile, that it's not because of hunger, or illiteracy or oppression, but it's because of envy and anger and pride. The more one becomes Westernized and has the stark contrast between a successful West and a failed Middle East... it's not Israel, it's not anything that we do. It's who we are. That was established in 2001. And then the seven years of calm has deluded us back into this period of recrimination and self-doubt, and he doesn't get it.

HH: Do you believe that Wahhabists and Salafists across the globe, those who are both in al Qaeda and affiliated with it, and those who are running their own operations, are emboldened by President Obama's rhetorical weakness, or soothed in their anger?

VDH: Oh, I think that they're emboldened, because after all, in 2009, we had more terrorist attempts than any year since 2001. In fact, one third of all attempts since 2001 occurred in 2009. This was a period with the al-Arabia interview, the reach out to Iran, the Cairo speech. And it sends a message that the real problem in America is the Bush-Cheney nexus and their anti-terrorism protocols, rather than radical Islam. That may be unfair, but that's what the enemy is beginning to conclude. And they think that this present administration either isn't up to it, or has no heart in fighting terrorism as in the past seven years.[13]

Our enemies have contempt for the president. Our most dangerous enemies, those with no hesitation about sacrificing their numbers in suicide attacks, must have the most contempt of all.

Gitmo is open, the Predators are flying, and bin Laden and al-Awlaki have been dispatched, but not because this president believes in what the war requires, but because he believes in his own reelection and in doing those things that if not done, would doom his already doomed presidency.

Of course he would order bin Laden killed—who would not?—but to strut about as though it was his courage or his policies that brought it about without ever acknowledging that it was the intelligence garnered from waterboarding that led the SEALs to bin Laden's lair—that is reprehensible, the most obvious evidence of his deep disassociation from the facts of the war, an unreality telegraphed by his pledges to close Gitmo and his staffing of DOJ with left-wing radicals. If President Obama believed in what the war requires—the long war, the one that will decide our fate—he would not have abandoned Iraq or be in the process of abandoning Afghanistan, selling the lie that we are safe because the SEALs and a missile have sent two of our worst enemies to their deaths.

Were he somehow to secure a second term, one can only guess what will happen to our defenses against the terrorists, and the murderers at Gitmo. Congress can do many things, but a president can simply act and defy a Congress to respond. Thus we have left Baghdad and are preparing to leave Kabul.

And thus we would leave Gitmo—without a thought to the consequences but with every consideration given to the president's own bizarre understanding of the world in which we live, the world he has made immeasurably more dangerous in three and a half short years.

III
LEADERSHIP
FAILURES

Chapter 21

The Hyperpartisanship of a Chicago Ward Heeler: Obama Is the Most Destructively Partisan President of the Past 40 Years

On some of these issues we're just going to have ideological differences. I won. So I think on that one, I trump you.
—President Obama, to then House GOP Whip Eric Cantor, at a White House meeting in January 23, 2009, as he rejected Cantor's suggestion for changes to the Stimulus package[1]

One vision has been championed by Republicans in the House of Representatives and embraced by several of their party's presidential candidates. It's a plan that aims to reduce our deficit by $4 trillion over the next ten years, and one that addresses the challenge of Medicare and Medicaid in the years after that. Those are both worthy goals for us to achieve. But the way this plan achieves those goals would lead to a fundamentally different America than the one we've known throughout most of our history.... These aren't the kind of cuts you make when you're trying to get rid of some waste or find extra savings in the budget. These aren't the kind of cuts that Republicans and Democrats on the Fiscal Commission proposed. These are the kind of cuts that tell us we can't *afford the America we believe in. And they paint a vision of our future that's deeply pessimistic.*

The fact is, their vision is less about reducing the deficit than it is about changing the basic social compact in America.... There's nothing serious about a plan that claims to reduce the deficit by spending a trillion dollars on tax cuts for millionaires and billionaires. There's nothing courageous about asking for sacrifice from those who can least afford it and don't have any clout on Capitol Hill. And this is not a vision of the America I know.

—from President Obama's speech about the deficit, while Congressman Paul Ryan, author of the plan denounced by the president, sat before him, on April 13, 2011[2]

Now, I know there's been a lot of skepticism about whether the politics of the moment will allow us to pass this jobs plan—or any jobs plan.... Regardless of the arguments we've had in the past, regardless of the arguments we will have in the future, this plan is the right thing to do right now. You should pass it. And I intend to take that message to every corner of this country. And I ask—I ask every American who agrees to lift your voice: Tell the people who are gathered here tonight that you want action now. Tell Washington that doing nothing is not an option. Remind us that if we act as one nation and one people, we have it within our power to meet this challenge.... These are difficult years for our country. But we are Americans. We are tougher than the times we live in, and we are bigger than our politics have been. So let's meet the moment.

—from President Obama's address introducing his Jobs Bill to a joint session of Congress, September 8, 2011[3]

So you've got their plan and we've got my plan. My plan says we're going to put teachers back into the classroom, construction workers back to work rebuilding America, rebuilding our schools, tax cuts for small businesses, tax cuts for hiring veterans, tax cuts if you give your worker a raise. That's my plan.

And then you've got their plan, which is, let's have dirtier air,
dirtier water, less people with health insurance. So far, at least,
I feel better about my plan.
—President Obama, at a North Carolina rally, October 17, 2011[4]

Presidents are by definition partisan. They run for the office
as nominees of a political party, and every one of them then
tries, with more or less energy, to increase their party's advantages in and outside of the Congress.

Even Ike, the least partisan of all modern presidents, took
his job as the head of the GOP seriously, and continued to work
on behalf of the Republicans even after he left office, even while
he supported John F. Kennedy and Lyndon B. Johnson through
many foreign crises.

Harry S. Truman was a fierce partisan, as were Kennedy,
Johnson, Richard Nixon, Gerald Ford, Ronald Reagan, and
both Bushes. It is our system and it works.

It is also the system of the most advanced democracies that
have endured the longest and with the strongest civic virtues.

Benjamin Disraeli, one of the greatest statesmen (and politicians) of British history, once unloaded on a fellow Tory who
had not promoted with an eye on political debts.

"Nothing is more ruinous to political connection than the
fear of justly rewarding your friends and a promotion of ordinary men of opposite opinions in preference to qualified adher-
ents," Disraeli wrote. "It is not becoming in any Minister to
decry party who has risen by party. We should always remember that if we were not partisans we should not be ministers."[5]

Each of the modern presidents has known, however, when
it was time to put partisanship aside, to work across the aisle,
and to aim for achievements that could genuinely be described
as bipartisan.

Not Barack Obama. He has proven to be the most relentless
partisan of them all, and to the country's great harm.

Had the president given any ground on the failed stimulus,

had he genuinely engaged on Dodd-Frank or Obamacare, had he really sought to meet John Boehner halfway in budget and debt-ceiling talks, much harm to the nation's economy and to its international position could have been avoided.

The practical sources of Obama's fierce partisan edge are certainly Chicago-based. His ruthlessness vis-à-vis his very first state senate opponent—knocking her off the ballot via a signature challenge—began a pattern which has never shifted. "If you can win, you should win and get to work doing the people's business," he said at that time, a neat summary of a Machiavellian focus useful in winning but not in good governing.[6]

There is no graciousness in him at all—as though he is wired to disdain and belittle his opponents. This is in fact the Alinsky way, the central tenet of "Rules for Radicals," wherein the old Chicago socialist wrote that it was necessary to isolate and then ridicule opponents, to divide and divide again, to create and thrive from crisis. "Never let a good crisis go to waste," is how Obama's first key hire, Rahm Emanuel, put it in one of the most famous phrases of the Chicago school of politics.[7]

His ruthlessness has surprised many, including me. Some saw it coming, and this particular foresight is one of the great indications of Rush Limbaugh's enduring political instincts. Rush knew no quarter would be given, and he shocked many by saying he hoped Obama would fail. Many Republicans recoiled a bit, sensing that the traditional rules of American politics would call for a new president to receive a honeymoon and indeed some large measure of his agenda.

What Rush and a few others saw coming—not I, I was wearing those rose-colored glasses—was that the traditional courtesies ought not to be extended to the new president because the new president would return courtesy with a sucker punch.

The blinders did not fall for many until two particular events occurred.

The first was the 2010 State of the Union address, delivered on January 27, 2010.

This speech was delivered after the United States Supreme Court handed down its 5–4 decision about *Citizens United*, a major blow to the left's control of campaign financing in the country because it removed the institutionalized advantages that allowed labor unions to operate in politics while preventing corporations, wealthy individuals, or associations from doing the same. Citing the First Amendment's strong protections of political speech, Justice Anthony Kennedy had written a strong opinion on behalf of robust political speech supported by large expenditures. Labor unions and left-wing advocacy groups would have the same rights as other institutions, of course, but they had enjoyed a tremendous advantage under the old regime—known as McCain-Feingold—and their bitterness and the bitterness of their leader was deep.

And focused.

On the justices of the Supreme Court sitting right in front of him.

This episode remains a shocking one for any fair-minded student of the Constitution and the history of the relationships between the Court and the chief executive.

Many of the justices of the Court make the trip to the Capitol for the State of the Union address each year. They listen respectfully. They do not applaud any particular provision of the president's speech. They are there to symbolize the unity of the government, honoring the balance of the three branches, reminding viewers that—like the military chiefs who also sit without applauding during the president's speech—there are parts of the government that are not political, thank God, judges and generals among them.

Presidents and other politicians of both parties have certainly attacked the Court's decisions and often vigorously.

But never in person. Never in that setting. Never in a way

calculated to bring scorn upon the justices before the American people. Here is what the president said:

> With all due deference to separation of powers, last week the Supreme Court reversed a century of law that I believe will open the floodgates for special interests—including foreign corporations—to spend without limit in our elections. I don't think American elections should be bank-rolled by America's most powerful interests, or worse, by foreign entities. They should be decided by the American people. And I'd urge Democrats and Republicans to pass a bill that helps to correct some of these problems.[8]

Justice Samuel Alito was seen by the cameras mouthing the words "not true" as the president misrepresented the essential holding of the case, demagoguing the decision with the intent of demonizing the Court—turning it into an agent of one party.[9]

Had the president not taught constitutional law at one of the nation's finest law schools—the University of Chicago—one might have forgiven his mangled presentation of the case's holding. But his supporters trumpet his grasp of the law, so his misrepresentation of it must be understood as willful.

The president is a dirty fighter—brass-knuckled—and willing to punch hard and below the belt, repeatedly. He is willing to demean and demonize, and is quite unrestrained by the most basic of courtesies.

He will fold temporarily when he has to, as he did when he accepted a two-year extension of the Bush tax rates in the aftermath of the 2010 congressional Democrat wipeout. This "deal" lulled the GOP into thinking that the president with a history of crazed pit-bull politics had changed his nature.

The real Obama returned in the spring, teeth bared and the trash talk flying. The single most glaring and disturbing display of this malicious streak came on April 13, 2011.

One of the country's sharpest young political minds, House

Budget Committee Chairman Congressman Paul Ryan, had given a major speech outlining a new approach to the deeply and dangerously insolvent Medicare program. The specifics do not matter here so much as the timing and nature of Ryan's speech. It came after the 2010 elections—a major political rebuke to the president—and it was sober, detailed, and delivered as an invitation to the president to engage on the most pressing domestic political issue of the day.

Many thought that when the president invited Republican leadership, including Congressman Ryan, to the Old Executive Office Building to listen to his speech on the deficit, that they would be hearing the opening bid by the president in a grand effort to gather both parties together to tackle the Medicare mess.

Instead the president used the occasion to deliver a verbal ambush, one that targeted the GOP generally, but Ryan specifically, and in highly personal terms. As Alinsky said, Obama did. I quoted him at the beginning of this chapter, and do so again for emphasis:

> One vision has been championed by Republicans in the House of Representatives and embraced by several of their party's presidential candidates. It's a plan that aims to reduce our deficit by $4 trillion over the next ten years, and one that addresses the challenge of Medicare and Medicaid in the years after that. Those are both worthy goals for us to achieve. But the way this plan achieves those goals would lead to a fundamentally different America than the one we've known throughout most of our history.... These aren't the kind of cuts you make when you're trying to get rid of some waste or find extra savings in the budget. These aren't the kind of cuts that Republicans and Democrats on the Fiscal Commission proposed. These are the kind of cuts that tell us we can't afford the America we believe in. And they paint a vision of our future that's deeply pessimistic.

The fact is, their vision is less about reducing the deficit than it is about changing the basic social compact in America.... There's nothing serious about a plan that claims to reduce the deficit by spending a trillion dollars on tax cuts for millionaires and billionaires. There's nothing courageous about asking for sacrifice from those who can least afford it and don't have any clout on Capitol Hill. And this is not a vision of the America I know.[10]

This was churlish behavior, and it marked an obvious point of no return. Obama did not intend to be turned from his course by the results of a congressional election. He saw the people's bet and raised the ante in a fashion that left no doubt about his lack of inner restraint.

When the summer of 2011 brought the debt-ceiling showdown and the prolonged dance between the president and John Boehner, many again allowed themselves to believe that the president would embrace compromise, putting aside his program of massive government expansion for the sake of ordinary Americans.

Many conservatives fretted that Obama would take the Speaker to the cleaners, and indeed he tried to—changing the essential terms of the sketchy deal he had struck with Boehner at the last minute, trying another jam down, playing a deceptive, partisan game that triggered a downgrade of the nation's credit.

Thereafter, the GOP would not be fooled again. A debt-ceiling deal was finally struck between congressional leadership without the involvement of a pouting president who was left glowering at 1600.

With no hope of his head-fake tactics' being successful, the president who cried "bipartisan wolf" one too many times shrugged off all pretense of good faith toward his opponents and launched one of the most cynical and cringe-inducing political campaigns in American history.

The president decided that his only hope is to win ugly, so ugly he went hard and fast. The result was an embrace of the economically illiterate but potentially potent class-warfare rhetoric, which soon combined with the absurdities of the Occupy Wall Street marchers into a toxic brew of resentment and castles built in the air.

The president hit the floor in the North Carolina speech quoted above. A longer excerpt:

> The Republican plan says that what's been standing in the way between us and full employment are laws that keep companies from polluting as much as they want. On the other hand our plan puts teachers, construction workers, firefighters, and police officers back on the job. Their plan says that the big problem we have is that we helped to get 30 million Americans health insurance. They figure, we should throw those folks off the health insurance roll, somehow that's going to help people find jobs. Our plan says we're better off if every small business and worker in America gets a tax cut. And that is what is in my jobs bill.
>
> Their plan says we should go back to the good old days before the financial crisis when Wall Street was writing its own rules, they want to roll back all the reforms that we've put in place. Our plan says we need to make it easier for small businesses to grow and hire and push this economy forward.
>
> So, you've gotten a sense, so you've got their plan and we've got my plan. My plan says we're going to put teachers back into the classroom, construction workers back to work rebuilding America, rebuilding our schools, tax cuts for small businesses, tax cuts for hiring veterans, tax cuts if you give your worker a raise. That's my plan. And then you've got their plan, which is, let's have dirtier air, dirtier water, less people with health insurance. All right, so, so far, at least, I feel better about my plan.[11]

This is just a succinct display of a campaign approach we will hear until November, one which we are guaranteed to hear reprised again and again from his retirement home in Chicago, New York, or D.C.

President Bush was often accused by the left of poisoning American politics because of the Florida recount and the invasion of Iraq.

This bankrupt line of reasoning has not been discouraged by the fact that Al Gore triggered the former and its result was confirmed by all but one of many post-election recounts, and the latter proceeded on a bipartisan basis under a U.N. mandate.

Neither has the essential graciousness of George W. Bush, in or out of office, done anything to soften the hatred often expressed for him. Bush was the very soul of country-ahead-of-party, and history will record and commend his essential decency toward even the most virulent of his citizen critics.

This will not be so of President Obama, at least for his time in office. Indeed there is no single memorable effort on his part to bridge the partisan gap. Plenty of words about bipartisanship are on record, yes, but these have usually been delivered just before an outrageous characterization or unmeetable demand. The president's unerring sense of moral superiority has never been corralled, never even been tamped down for public consumption. He is all scorn for his opponents, in victory and defeat. When he is turned out, his "concession" will make Jimmy Carter's of thirty-two years earlier seem dignified, and his post-presidency will almost certainly be defined by carping, and almost as certainly by a bid for the presidency he lost, because he would not, could not, be other than who he is—a Chicago man, though and through.

"We won," President Obama said to then House GOP Whip Eric Cantor on January 23, 2009, when he invited Republicans to the White House for talks on what would become the disastrous Stimulus. Cantor had put on the table some alternative ideas, which the president, in an early display of his style, dismissed with a verbal smackdown that his hard-left base loved. "We won" became a defining phrase because it summed up an arrogance that took the president further and further to the left, and further and further into acrimony, even as the public turned against his radical restructuring of the American economy.

My review of Obamacare began this book, but it is important to remember, as Obama's defeat grows nearer, that this millstone around his neck could have been avoided.

The gubernatorial elections of 2009 in New Jersey and Virginia, which brought Chris Christie and Bob McDonnell to their statehouses, were in large part referenda on Obama's first year of governing and especially on the merits of Obamacare, and these results confirmed what the summer of Tea Parties and contentious town halls had demonstrated—that American people did not want Obamacare jammed down their throats, and certainly not in a one-sided hyperpartisan process.

That message was delivered again, and in unmistakable fashion, when Republican Scott Brown defeated Democrat Martha Coakley to take the Massachusetts Senate seat that had become vacant when Ted Kennedy died.

No more striking message could have been more bluntly delivered than to lose the seat of the Lion of the Senate (and of the Left) to a Republican who campaigned explicitly against Obamacare.

For days after the Bay State's vote, the fate of the obviously toxic Obamacare hung in the balance as party leaders discussed and maneuvered. When Obama emerged from that evaluation he chose to jam down an economically disfiguring scheme that was wildly unpopular, but advanced his cherished agenda of government expansion to previously unimaginable levels, with a price tag that could never be paid.

What's important to see in retrospect is that the president has never been anything other than a fierce hyperpartisan.

He was hyperpartisan when he dismissed Cantor. He was hyperpartisan when he spent hundreds of billions on favored friends and turned General Motors and Chrysler over to the United Auto Workers. He was hyperpartisan when he assaulted the Supreme Court from the well of the Senate. He was hyperpartisan when he savaged Paul Ryan. He was hyperpartisan when he attempted to punk John Boehner. He was hyperpartisan when he chose low-blow and straw-man rhetoric in his North Carolina stump speech, accusing Republicans of favoring deadly levels of pollution and hoping for an explosion of medically uninsured Americans.

This will be a brutal campaign waged by a desperate and cornered hyperpartisan who will use any means he can, supported by enormous amounts of money.

Just imagine how he will act if he, by some stroke of fate, wins a second term.

Chapter 22

The Unilateralism of an Anti-Constitutional President

*I hope that the conversation we begin here doesn't end here;
that we can continue our dialogue in the days ahead. It's
important to me that we do so. It's important to you, I think,
that we do so. But most importantly, it's important to the
American people that we do so.*

*I've said this before, but I'm a big believer not just in the
value of a loyal opposition, but in its necessity. Having differences of opinion, having a real debate about matters of
domestic policy and national security—and that's not something that's only good for our country, it's absolutely essential. It's only through the process of disagreement and debate
that bad ideas get tossed out and good ideas get refined and
made better. And that kind of vigorous back-and-forth—that
imperfect but well-founded process, messy as it often is—
is at the heart of our democracy. That's what makes us the
greatest nation in the world.*

—President Obama, speaking at a House
Republican Caucus retreat, March 2010[1]

"With much of his legislative agenda stalled in Congress,
President Obama and his team are preparing an array of actions
using his executive power to advance energy, environmental,
fiscal and other domestic policy priorities," Peter Baker wrote
in the February 12, 2010, *New York Times.*[2]

President Obama's evolution to an imperial presidency came at a cost to his credibility, as Baker explained:

The use of executive authority during times of legislative inertia is hardly new; former Presidents Bill Clinton and George W. Bush turned to such powers at various moments in their presidencies, and Mr. Emanuel was in the thick of carrying out the strategy during his days as a top official in the Clinton White House.

But Mr. Obama has to be careful how he proceeds because he has been critical of both Mr. Clinton's penchant for expending presidential capital on small-bore initiatives, like school uniforms, and Mr. Bush's expansive assertions of executive authority, like the secret program of wiretapping without warrants.

Already, Mr. Obama has had to reconcile his campaign-trail criticism of Mr. Bush for excessive use of so-called signing statements to bypass parts of legislation with his own use of such tactics. After a bipartisan furor in Congress last year, Mr. Obama stopped issuing such signing statements, but aides said last month that he still reserves the right to ignore sections of bills he considers unconstitutional if objections have been lodged previously by the executive branch.[3]

As with so many of the "Hope and Change" president's promises, the ideas of a restrained executive authority, transparency in government, and comity with the two other branches went flying out the window at 1600 Pennsylvania soon after President Obama moved in—it just took Mr. Baker a couple of years to notice.

A year and a half after Mr. Baker saw what was coming, *The Hill*'s Jordy Yager also reviewed Obama's unilateralism, on July 12, 2011:

President Obama increasingly is using his executive authority to move his policies forward when confronted with congressional opposition.

The administration chose not to defend the federal Defense of Marriage Act banning gay marriage, and Obama bypassed military tribunals and the Guantánamo Bay prison in Cuba to send an accused terrorist from Somalia to a U.S. civilian court.

The latter effort was seen as a backdoor way to circumvent congressional opposition to civilian trials for terrorism suspects.

The president also has granted immigration officers greater latitude when deciding whether to deport illegal immigrants, and has determined the War Powers Resolution requiring congressional authorization for military actions does not apply to the intervention he ordered in Libya.

Most recently, Congress has been abuzz with the possibility that Obama could bypass its authority altogether and raise the debt ceiling using the so-called 14th Amendment solution.[4]

While the president did not use the "14th Amendment solution," there is no reason to believe that he won't in the future. He has aggressively expanded the powers of the presidency to Nixon-era levels, and a second term would almost certainly see Nixon-era abuses flourish as the consequences of his first-term scandals, like Solyndra and Fast and Furious, catch up with him.

No one should be surprised, not after the "March of the Czars" early in the president's tenure. Not after "recess appointments" made when the Senate wasn't in recess.

The left now likes to mock the idea that President Obama did anything untoward with his appointment of unaccountable policy czars who were beyond the reach of congressional oversight and media scrutiny, but at the beginning of his term, the elite media was aglow with praise for his bold appointments and willingness to bypass the traditional constitutional structures. On March 5, 2009, *Los Angeles Times* reporters Tom Hamburger and Christi Parsons applauded the president's new staffing patterns in print:

> As President Obama names more policy czars to his White House team—high-level staff members who will help oversee the administration's top initiatives—some lawmakers and Washington interest groups are raising concerns that he may be subverting the authority of Congress and concentrating too much power in the presidency.
>
> The idea of these "super aides," who will work across agency lines to push the president's agenda, is not a new one. President Nixon may have named the first "czar" with his appointment of William E. Simon to handle the 1970s energy crisis. Other presidents have followed suit.
>
> But none has embraced the concept, presidential scholars say, to the extent that Obama has.
>
> He has appointed special advisors who will work from inside the White House on healthcare, the economy, energy and urban issues, with more to come.[5]

Glenn Beck famously counted thirty-two czars appointed to the Obama administration by July 2009, with reports of three more on the way.[6]

It was Beck who drove this story, and who also drove out one of the administration's most radical czars, Van Jones, thus demonstrating to all that no one else in the media had vetted Obama's appointments very much, and of course the Senate had no opportunity to do so in confirmation hearings.

Here's a list of the thirty-two czars Beck identified and their areas of policy:

1. Afghanistan Czar—Richard Holbrooke
2. AIDs Czar—Jeffrey Crowley

3. Auto Recovery Czar—Ed Montgomery
4. Border Czar—Alan Bersin
5. California Water Czar—David J. Hayes
6. Car Czar—Ron Bloom
7. Central Region Czar—Dennis Ross
8. Climate Czar—Todd Stern
9. Domestic Violence Czar—Lynn Rosenthal
10. Drug Czar—Gil Kerlikowske
11. Economic Czar—Paul Volcker
12. Energy and Environment Czar—Carol Browner
13. Faith-Based Czar—Joshua DuBois
14. Government Performance Czar—Jeffrey Zients
15. Great Lakes Czar—Cameron Davis
16. Green Jobs Czar—Van Jones
17. Guantanamo Closure Czar—Daniel Fried
18. Health Czar—Nancy-Ann DeParle
19. Information Czar—Vivek Kundra
20. Intelligence Czar—Dennis Blair
21. Mideast Peace Czar—George Mitchell
22. Pay Czar—Kenneth Feinberg
23. Regulatory Czar—Cass Sunstein
24. Science Czar—John Holdren
25. Stimulus Accountability Czar—Earl Devaney
26. Sudan Czar—J. Scott Gration
27. TARP Czar—Herb Allison
28. Technology Czar—Aneesh Chopra
29. Terrorism Czar—John Brennan
30. Urban Affairs Czar—Adolfo Carrion Jr.
31. Weapons Czar—Ashton Carter
32. WMD Policy Czar—Gary Samore[7]

When he wrote this in July 2009, Beck also reported the imminent arrival of a "cyber czar," a "health insurance czar," and a "copyright czar," though none to my knowledge were ever reported.

In compiling his list Glenn used a mix of positions, some established by law and not subject to congressional review, and some just established by the president and not subject to congressional review. What even this mixed list of legitimate, long-standing positions within the executive branch and new creations of Team Obama represents, however, is much more than a chaotic personnel structure and a desire to place powerful political friends and allies in positions of authority not accountable to Congress or the media.

It represents a theory of government that has a tradition in American history, but not one that is held in high regard.

Wilson, FDR, JFK, LBJ, and Nixon were the biggest users of the latent power of the presidency, stretching the ambiguities of the document to the max and only occasionally finding themselves rebuked, as when the Supreme Court struck down Harry Truman's seizure of the steel mills during the Korean War and, of course, with Nixon's impeachment.

Presidents of a certain personality grasp for power, take as much as they can, hoard it, and use it. Frequently they use it chiefly to reward friends and allies and thus accumulate more power, but sometimes they simply increase their own vision of themselves and their place in history.

The more histrionic the president, the more unilateral his governing style. Perhaps his Nobel Peace Prize in October 2009—nine months into his presidency—took an already overflowing ego and warped it into something previously unseen in the Oval Office, but the president's certitude about himself has led to a willingness to embrace any means that can be dressed up in remotely constitutional garb. Since past presidents used executive orders and the president's appointing power to create czars, Obama just took the precedents and stretched and stretched them.

No president has ever shown as complete a disregard for the War Powers Act as President Obama did with the Libyan conflict. We conservatives tend to think of the War Powers

Act as an unconstitutional attempt to restrain the president's authority as commander in chief.

President Obama was a critic of President Bush's "unilateralism," which always came with congressional backing and international support, whether deployed against the Taliban, Saddam Hussein, or North Korea.[8]

Obama certainly had NATO with him on Libya, but not Congress. He didn't blink. He just ordered the bombs dropped and the Special Forces deployed when necessary. And when it came time to use drones to dispatch terrorists, he did so. When it came time to dispatch Osama bin Laden without Pakistan's knowledge or approval, he did so.

Conservatives applaud these last actions, and understand them as the necessary exercise of the president's oath to protect and defend the Constitution of the United States.

But we worry, and the country should worry, about the ease with which Obama has abandoned all his previous positions on the use of executive branch authority, has forgotten his criticisms of George W. Bush, and has run roughshod over the rights and responsibilities of Congress in the making of domestic policy.

Americans have to ask themselves: If this is his love of unchecked power in a first term with a reelection campaign looming, what will he do if given a second four years?

Chapter 23

The Smartest President Ever? The Fumbler-in-Chief and His Lazy, Soft Countrymen

This is a great, great country that had gotten a little soft, and we didn't have the same competitive edge that we needed.
—President Obama, September 30, 2011, to WESH TV's Jim Payne, Orlando, Florida[1]

We have lost our ambition, our imagination, and our willingness to do the things that built the Golden Gate Bridge and Hoover Dam.
—President Obama, at a fund-raiser in San Francisco, October 25, 2011[2]

We've been a little bit lazy over the last couple of decades.
—President Obama, at an Asia-Pacific Economic Co-Operation (APEC) summit in Hawaii, November 12, 2011[3]

Overt opposition to what would become the full—and fully disastrous—Obama agenda was limited and muted at first. Rush Limbaugh was the first to the rhetorical ramparts—and loud upon arriving there. Sean Hannity, Mark Levin, and Laura Ingraham soon joined him. (None of these extraordinary talents work for the same network as I do. We compete in the marketplace, but they are allies in the war of ideas and completely committed to the Constitution.)

My own colleagues on the Salem Radio Network—Bill Bennett, Mike Gallagher, Dennis Prager, and Michael Medved—joined the effort quickly afterward, to turn back the worst features of the Obama program. Scores of local talk show hosts around the country—Mike Rosen in Denver, Frank Pastore in Los Angeles, and Mark Larson in San Diego are just three of a hundred examples—joined in the effort, as did Townhall.com (with its extraordinary team of political reporters led by Guy Benson), HotAir.com (with Ed Morrissey and Allahpundit), the *Washington Examiner*'s superb team, the vastly rightly influential NationalReview.com, the Jason Mattera–led *Human Events*, a hundred different bloggers (led as they have been for a decade by Powerline, Instapundit, PJMedia, the incredible team of writers at *National Review* and now at *Commentary*), and new stars emerged via the Fox News Channel (Megyn Kelley, Mary Katharine Ham, Monica Crowley, Dana Perino, and Greg Gutfeld) and Andrew Breitbart's many platforms to make great arguments using humor and irony.

Compared, however, to the MSM—the entrenched Manhattan-Beltway media elite, or the "drive-by media," as Rush likes to call it—all of these voices and platforms were initially as effective as shouts in a hurricane. The hurricane was praise for President Obama, an unquestioning adoration that swept away the theory and practice of real journalism, and many alleged journalists simply fell for the president's astonishing promises, premises, and presumptions.

Objectivity about the president's plans and, crucially, his abilities vanished in the aftermath of his declaration of candidacy and then his election. Even the astonishing absurdity of receiving a Nobel Prize in October 2009 stunned only a few among the Manhattan-Beltway media elite. They adjusted, smiled, and continued clapping, clapping, and clapping even as Obamacare gathered its momentum and the economy didn't.

Conservative journalism found one significant ally, however. It was unlooked for and unexpected, but powerful in the undoing of Obama's agenda and the effort to reverse his momentum from the very beginning of his term:

President Obama himself.

Never has a president been so ubiquitous and never has one been so unsuccessful in turning face time into public support.

Early in his presidency it became obvious that Obama believed he could crowd out bad news and criticism by simply being available to the media, although always in highly structured circumstances where he would have the first, last, and middle word.

Rarely would he engage a critic or even a moderately aggressive journalist, like Fox News' Bret Baier, as he did on March 17, 2010, in what has proven to be the only real interview of his presidency.[4]

This one-time sit-down with a prepared and respectfully aggressive journalist ended the practice for the president. It did not go well for President Obama, because Baier asked obvious but pointed questions and would not be filibustered.

After that, when the president wanted to pretend to do an interview, he would pick a setting like Super Bowl Sunday, and a gentleman like Bill O'Reilly, and then arrange circumstances to avoid the prolonged give-and-take that would easily puncture his pretensions to be on top of things and working a plan toward a successful conclusion. Fortunately, O'Reilly used his fifteen minutes to set up the one question that counted, to ask whether the president was bothered by the hate that always focuses on the president. (This Fox News anchor and the most watched man in cable-land had asked the same question of George W. Bush a few years earlier.)

"The folks who hate you don't know you," the president told O'Reilly. "What they hate is the funhouse mirror image of you that's out there."[5]

What ought to have been an opportunity for the president

to show disdain or even understanding for the economic ravages was instead a revelation of the overwhelming self-pity he can feel for himself that would, over the year, harden into contempt for the American people as evidenced by the three separate quotations from three separate occasions that were given at the beginning of this chapter.

The president has responded to mounting criticism—the "funhouse mirror image"—very, very personally. O'Reilly scratched the surface, and over the course of 2011 and now into 2012 we have seen the real President Obama revealed again and again: the one that doesn't like the average American; the one with contempt for the work ethic, ambition, and drive of the average American; the one that thinks this people isn't good enough for this president.

To be sure the president tries to hide his inner elitist—this contemptor in chief—right next to his inner Alinskyite.

To that end, his press conferences changed from the rapid-fire question-and-answer sessions that dated back to FDR into a long series of Obama soliloquies. The eight- to ten-minute answers that are routine with President Obama, for which past presidents would have been ruthlessly mocked, are now routinely accepted by a meek and adoring White House press (ABC's Jake Tapper and Fox's Ed Henry excepted).

And the president gives speeches. Again and again and again. His campaign, which never stopped even after his victory in 2008, just kept going, but the president's contempt also just kept slipping through.

I am not talking about his famous gaffes, which include "I have now been in fifty-seven states," mixing up the names of the dead and the living Medal of Honor recipients, mispronouncing *corpsmen*, not knowing how to speak "Austrian," referring to the fact that "John McCain has not talked about my Muslim faith," etc., etc., etc.[6]

The president can thank his vice president, Joe Biden, who is the record holder when it comes to embarrassing gaffes, for keeping him from prolonged ridicule on the verbal pratfall front—the president's silver medal is secure.

No, what wore the people down was the endless hectoring, the endless speechifying, the refusal to leave us alone—even those of us who love politics and public policy.

The president has worn out his welcome with the middle of America—the physical and political middle of America. And he did so by becoming the insurance salesman who never goes away.

My insurance guy, Jerry Tardie, has never tried to sell me anything over the twenty years that I have bought products from him. He's the best salesman I know. If I asked a question within his world, he was instantly on his game—providing information and options—but he never oversold. Actually, he never sold at all. He was of service to me, his client. I like to think my law partners and I approach our clients in the same fashion.

President Obama, of course, has never sold anything in his life except himself, and that via campaigns that operate for defined periods of time along a building arc, which culminates in an intense period of very high public-politician interaction. He doesn't have any sense of the danger of overselling. He never did, nor did Axelrod or Emanuel or all the other sharpies from Chicago who didn't realize that the attention you have to work for in Chicago is part of the furniture in the White House. They never hit the off button. They didn't know it existed.

We overdosed on Obama. Very early on. We consumed a toxic amount of the president.

People generally want campaigns to end. To be done. Finished. Go away and bother us again in two years or, if you are the president, four.

The president never stopped bothering us, never went away, invading the living room night after night, and the cable networks loved it. The Beltway loved it. But out in the country he wore out his welcome quickly, and when the economy refused to grow and in fact withered under his ministrations, his every appearance became a reminder of his incompetence.

Except for his rock-solid support among African-Americans, President Obama's approval rating would be close to Nixon's right before his resignation, right around Clinton's after the dress, or W's after the 2006 election before the surge deployed and worked. His quite understandable standing among blacks and to a lesser extent other minorities—exactly what one would expect given all that the president represents to every American, but especially for those who have suffered racism, about the triumph of opportunity—that standing has masked a deep political weakness. His numbers will rise a bit with the staging of a convention, the tweaking of polling samples and turnout models, and all the other tricks that the Manhattan-Beltway media elite will deploy on behalf of their prince, but the president is in a box.

We are tired of him. Worn out by his hectoring. Offended by his tone. Respectful of the office but quite done with being lectured to by a man quite obviously in over his head and struggling to understand basic concepts of economics and the costs of regulation, confused about Israel, and just as befuddled as Jimmy Carter by the fact that our enemies cannot be charmed.

A president comfortable telling the president of Russia that he can be more "flexible" after November 2012 but a president unwilling to tell voters what that means.

The president seems to understand the situation even while he is unable to figure out how to fix it, so he keeps playing the same card again and again—more appearances, more appeals to trust him, more assaults on the Republicans, and more increasingly vehement class-warfare rhetoric.

And as I noted above, his anger is growing, slipping out in asides that communicate his contempt. "Soft," "lazy," "lost our ambition and our imagination." Those are bitter words from a bitter man feeling the approach of a massive rejection.

Chapter 24

Avoiding the Fecklessness Argument: Martha's Vineyard, Presidential Bracketology, and Commander-in-Chief Golf

Obviously we are going through incredible changes through-out the world, most recently obviously, our hearts go out to the people of Japan. One thing I wanted to make sure the viewers who are filling out their brackets, this is a great tradi-tion, we have fun every year doing it, but while you are doing it...go to usaid.gov. I think that would be a great gesture as you are filling out your brackets, they can help out some peo-ple who are really having a tough time.

It's a great tradition. I have to say, last year I got deci-mated, the year before that we did okay...so I'm hoping that I can make some progress.

—President Obama filling out his 2011 NCAA bracket with ESPN's Andy Katz, for the second year in a row[1]

President Obama played golf seventy-five times in his first thirty months as president and more since, but this is a num-ber I could write down as I went to press. While that may seem like a lot of golfing—five rounds every two months isn't much to a golf addict—and Dwight Eisenhower may have put that swinging pace to shame, it is a considerable number of swings.[2]

George W. Bush also started his time in the White House as an avid golfer, but then he stopped. The *Washington Post*'s Dan Eggen explained why in a 2008 story:

> President Bush said yesterday that he gave up golfing in 2003 "in solidarity" with the families of soldiers who were dying in Iraq concluding that it was "just not worth it anymore" to play the sport in a time of war.
>
> "I don't want some mom whose son may have recently died to see the commander in chief playing golf," Bush said in a White House interview with the *Politico*. "I feel I owe it to the families to be as—to be in solidarity as best as I can with them. And I think playing golf during a war just sends the wrong signal."
>
> Bush said he decided to stop playing golf on Aug. 19, 2003, when a truck bomb in Baghdad killed U.N. special representative Sergio Vieira de Mello and more than a dozen others.
>
> He said he received word of the attack while playing golf during a stay at the family ranch near Crawford, Tex. Press reports at the time indicate he took the call from Condoleezza Rice, then his national security adviser.
>
> "They pulled me off the golf course, and I said it's just not worth it anymore to do," Bush said in yesterday's interview.[3]

There is no law or regulation regulating a president's pastimes, and every president needs recreation and leisure in order to be better equipped to deal with the monumental stresses of the office.

Golf is uniquely a sport that suggests a life of leisurely pleasure—an abundant life—especially when it is played at the finest courses in the world at a moment's notice and in the company of enough eyes never to lose a ball. It is not a game that binds politicians to the people struggling through difficult times. Access to golf courses appears infrequently on the Service Employees International Union's agenda.

Basketball, on the other hand, is a game of the people. Well, at least watched by the people. Millions of Americans love college basketball, and filling out the annual brackets in the NCAA tournament is a beloved ritual in homes, businesses, and places of education around the country.

President Obama, a serious basketball fan, brought bracketology to the White House:

"In what has become a much-anticipated annual ritual, Obama joined in on the March Madness and filled out his bracket on ESPN's *SportsCenter*," reported Reuters on March 16, 2011. "He picked Kansas to go all the way, beating Ohio State in the final game."[4]

Anticipated by whom? Certainly ESPN loves the ratings that come from having one of their correspondents watch as the president fills out a white board with his guesses on which college hoopsters will advance and when.

A fan of Greg Gutfeld and his late-night Fox show came to the president's defense in this matter, in a *Red Eye* kind of way:

i don't know how conservatives in general walks of life feel about this, but i have a problem with the usual suspects of conservative punditry piling on obama for taking time out on national tv to fill out his ncaa tourney brackets...i'm a conservative and i'm totally fine with it...in fact, the president ought to take part in march madness, it's become a great american spectacle...criticize him, if you will, for dropping the ball on egypt, dithering on libya or being clueless on japan...but there will always be turmoil of some sort, somewhere...and unless we are under a threat of imminent destruction, american presidents should have the opportunity to take part in events that make this country great...

what i do have a problem with is obama's feigning knowledge of the teams taking part in the tourney...his bullcrap along the lines of "this team has depth", "this team can play defense" and "this team can fill the hoop" is obviously researched by some low ranking lackeys...i guess politicians just can't help themselves, but gimme a break... they call it march madness for a reason, and it's not because things shake out as the experts predict...while obama is [bull$#%] us with his alleged knowledge of this year's field, analysts on espn, who do this [&*^%] for a living, are giving the reasons for their picks...such as, "i like their uniforms", "it's my alma mater", "my college roommate is on the coaching staff", and so forth...when 12's are beating 5's all logic goes out the window...so mr president, i know you got game and can ball...but please, spare me your fake insight into these teams and save the analysis for the final four...until then, put on a blindfold and start throwing darts like everyone else...[ellipses in the original][5]

My apologies to the author for a mild edit to protect younger readers and the easily offended.

So there are defenders of the president's bracketology, just like there are defenders of his golfing, or his Martha's Vineyard vacations, or his big Canadian-made bus.

The president enjoys being president, likes the perks, likes the attention, and loves building the image of the cool guy who is always on top of things even as he stays loose while the country is on edge.

President Obama has suffered very little criticism for his personal pursuits, and GOP leaders have been wise to leave these subjects alone. It is not a point of policy, not a burning issue, and attempting to raise these issues would backfire because Obama is skilled in dealing blowback when attacked—personal attacks are the most easily dismissed and then turned. Obama's model has been Franklin Roosevelt, and no doubt one of his guidebooks to FDR is Jonathan Alter's very fine book *The Defining Moment: FDR's Hundred Days and the Triumph of Hope.*

Alter writes about FDR coming under attack because of his wealth and class from, of all people, Al Smith, the 1928 Democratic nominee who hoped to push aside FDR and run again in 1932. Roosevelt brushed the attacks away, "showing a national audience," writes Alter, "how to deflect attacks with a bit of humor; nothing especially witty, just light and dismissive....

"This natural skill would serve him well in the years ahead," Alter concluded, noting the Fala story from further along in FDR's saga. "The difference between first-rate politicians and ordinary ones is often no more than their capacity to deprive a big story of oxygen, and to disarm an opponent or score on him with a quip."[6]

The double standard at work here drives some conservatives crazy. Even a lefty like Jon Meacham knows the score, commenting on MSNBC after one Obama bracketology exercise that "Bush would have gotten more barbecued for this," as he and his fellow talking heads debated the merits of making nationally televised basketball picks as the Libyan crisis unfolded in 2011. "Anyone who thinks that he didn't—he wouldn't—is crazy."[7]

Meacham is right, of course, but the reality of the double standard is the reality of the double standard. The GOP and any of its elected officials can only lightly remind voters of golfing and brackets and the Vineyard, and only in a humorous way, perhaps in combination with a reminder that the president and his team had great sympathy for the Occupy Wall Street movement's attacks on the fabled 1 percent.

Sometimes the best arguments, even the most obvious ones, cannot be used. The president's fundamental lack of seriousness about his job is an easily made case, his refusal to try and master it is obvious, and his willingness to abandon even the most pressing of problems for some "me time" may or may not resonate with voters, but the GOP must let the ball play as it lays.

Chapter 25

The "Decline and Despair" President

The way I think about it is, this is a great, great country that had gotten a little soft and we didn't have that same competitive edge that we needed over the last couple of decades. We need to get back on track.
   —President Obama, September 30, 2011, to WESH TV's
Jim Payne, Orlando, Florida[1]

We have lost our ambition, our imagination, and our willingness to do the things that built the Golden Gate Bridge.
   —President Obama, at a Democratic Party fund-raiser in San
Francisco, October 25, 2011[2]

But, you know, we've been a little bit lazy, I think, over the last couple of decades. We've kind of taken for granted, well, people will want to come here. And we aren't out there hungry, selling America.
   —President Obama, at an Asia-Pacific Economic Co-Operation
(APEC) summit in Hawaii, November 12, 2011[3]

You have to love a president who believes in America. Or not.

President Obama has made statements such as this triple play of contemptuous disdain for America a recurring theme of his speeches all the way back to his campaign, though it isn't clear whether they just pop out of his inner Alinksy or whether they cross the teleprompter in front of him.

In Mumbai, India, in 2010 he said the United States was no longer in a position to "meet the rest of the world economically on our terms."

"The fact of the matter is that for most of my lifetime, and I'll turn fifty next year—the U.S. was such an enormously dominant economic power, we were such a large market, our industry, our technology, our manufacturing was so significant that we always met the rest of the world economically on our terms," the president told his foreign audience.

"And now because of the incredible rise of India and China and Brazil and other countries, the U.S. remains the largest economy and the largest market, but there is real competition."[4]

Apple faces real competition, but it hasn't declined. It is thriving. But our president assumes American decline instead of assuming that we could win a competition, and handily.

In the UK, *Telegraph* columnist Nile Gardiner called Obama "the decline and despair president."[5]

Gardiner writes after sourcing several recent studies indicating pessimism about America's future being on the rise, both domestically and abroad:[6]

> Instead of hope and change, the Obama presidency has delivered decline and despair on a scale not seen in America since the dying days of the Carter administration. Both at home and abroad, the United States is perceived to be a sinking power, and with good reason.... The liberal experiment of the past few years has knocked the stuffing out of the American economy. Job creation has been barely non-existent, and millions of Americans are now significantly worse off than they were a few years ago. Even the *New York Times* has acknowledged "soaring poverty" in Obama's America, citing a Census Bureau report showing

the number of Americans officially living below the poverty line (46.2 million) at its highest level for more than half a century, since 1959.

Despite the bleak outlook, America can and must rebound later this decade, but it certainly won't be capable of doing so in the hands of the current president. Levels of public disillusionment with the federal government have never been higher, and almost everything the current White House touches ends in failure. It will require another epic Reagan-style revolution to turn this great nation around and get it off its knees.[7]

The most famous expression of the president's disdain for the notion that America is a superpower, and exceptionally situated and equipped to lead the world, came a year before his remarks in India, when at the European summit of the Group of 20 in 2009, he quipped, "I believe in American exceptionalism, just as I suspect that the Brits believe in British exceptionalism and the Greeks believe in Greek exceptionalism."[8]

Andrew Sullivan, for one, denied that the president meant what he said here, and rose to his defense in 2010 with an extended quote from this same "Greek exceptionalism" speech in which the president professes pride in the United States and its core values, but he misses the point of what the president believes to be the arc of American history right now: "What cannot be done honestly, in my view," Sullivan wrote, "is to create a narrative from all of [the president's moves] to describe Obama as an anti-American hyper-leftist, spending the U.S. into oblivion."[9]

By now the president's talk of lost ambition and ruined imagination ends the debate that Sullivan attempted to sway. The president keeps providing those whom Sullivan criticizes with more evidence of his bleak view of the American future, and the left is helpless to defend him when the president simply insists on telling it the way he sees it.

"What's especially remarkable about this hackery," wrote

Sullivan a year ago, "is that these conservative authors don't just egregiously misrepresent the president's actual position. It's that all of them actually cite, as evidence, an out of context line from the very speech that proves their analysis is wrong.

"You can call this truthiness if you like," he concluded. "Better, the Dish believes, to call it what it is. A deliberate campaign of misinformation. A Big Lie."[10]

The trouble for Sullivan's argument is the evidence. The president went abroad early in his presidency, and the result is what is widely known as "the apology tour."

"President Barack Obama has finished the second leg of his international confession tour," Karl Rove wrote in the *Wall Street Journal* on April 23, 2009. "In less than 100 days, he has apologized on three continents for what he views as the sins of America and his predecessors."[11]

Rove continued:

> Mr. Obama told the French (the French!) that America "has shown arrogance and been dismissive, even derisive" toward Europe. In Prague, he said America has "a moral responsibility to act" on arms control because only the U.S. had "used a nuclear weapon." In London, he said that decisions about the world financial system were no longer made by "just Roosevelt and Churchill sitting in a room with a brandy"—as if that were a bad thing. And in Latin America, he said the U.S. had not "pursued and sustained engagement with our neighbors" because we "failed to see that our own progress is tied directly to progress throughout the Americas."[12]

In June 2011 Obama gave a speech announcing the withdrawal of American troops in Afghanistan. It is titled, "Remarks by the President on the Way Forward in Afghanistan."

His speech makes clear that the "way forward in Afghanistan" is not by creating a secure, sustainable government and ally in Central Asia, but by focusing on domestic issues in lieu of foreign ones: "America, it is time to focus on nation building here at home."[13]

He tried to reconcile this obvious contradiction by an elaborate appeal to America's founding values:

> In all that we do, we must remember that what sets America apart is not solely our power—it is the principles upon which our union was founded. We're a nation that brings our enemies to justice while adhering to the rule of law, and respecting the rights of all our citizens. We protect our own freedom and prosperity by extending it to others. We stand not for empire, but for self-determination. That is why we have a stake in the democratic aspirations that are now washing across the Arab world. We will support those revolutions with fidelity to our ideals, with the power of our example, and with an unwavering belief that all human beings deserve to live with freedom and dignity.
>
> We are bound together by the creed that is written into our founding documents, and a conviction that the United States of America is a country that can achieve whatever it sets out to accomplish. Now, let us finish the work at hand. Let us responsibly end these wars, and reclaim the American Dream that is at the center of our story. With confidence in our cause, with faith in our fellow citizens, and with hope in our hearts, let us go about the work of extending the promise of America—for this generation, and the next.[14]

Compare Obama's rhetoric to this excerpt from a speech given by Margaret Thatcher in 1991:

> Americans and Europeans alike sometimes forget how unique is the United States of America. No other nation has been created so swiftly and successfully. No other nation has been built upon an idea—the idea of liberty. No

other nation has so successfully combined people of different races and nations within a single culture. Both the founding fathers of the United States and successive waves of immigrants to your country were determined to create a new identity. Whether in flight from persecution or from poverty, the huddled masses have, with few exceptions, welcomed American values, the American way of life and American opportunities. And America herself has bound them to her with powerful bonds of patriotism and pride.[15]

Obama's vision of American prosperity is clear from his rhetoric and policy priorities: "Over the last decade, we have spent a trillion dollars on war, at a time of rising debt and hard economic times. Now, we must invest in America's greatest resource—our people. We must unleash innovation that creates new jobs and industries, while living within our means. We must rebuild our infrastructure and find new and clean sources of energy."[16]

But, as we have already seen, these policies have exacerbated, not reversed, the sense of fatigue and misdirection that has plagued the country during the Obama years. They have made the economy worse and turned public opinion sour.

Despite his repeated[17] claims[18] that he is open,[19] and even "eager"[20] "to hear other ideas from all ends of the political spectrum,"[21] it has become clear that Obama means "hear" only in the most literal sense.

In a speech before the Conservative Political Action Committee, Representative Mike Pence from Indiana—soon to be that state's governor—said, "You know, I'm told that officials in this administration will actually admit in private that they see their job as managing American decline. Well, let me say from my heart: the job of the American president isn't to manage American decline. The job of the American president is to reverse it.[22]

Mitt Romney said as much on my show, after I quoted for

him the three statements made by President Obama which
opened this chapter:

You know, I don't think that President Obama understands America. I don't think he understands what makes
America work. I think his failure to get this economy going
flows from the fact that he doesn't understand how free
individuals and free enterprise drive the American economy. He is under the mistaken impression that government
is what makes America work. And so he's done the governmental things he wanted to do, and not surprisingly, they
have not worked to help the economy, so he's trying to find
someone to blame. And having begun by blaming President Bush, and then blaming Congress and Republicans
and ATM machines, he's finally come down to blaming
the American people. And the truth is, as Harry Truman
pointed out, the buck stops at his desk. His desk is where
the mistakes have been made, and it is not the American
people that don't know what to do. It's American people
who are being oppressed and overwhelmed by a government that is simply too intrusive in our lives. We've got to
scale back the size of the federal government. And if we
do that, America will be cooking again, and he's simply
wrong to suggest it's the American people's fault.[23]

Despite occasional bursts of President Obama's high-flying
rhetoric about American potential from the president—"The
America I know is generous and compassionate. It's a land of
opportunity and optimism.... We have led the world in sci-
entific research and technological breakthroughs that have
transformed millions of lives. That's who we are. This is the
America that I know. We don't have to choose between a future
of spiraling debt and one where we forfeit our investment in
our people and our country"[24]—the evidence of the president's
pessimism has built up throughout his term.

After the first apology tour came the "Greek exceptionalism" moment, after that his Mumbai confession, then his "way forward in Afghanistan," and then his San Francisco sigh. When one evaluates Obama's apologies in conjunction with his dire assessments, one easily concludes that his comments have evolved into explicit pessimism:

> We have lost our ambition, our imagination, and our willingness to do the things that built the Golden Gate Bridge.[25]

This is not the man to lead an American renaissance, any more than Jimmy Carter could be expected to rise above his personal sense of malaise, which he projected onto the country more than thirty years ago.

Conclusion
Back to the Future of 1980 and 1981

Yes we can!
> —President Obama, throughout the 2008 campaign[1]

No, sad to say, he couldn't.

Neither could "they," the gang he brought with him from Chicago, do "it," either.

Neither could all the Obamians in the Manhattan-Beltway media elite, pulling hard on every oar they could find and pulling still, and all the left-wing ideologuges who flocked to D.C. and into the DOJ, the EPA, and every other part of the Executive Branch.

Nor could Nancy Pelosi and Harry Reid, Barney Frank and Chris Dodd, Charles Rangel and Maxine Waters, Henry Waxman and Patrick Leahy, and all the king's horses and all the king's men of this epic fail we call the Obama presidency.

What he and they did do is prove you cannot kill America because our Framers put together a self-correcting, beautifully balanced, and enduring Constitution, one which allowed for a powerful rebuke to be delivered to President Obama in November 2010, and one which will send him packing in a few short months.

What he and they will also end up doing is proving the

resilience of the American system, of free enterprise combining with faith-driven traditional values to power freedom and prosperity not only here in America but around the globe.

We have been here before. In 1980. Under Jimmy Carter.

Some will argue we are much worse off now because of our debt, but then there was roaring inflation, sky-high interest rates and high unemployment; an aging, dangerous Soviet empire, armed to the teeth with nukes, excellent weaponry, and a real navy; and the expeditionary forces of a middle-aged as opposed to a dying (and perhaps dead by the time this book appears) Castro, spreading out across Africa and Central America. True, the fanatics who had taken over Iran under Carter and flourished there under Obama are now on the brink or already in possession of nukes, and many of them are messianic martyrs hoping to the induce the "Hidden Imam" from his well, but we are much stronger militarily vis-à-vis them than we were vis-à-vis the Soviets.

Okay, hard to say which is worse, then or now. Both are low points in modern American history. There will be more low points in the future.

I was a young man in 1980, just begun on my law school studies at the University of Michigan after two years on the staff of Richard Nixon, first at the Elba of America in San Clemente and then in New York City. Now I am fifty-six and wondering if my optimism is justified. *Commentary* magazine ran a symposium on optimists versus pessimists for its November 2011 issue, and I was among the optimists. Here is what I wrote for the issue, an issue which should be read in its entirety because its contributors are so much more qualified to write on such a subject than I am, and they are equally divided:

> Our abundant national energy, unrivaled technological genius, and history's most powerful military ought to leave me and everyone else an optimist about our country's future.

There is simply no better place or time to live than America at the end of 2011, even with the most incompetent president since the discovery of electricity, even after a horrific decade of tears and sacrifices made by the innocent at home and the best and brightest of America on battlefields across the world.

The widespread tentativeness, the gnawing doubt felt by all parents and grandparents, is due to government never having been this large, with burdens so sclerosis-inducing in all aspects of national life.

Out here in California—once the best place of all when measured by freedom and creativity, plentitude, and sheer exuberant living—the arteries have already closed, and the political class seems simply incapable of doing anything to reverse the disease. Asking the California legislature to repeal what must be repealed and slash the tax burdens that must be slashed is akin to asking a third grader to do calculus.

There simply isn't the capacity. Jerry Brown knows it. We all know it. The goose is on life support.

The California disease, like the deadly "greyscale" sickness in George R. R. Martin's Song of Ice and Fire novels, spreads slowly and inexorably across the country. Stupidity and power is a bad combination, and it seems as though the country has now touched the bottom California hit long ago. Again and again, interviews of people with power, from both parties and across all three branches, reveal they simply don't read, think, or analyze.

They don't know anything. And most of the media that covers them knows less.

Epic incompetence didn't matter so much when government was smaller. Now, penetrating every aspect of the economy and encroaching on what had previously been the private sphere, government incompetence is poisoning everything. Of all the hats I wear—law school professor, practicing lawyer, broadcaster, and writer—my experience

practicing law before federal regulatory agencies, witness-
ing the defense of businesses against trial lawyers with
absurd claims, constitutes the wellspring of my pessimism.

There are so many destroyers of wealth and produc-
tivity, legions of dim-witted and credentialed bullies, that
even the sunniest optimist may eventually pull down the
blinds.

But...young people loathe government. Many millions
who fell for Obama have learned a hard and necessary
lesson.

Amazing veterans of the wars are returning to take up
public life. They are smarter than can be imagined, wise
beyond their years, courageous, and ready to lead in politics as they have in combat.

And the relentless hum of technology mixing with freedom, still vastly more prevalent here than anywhere else, is
at work 24 hours a day in every corner of the country, from
the tiniest hamlet to New York City, all linked by a net of
astonishing power.

If upcoming elections deliver the rebuke to the tenured
overlords of government, media, and academia, it will be
enough to salvage the situation, just as the election of 1980
did 32 years ago.

If not, well then, I offer another George R. R. Martin
reference: "Winter is coming."[2]

What matters at this precise moment, in the months, weeks
and days leading up to the election of 2012, is that Americans
not look away, not pretend we are not in trouble, but instead
take up the task of rebuilding and renewal. Ronald Reagan led
the last reconstruction. Mitt Romney can lead the next, especially if voters across this country massively repudiate the stat-
ists and left-wing extremists of the Democratic Party at every
level of government, but especially within the House and Senate. Obamacare can be repealed, unemployment can return
to 5 percent or even slightly lower, home prices can rise, and

America's military can be re-equipped and funded to remain the best friend and worst enemy in history.

This book is something of a long "brief," but it takes as a model for breaking the rules of "briefs" the original "Brandeis brief," filed in the 1908 Supreme Court case of *Muller v. Oregon.* The case involved whether the hours women were obliged to work could be constitutionally limited, and Louis D. Brandeis, later a great Supreme Court Justice, turned in a brief of 113 pages packed with nonlegal data of the sort the Supreme Court was not used to reviewing.

"The brief was a masterpiece," wrote George Mason University School of Law professor David Bernstein in an essay titled "Brandeis Brief Myths" last year.[3]

"Relying on the able research talents of his sister-in-law, Josephine Goldmark, Brandeis presented a lengthy brief showing that long hours of labor harmed women's health," Bernstein continued. "The result was a unanimous decision by the Court upholding the law. Justice Brewer, one of the leading pro-laissez-faire Justices, was so taken by Brandeis's handiwork that he not only wrote the majority opinion, he also took the extraordinary step of acknowledging the influence of Brandeis's brief.

"Since then," Bernstein concluded, before going on to illuminate some of the myths around the famous brief, "the 'Brandeis Brief'—heavy on social science data and policy analysis, light on legal citation—has been a staple of American argument."

I would be happy if anyone was influenced by this book, much less influencers as lofty as the justices of the Supreme Court. I am hoping you have been and that you will press it on your friends, family and coworkers.

Smart politicians always *ask* voters for their votes, and then *thank* them for them.

I thank you for reading this book and ask you to provide it to others, soon. By the carton, if you will, or via links to the eBook or audio edition.

And that you do more than read and distribute. That you go to MittRomney.com and contribute as much as you can—the maximum contribution of $2,500 if you are blessed, $25 or $50 or $100 if money is tight—and sign up to work between now and the election on a daily and nightly basis to persuade, cajole, and push people to the polls for the purpose of retiring President Obama.

Pray for a long and happy life for the president and his wife, children, and eventually grandchildren. Pray that he finds good and important work to do.

But also pray that we never ever again indulge such an unserious campaign and such an unprepared individual with the Oval Office. The Republic is great and strong. But it cannot take another such term or president, and the Supreme Court cannot handle another set of nominees who believe they are superior to the Framers.

In September 2011, Justice Stephen Breyer did me a great honor and came to my radio studio in California and sat down for a long talk about the Court, the Constitution, and his book *Making Our Democracy Work*. I want to close this book by referencing that conversation because, as noted earlier, Justice Breyer is a gracious and very able exponent of President Obama's understanding of America and of the Constitution.

Here is the key exchange from that interview:

SB: I mean, some people think the answers are all found in history. Justice Scalia says that's originalism. And the motive of that is a good motive, because I think that they want to control the subjective influence of the judge. They think that what I do, for example, or by looking more to Congressional purposes, or trying to figure out what the values are underlying, say, the freedom of speech, underlying parts of the Constitution, they think it's too subjective. I don't think it's too subjective. I think I write down my reasons, and I think people are free to criticize them, and you have. There's nothing wrong with that. We're used to criticism. And that's fine. People certainly can criticize and pay attention to it in general. Of course they can criticize. But there are different approaches to these very grand problems, very different. And I think, for example, originalism doesn't work very well. I think it's pretty hard. I don't think George Washington knew about the Internet. I think our basic job there is to take the values in the Constitution, which don't change. They're virtually the same now as they were in the 18th Century. They're the values of the enlightenment, and apply them to today's world which changes every five minutes. I mean, yes, George Washington didn't know the Internet, nor did James Madison know about television, et cetera. And this world keeps changing.

HH: They knew liberty. That's what they knew. They knew liberty.

SB: Correct.

HH: Let me give you my favorite approach to the Constitution.

SB: All right.

HH: It's from the Massachusetts ratification convention, January 25th, 1788. Mr. Smith rises up and says "Mr. President, I am a plain man, and I get my living by the plow. I'm not used to speaking in public, but I beg your leave to say a few words to my brother plow joggers in this house." And he goes on to say "[W]hen I saw this Constitution, I found that it was a cure for these disorders. It was just such a thing as wanted. I got a copy of it and read it over and over. I had been a member of the convention to form our own state constitution, and learnt something of the checks and balances of power, and I found them all there, and I did not go to any lawyer to ask his opinion. We have no lawyers in our town, and we do well enough without. I form my own opinion, and I'm pleased with this Constitution."[4]

Justice Breyer's simple statement, "And this world keeps changing," cannot be denied. So it is, and so it will continue to do until the end of days.

But the implication—almost, though not quite, explicit—is that because the world changes judges and elites must have the power to change the rules to make do, to adjust, to cope with the "Internet" and "television," and one could say terrorism and the PRC and a thousand other things.

But that doesn't mean we should change the way we deal with those changes, or the principles on which we develop our solutions to the challenges they present. It shouldn't mean more agencies, and more spending, and less faith in "Nature and Nature's God." Just the opposite, in fact. We need more liberty and more allegiance to the Constitution, more of the free market, and a lot more of faithfulness to God's design as revealed in Scripture and in nature.

Unlike Farmer Smith, I am a lawyer, and proud to be one. But just as when he rose to address his state's ratification convention, still we can say with confidence that our Republic does not require lawyers—or media elites, public intellectuals, talking heads, or anybody other than you—to review the record of this president, the absolute, disastrous record of his time in office, and to conclude that he must be turned out and a new start begun.

Like Farmer Smith, I am pleased with the Constitution, including the many and crucial improvements made to it by formal amendment, including those to bring about equality and due process for all American regardless of the color of their skin, and extending the franchise to women and younger Americans. I want the Constitution to endure and the people it governs to prosper.

And that will require a change of address for President Obama next winter, and a very busy 2013 for President Romney and new Senate and House, as well as wisdom from the Supreme Court, energy in the states, and a renewed and liberated private sector free to produce energy and the wealth that energy brings that will benefit every American and the entire globe.

It can be done, and we know that because it has been done before. Because 1981 was as great as 1980 was awful, and President Reagan as successful as President Carter was failed.

It will be so again.

Acknowledgments

When my agent, Craig Wiley, suggested a book about the failure of the Obama presidency, I hesitated. There are scores of political books every election season, and I have pulled my oar in that water before. He pointed out, however, that if a book could help in the defeat of Obama even a bit, it was worth the effort. Constructed the right way, he later added, it could also serve as a first assessment of the many reasons why President Obama failed in such a spectacular fashion. So to Craig goes the credit for first mover.

And right there with Craig, Jack and Pina Templeton. Jack and Pina are patriots, and Jack's consistent encouragement to stay focused on the biggest issues has been invaluable, as have Pina's admonitions to leave off after a couple of hours of conversation.

As she has since 1989, Lynne Chapman shepherded the manuscript, this time ably assisted by researcher and editor extraordinaire Frederick Alexander Elmore, a man I name this way because he goes by Fred to some, Alex to others, and "indispensable" to me. Thanks as well to Snow Philip, who has, once again, brought her considerable copywriting skills to my errant prose and spelling.

The team at Center Street Books, led by senior editor Kate Hartson, has been a joy to work with on this first of our collaborations.

Over at radio central, the team of Duane Patterson and Adam Ramsey have been manning the controls since our launch in July 2000, with Anthony Ochoa in the background making the hamsters run, and Danielle Howe holding down the eastern border, a booker without parallel. Del has made a hobby of the show since his retirement, and he has brought us many smiles and snacks. Thanks to them all, but especially Duane, easily the best producer the world of radio has ever seen.

The interns, Nick, Breck, Sean, Zach, Collin, and Holly… well, they are interns, but much loved, as was Jerry Kushner, who while never an intern was always an enouragment and an inspiration.

And to our online legion, the "Tribbles," long may you noisily engage.

Salem Communications remains an extraordinary force for the good in the country, led by Edward Atsinger and Stuart Epperson, and assisted by, among many others, Greg Anderson, Tom Tradup, and Dave Sentrella. Russ Hauth carries the burden of having asked me to come to work at Salem, and his colleagues in the National News and Public Affairs division, Russ Shubin, David Spady, and their rising star pals, Greg Hengler and Derek Fowler, help each and every week to produce the content that drives the show, as well as the *Townhall Weekend Journal*. Lee Habeeb is a joy to work with. And to my editors at Townhall.com, especially the long-suffering Helen Whalen Cohen and John Hanlon, and to Mark Tapscott at the *Washington Examiner*, many thanks.

I am also in the debt of those among the Salem ranks who sell my show to affiliates, and the commercials within it to advertisers. "Nothing happens," it is often and truly said, "until somebody sells something." This is so true in the world of radio, buffeted by the new media revolution, but still here and now growing again as listeners look for the content that educates, encourages, and inspires. My thanks to my colleagues Bill Bennett, Mike Gallagher, Dennis Prager, and Michael

Medved, and to our competitor friends across the radio dial, especially Rush, who invented our medium; and Mark Levin and Sean Hannity, whose generous support of me has been particularly kind.

No one is paid a dime to appear as a guest on the radio show, but some do so week in and out just to help renew and restore the spirit of the audience. My thanks especially to these weekly or near-weekly regulars: Mark Steyn, James Lileks, Fred Barnes, Jim Geraghty, Chris Cillizza, Mike Allen, the "Smart Guys" Erwin Chemerinsky and John Eastman, Guy Benson and Mary Katharine Ham, Congressmen John Campbell and David Dreier, Michael Barone, Brian Wesbury, Emmett of the Unblinking Eye, and Tarzana Joe. Some gentlemen of the left have been willing to return agan and again over the years, and I salute them: Jonathan Alter, Jonathan Chait, E. J. Dionne, and Ryan Lizza have been particularly generous in their time. Many, many others appear and entertain and inform. Thank you.

Five of the program's most popular guests died far too young: Dean Barnett, Andrew Breitbart, Christopher Hitchens, Michael Kelly, and Tony Snow. Dean and Andrew were among my guest hosts, but all five were among the greatest controversialists of their age, and all are much missed.

My colleagues on the faculty and staff at Chapman University Law School, even those from across the political aisle, are unfailingly encouraging and usually willing to come on air to mix up the ideas which they believe and I reject. Chapman University president Jim Doti, provost Dr. Daniele Struppa, and Law School dean Tom Campbell are ever encouraging of this sort of sustained civic engagement and in the best ways.

My partners at Hewitt Wolensky LLP—Joseph Timothy Cook, Janet Hickson, Liz McNulty, and Gary Wolensky—as well as my old friends at O'Neil LLP are among the country's finest lawyers, and it remains an honor and a privilege to have worked alongside them. Even the people to whom I have sent the bills these many years, especially Mike McGee, Amy Glad, and Len Frank, have always been encouraging and have made lawyering a great joy.

And to my friends at the Semper Fi Fund, who each Memorial Day and Veterans Day bring me and the audience into the company of the best this country has ever produced, thank you for your service to them.

My radio audience is unique. For a dozen years now, beginning on July 10, 2000, they have walked with me through four presidential elections and one Florida recount, through a terrible September morning and the decade of war it launched, through economic booms and financial busts, and through a series of horrific days and beautiful, moving inspirations. You have been very kind in your support, and I am thankful for it, those who have called, those who have written, and those who have just listened and thrown in with various causes and candidates all these years.

Family and friends are endlessly patient with the unpredictable life of a talking head, especially Diana and Damon, Will and Jamie, and of course Elisabeth Lucy. I am so richly blessed by your encouragement, good humor, and faith. To Mark and Linda Roberts and Scott and Britta Bullock, thanks for your prayers.

And to Betsy, the light of my life and so many others, my greatest thanks and love.

Notes

Introduction. From "Hope and Change" to Epic Fail

1. Barack Obama. "A Defining Moment for Our Nation." *RealClearPolitics*. [June 4, 2008] http://www.realclearpolitics.com/articles/2008/06/obamas _victory_speech_in_st_pa.html [accessed November 8, 2011].
2. Personal Communication.
3. United States Department of Labor. Bureau of Labor Statistics. Seasonally adjusted. http://www.bls.gov/home.htm [accessed August 25,2011].
4. "30 Years of Spending Priorities." *Washington Post*. [February 14, 2011] http://www.washingtonpost.com/wp-srv/special/politics/30-years-spending -priorities-federal-budget-2012/ [accessed August 25, 2011].
5. Ibid.
6. Ibid.
7. Ibid.
8. Ibid.
9. Damian Paletta. "Deficit Is Again Set to Top $1 Trillion." *Wall Street Journal*. [February 1, 2012] http://online.wsj.com/article/SB1000142405297020474 0904577194872392678482.html [accessed February 10, 2012].
10. "30 Years of Spending Priorities."
11. Office of the Under Secretary of Defense (Comptroller). "National Defense Budget Estimates for FY 2012," p. 7. [March 2011] http://comptroller .defense.gov/defbudget/fy2012/FY12_Green_Book.pdf [accessed February 10, 2012].

Chapter 1. The Nightmare of Obamacare

1. *American Morning*. Super Tuesday. Transcript. [February 5, 2008] http:// transcripts.cnn.com/TRANSCRIPTS/0802/05/ltm.02.html [accessed October 10, 2011].
2. "Obama At House Republican Retreat in Baltimore: FULL VIDEO, TEXT." *Huffington Post*. [March 31, 2010] http://www.huffingtonpost .com/2010/01/29/transcript-of-president-o_n_442423.html [accessed October 10, 2011].

3. "Obama AMA Speech: Full Video, Full Text." *Huffington Post.* [June 15, 2009] http://www.huffingtonpost.com/2009/06/15/obama-ama-speech-full -tex_n_215699.html [accessed October 25, 2011].
4. Nicholas Ballasy. "Gov. Christie: Obamacare's Medicaid Mandates Are 'Drowning' States." *CNS News.* [May 9, 2011] http://www.cnsnews.com/ news/article/gov-christie-obamacare-s-medicaid-mandates-are-drowning -states [accessed October 20, 2011]. Also, see Kendra Marr. "Experts: Chris Christie's moment is now." *Politico.* [February 16, 2011] http://www.politico .com/news/stories/0211/49701.html [accessed October 20, 2011].
5. Toby Romm. "Some States Already Poised to Opt Out of Government-Run Public Health Plan." *The Hill.* [November 21, 2009] http://thehill.com/ homenews/senate/68967-some-states-already-poised-to-opt-out-of-public-plan [accessed October 22, 2011].
6. "Gov. Bob McDonnell (R-VA) Responds to State of the Union." CSPAN video. [January 27, 2010] http://www.youtube.com/watch?v=LeSLVnAQ SYo&feature=player_embedded# [accessed October 22, 2011], 2:35–55; 4:05–5:20; Olympia Meola. "McDonnell chides White House on Spending, Health Care." *Richmond Times-Dispatch.* [January 28, 2010] http:// www2.timesdispatch.com/news/2010/jan/28/mcdogat27_20100127 -224202-ar-13715/ [accessed October 22, 2011]; and Steve Padilla. "Republican response: Gov. Bob McDonnell invokes Jefferson." *Los Angeles Times.* [January 27, 2010] http://latimesblogs.latimes.com/washington/2010/01/ republican-response-x.html [accessed October 22, 2011].
7. "Governor McDonnell Signs Virginia Healthcare Freedom Act Legislation." Press Release. *Virginia.gov.* [March 24, 2010] http://www.governor .virginia.gov/news/viewRelease.cfm?id=88 [accessed October 22, 2011].
8. Publius. "Scott Brown: Remarks from Sunday's Campaign Rally in Worcester." *BigGovernment.* [January 17, 2010] http://biggovernment.com/ publius/2010/01/17/scott-brown-remarks-from-sundays-campaign-rally -in-worcester/ [accessed October 24, 2011].
9. David M. Halbfinger and Ian Urbina. "G.O.P. Wins Two Key Governors' Races; Bloomberg Prevails in a Close Contest." *New York Times.* [November 4, 2009] http://www.nytimes.com/2009/11/04/nyregion/04elect.html?pagewanted =all [accessed October 20, 2011].
10. "2009 Elections Results." *New York Times.* [November 9, 2009] http://elections .nytimes.com/2009/results/other.html [accessed October 24, 2011].
11. "Presidential Election of 2008, Electoral and Popular Vote Summary" *infoplease.com.* http://www.infoplease.com/us/government/presidential -election-vote-summary.html [accessed October 20, 2011].
12. Michael Cooper. "G.O.P. Senate Victory Stuns Democrats." *New York Times.* [January 19, 2010] http://www.nytimes.com/2010/01/20/us/politics/20election .html [accessed October 24, 2011].
13. NACo Video. "Pt. 2/2—Speaker Pelosi addresses NACo." Video. *YouTube.* [May 7, 2010] http://www.youtube.com/watch?v=nWEeP7bY9Lw [accessed October 20, 2011], 7:30-40.
14. Paula Span. "Congress Tackles Long-Term Care." *New York Times.* [July 22,

2009] http://newoldage.blogs.nytimes.com/2009/07/22/congress-tackles-long
-term-care/ [accessed October 25, 2011]; "CLASS Act Information."
American Association for Long-Term Care Insurance. [October 10, 2011]
http://www.aaltci.org/long-term-care-insurance/learning-center/CLASS
-Act.php [accessed October 25, 2011].

15. Ibid.
16. National Commission on Fiscal Responsibility and Reform. Commission
Members. *FiscalCommission.gov.* http://www.fiscalcommission.gov/members
[accessed October 25, 2011].
17. National Commission on Fiscal Responsibility and Reform. "The Moment of
Truth: Report of the National Commission on Fiscal Responsibility and Reform."
FiscalCommission.gov. [December 1, 2010] http://www.fiscalcommission.gov/
sites/fiscalcommission.gov/files/documents/TheMomentofTruth12_1_2010.pdf
[accessed October 25, 2011], 36.
18. Ibid., 37.
19. Kathleen Sebelius. "Kaiser Family Foundation Briefing on Long-term Care."
U.S. Department of Health & Human Services. [February 7, 2011] http://
www.hhs.gov/secretary/about/speeches/sp20110207.html [accessed October
25, 2011]; J. Lester Feder. "Kathleen Sebelius Gets Ahead of CLASS
debate." *Politico.* [February 7, 2011] http://www.politico.com/news/stories/
0211/49001.html [accessed October 25, 2011].
20. Brett Norman. "End of CLASS Act Marks Rapid Change for White
House." *Politico.* [October 14, 2011] http://www.politico.com/news/stories/
1011/66015.html [accessed October 25, 2011].
21. Ibid.
22. Ibid.
23. Paula Span. "Congress Tackles Long-Term Care." *New York Times.* [July 22,
2009] http://newoldage.blogs.nytimes.com/2009/07/22/congress-tackles-long
-term-care/ [accessed October 25, 2011].
24. Jordan Rau. "Poll Finds Americans Gloomy on Some Promises In Health
Law." [July 28, 2011] http://www.kaiserhealthnews.org/Stories/2011/July/
28/kff-poll-americans-gloomy-health-law-promises.aspx[accessedOctober25,
2011]. The poll results can be found at http://www.kff.org/kaiserpolls/8209
.cfm [accessed October 25, 2011].
25. Janet Adamy. "Health Insurers Plan Hikes." *Wall Street Journal.* [September-
ber 7, 2010] http://online.wsj.com/article/SB10001424052748703720004575
5478200948908976.html [accessed October 25, 2011]; and Hewitt Associates. "U.S. Health Care Cost Rate Increases Reach Highest Levels in Five
Years, According to New Data from Hewitt Associates." Hewitt News
Release Archive. [September 27, 2010] http://aon.mediaroom.com/index
.php?s=114&item=89 [accessed October 25, 2011].
26. Aaron Yelowitz. "ObamaCare: A Bad Deal for Young Adults." The Cato
Institute, Briefing Paper no. 115. [November, 5, 2009] http://www.cato.org/
pubdisplay.php?pub id=10933 [accessed August 18, 2011], 3.
27. Linda Blumberg et al., "Age Rating Under Comprehensive Health Care
Reform: Implications for Coverage, Costs and Household Financial Burdens,"

Urban Institute/Robert Wood Johnson Foundation. [October 07, 2009] http://www.rwjf.org/files/research/49470.pdf [accessed August 18, 2011]; and Carla Johnson. "Health Premiums Could Rise 17 Percent for Young Adults." Associated Press, *Seattle Times*. [March 29, 2010] http://seattletimes .nwsource.com/html/nationworld/2011474724_healthage30.html [accessed August 20, 2011].

28. Tarren Bragdon. "Command and Control: Maine's Dirigo Health Care Program." Heritage Foundation Backgrounder no. 1878. [September 19, 2005] http://www.heritage.org/Research/Reports/2005/09/Command -and-Control-Maines-Dirigo-Health-Care-Program [accessed August 22, 2011].

29. U.S. Census Bureau. "Health Insurance Historical Tables," Table HIA-6. http://www.census.gov/hhes/www/hlthins/data/historical/files/hihistt6.xls [accessed August 22, 2011].

30. Tarren Bragdon and Joel Allumbaugh. "Health Care Reform in Maine: Reversing 'Obamacare Lite.'" [July 19, 2011] http://www.heritage.org/ Research/Reports/2011/07/Health-Care-Reform-in-Maine-Reversing -Obamacare-Lite#ftn6 [accessed August 22, 2011].

31. America's Health Insurance Plans, Center for Policy Research. "Individual Health Insurance 2009: A Comprehensive Survey of Premiums, Availability, and Benefits." [October 2009] http://www.ahipresearch.org/pdfs/2009Indiv idualMarketSurveyFinalReport.pdf, p. 19 [accessed August 22, 2011].

32. Paul D. Jacobs. "The Patient Protection and Affordable Care Act's Effects on Employers' Decisions to Offer Health Insurance." Presentation at the Eighth World Congress of the International Health Economics Association. [July 2011] http://www.cbo.gov/doc.cfm?index=12374 [accessed August 18, 2011].

33. Shubham Singhal, Jeris Stueland, and Drew Ungerman. "How US Health Care Reform Will Affect Employee Benefits." *McKinsey Quarterly*. [June 2011] http://www.mckinseyquarterly.com/How_US_health_care_reform _will_affect_employee_benefits_2813 [accessed August 18, 2011].

34. "The Impact of Health Care Reform on Employers." A survey of 650 mid- to senior-level benefit professionals. [May 2010] http://www.towerswatson .com/united-states/research/1935 [accessed August 20, 2011].

35. "Bargaining Facts." 2011 Bargaining Information. *Verizon*. http://newscenter .verizon.com/2011-bargaining/bargaining-facts.html [accessed October 25, 2011].

36. Lachlan Markay. "In Verizon Strike, Unions Protest Obamacare Law They Supported." [August 19, 2011] http://blog.heritage.org/2011/08/19/in-verizon -strike-unions-protest-obamacare-law-they-helped-pass/ [accessed August 20, 2011].

37. John C. Goodman. "Goodbye, Employer-Sponsored Insurance." *Wall Street Journal*. [May 21, 2010] http://online.wsj.com/article/SB100014240527487 03880304575236602943319816.html [accessed August 20, 2011].

38. Duff Wilson. "Industry Aims at Medicare Board." *New York Times*. [November 4, 2010] http://prescriptions.blogs.nytimes.com/2010/11/04/ industry-targets-medicare-board/ [accessed October 20, 2011].

Chapter 2. A Failed *"Stimulus"*

1. Mike Allen. "Obama Sounds Economic Warning." *Politico.* [January 8, 2009] http://www.politico.com/news/stories/0109/17208_Page2.html [accessed October 10, 2011].
2. The Recovery Act. *Recovery.gov.* http://www.recovery.gov/about/pages/the_act.aspx [accessed February 5, 2012].
3. The White House. Office of the Press Secretary. "Administration Kicks Off 'Recovery Summer' with Groundbreakings and Events Across the Country." [June 17, 2010] http://www.whitehouse.gov/the-press-office/administration-kicks-recovery-summer-with-groundbreakings-and-events-across-country [accessed November 2, 2011].
4. Simmi Aujla. "Pelosi: Stimulus 'Definitely Worth It.'" *Politico.* [February 17, 2011] http://www.politico.com/news/stories/0211/49763.html [accessed February 13, 2012].
5. "*Newsweek*'s Jonathan Alter on Barack Obama, the Savior of Route 3 in New Jersey." *HughHewitt.com.* [September 15, 2010] http://www.hughhewitt.com/transcripts.aspx?id=6a1adbf5-a049-438e-81d5-ac33cab50371 [accessed February 5, 2012].
6. Jonathan V. Last. "Being Obama." *Weekly Standard.* [September 5, 2011] http://www.weeklystandard.com/articles/being-obama_591426.html [accessed September 15, 2011].
7. Garrett Jones and Daniel M. Rothschild. "No Such Thing as Shovel Ready." Working paper. Mercatus Center. [August 30, 2011] http://mercatus.org/publication/no-such-thing-shovel-ready [accessed September 15, 2011].
8. It is worth noting that when the Stimulus passed, the administration created http://www.recovery.gov, which attempts to both make stimulus spending transparent and to measure its effect on the economy. In some way, then, someone can point and say, "The stimulus went here and did that."
9. In addition to the obvious logic that any jobs directly created by Stimulus money are threatened as soon as the Stimulus is spent—thus providing only temporary employment—a recent study indicates that only about half of the jobs created by the Stimulus were filled with someone who was previously unemployed. See Garett Jones and Daniel M. Rothschild. "Did Stimulus Dollars Hire the Unemployed?" Working paper. Mercatus Center. [August 30, 2011] http://mercatus.org/publication/did-stimulus-dollars-hire-unemployed [accessed September 15, 2011]. As Veronique de Rugy points out at *National Review*, poaching employees from another firm potentially creates job opportunity at that other firm, but it does not guarantee that, and all such transfers cost both companies money. See "Why Didn't Stimulus Spending Deliver the Promised Jobs?" *National Review.* [August 31, 2011] http://www.nationalreview.com/corner/275947/why-didnt-stimulus-spending-deliver-promised-jobs-veronique-de-rugy [accessed September 15, 2011].

Chapter 3. Doubling Down on Failure: *"Stimulus 2.0"*

1. "Text: Obama's Job Speech: 'There are Steps We Can Take Right Now.'" *National Journal.* [September 9, 2011] http://www.nationaljournal.com/

whitehouse/text-obama-s-jobs-speech-there-are-steps-we-can-take-right
-now—20110908 [accessed September 14, 2011].

2. Congressional Budget Office. "CBO's Economic Projections for Calendar
   Years 2012 to 2022. Testimony on the Budget and Economic Outlook:
   Fiscal Years 2012 to 2022." Table 2. [February 2, 2012]. http://www.cbo
   .gov/ftpdocs/127xx/doc12713/02-02-TestimonyOutlook-Senate.pdf
   [accessed February 11, 2012].

3. The White House. Office of the Press Secretary. "Address by the President
   to a Joint Session of Congress." [September 8, 2011] http://www.whitehouse
   .gov/the-press-office/2011/09/08/address-president-joint-session-congress
   [accessed November 2, 2011].

4. "Obama Calls on Congress to Quickly Pass His 'American Jobs Act.'"
   CNN. [September 8, 2011] http://articles.cnn.com/2011-09-08/politics/
   obama.jobs.plan_1_president-obama-deficit-reduction-political-circus?
   _s=PM:POLITICS [accessed November 2, 2011].

5. Ibid.

6. Ibid.

7. Zachary A. Goldfarb. "Obama Announces $447 Billion Plan to Boost Econ-
   omy." Washington Post. [September 8, 2011] http://www.washingtonpost
   .com/business/economy/obama-lays-out-447-billion-plan-to-boost-nations
   -economy/2011/09/08/gIQAk3ELDK_story_1.html [accessed November 2,
   2011].

8. Devin Dwyer. "First Glimpse inside Obama's Armored Tour Bus." ABC
   News. [August 17, 2011] http://abcnews.go.com/blogs/politics/2011/08/
   first-glimpse-inside-obamas-armored-tour-bus/ [accessed November 2,
   2011].

9. Glenn Kessler. "Biden's Absurd Claims about Rising Rape and Murder
   Rates." Washington Post. [October 21, 2011] http://www.washingtonpost
   .com/blogs/fact-checker/post/bidens-absurd-claims-about-rising-rape-and
   -murder-rates/2011/10/20/gIQAkq0y1L_blog.html [accessed November 3,
   2011].

10. Lois Lee. "Vice President Joe Biden Talks Jobs Act at Penn." Daily Penn-
    sylvanian. [October 18, 2011] http://thedp.com/index.php/article/2011/10/
    joe_biden_talks_jobs_act [accessed November 2, 2011]; HumanEvents.
    "All Huffy, Joe Biden Stands by Rape Reference to GOP." Video. YouTube
    .com. [October 19, 2011] http://www.youtube.com/watch?v=fxxotkX9ZOo
    [accessed November 2, 2011].

11. "Biden Now Pitching Obama's Dead 'Jobs' Bill to 4th Grade Class." Fox
    News. [October 19, 2011] http://nation.foxnews.com/joe-biden/2011/
    10/19/biden-now-pitching-obamas-dead-jobs-bill-4th-grade-class [accessed
    November 2, 2011].

12. "Mark Steyn on Democratic Rhetoric and the Coming Raping of Cowboy
    Poets Everywhere." HughHewitt.com. [October 21, 2011] http://www
    .hughhewitt.com/transcripts.aspx?id=5880ddfc-f147-4ffa-afa6
    -f481b4db7bf6 [accessed November 2, 2011].

13. David Jackson. "Obama's Call For Jobs Vote Requires Democrats." USA-
    Today. [October 5, 2011] http://content.usatoday.com/communities/theoval/

post/2011/10/obamas-call-for-jobs-vote-requires-democrats/1 [accessed February 6, 2012].

14. The White House. Office of the Press Secretary. "Remarks by the President on Economic Growth and Deficit Reduction." [September 19, 2011] http://www.whitehouse.gov/the-press-office/2011/09/19/remarks-president-economic-growth-and-deficit-reduction [accessed November 2, 2011].

15. The White House. Office of the Press Secretary. "President Obama News Conference." [June 29, 2011] http://www.whitehouse.gov/photos-and-video/video/2011/06/29/president-obama-news-conference#transcript [accessed November 2, 2011].

16. David Nakamura. "Obama on *Tonight Show with Jay Leno*: Full Video and Transcript." *Washington Post*. [October 26, 2011] http://www.washingtonpost.com/blogs/44/post/obama-on-tonight-show-with-jay-leno-full-video-and-transcript/2011/10/26/gIQAHXJjIM_blog.html [accessed November 3, 2011].

17. The White House. Office of the Press Secretary. "Press Briefing by Press Secretary Jay Carney." [October 28, 2011] http://www.whitehouse.gov/the-press-office/2011/10/28/press-briefing-press-secretary-jay-carney [accessed November 3, 2011].

18. Devin Dwyer. "Biden: Occupy Wall Street, Tea Party Have Frustration in Common." *ABC News*. [October 6, 2011] http://abcnews.go.com/blogs/politics/2011/10/biden-occupy-wall-street-tea-party-have-frustration-in-common/ [accessed November 3, 2011]; James Oliphant. "Biden Likens Occupy Wall-Street to Tea Party, Blasts BofA." *Los Angeles Times*. [October 6, 2011] http://articles.latimes.com/2011/oct/06/news/la-pn-biden-wall-street-20111006 [accessed November 3, 2011].

19. Jessica Desvarieux. "Pelosi Supports Occupy Wall Street Movement." *ABC News*.[October 9, 2011]http://abcnews.go.com/Politics/pelosi-supports-occupy-wall-street-movement/story?id=14696893 [accessed November 3, 2011].

20. "Reid Invokes Occupy Wall Street on Senate Floor." *Politico*. [October 31, 2011] http://www.politico.com/blogs/glennthrush/1011/Reid_sympathetic_to_Occupy_Wall_Street.html [accessed November 3, 2011].

21. The White House. Office of the Press Secretary. "Administration Kicks Off 'Recovery Summer' with Groundbreakings and Events across the Country." [June 17, 2010] http://www.whitehouse.gov/the-press-office/administration-kicks-recovery-summer-with-groundbreakings-and-events-across-country [accessed November 2, 2011].

Chapter 4. The Biggest Spendthrift—in History

1. "Flashback: Obama Calls Adding $4 Trillion to the National Debt 'Unpatriotic.'" *Hotair.com*. [August 24, 2011] http://hotair.com/archives/2011/08/24/flashback-obama-calls-adding-4-trillion-to-national-debt-unpatriotic/ [accessed February 6, 2011].

2. Christopher Chantrill. "Time Series Chart of US Government Spending." http://www.usgovernmentspending.com/downchart_gs.php?year=&chart=G0-fed&units=b [accessed September 21, 2011].

3. Ibid.
4. "30 Years of Spending Priorities." *Washington Post.* [February 14, 2011] http://www.washingtonpost.com/wp-srv/special/politics/30-years-spending-priorities-federal-budget-2012/ [accessed February 13, 2012].
5. Kate Phillips. "Obama Rallies Democrats on Stimulus Package." *New York Times.* [February 5, 2009] http://thecaucus.blogs.nytimes.com/2009/02/05/obama-rallies-democrats-on-stimulus-package/ [accessed September 9, 2011].
6. John Steele Gordon. "A Short Primer on the National Debt." [August 29, 2011] *Wall Street Journal.* http://online.wsj.com/article/SB10001424053111903480904576510660976229354.html?mod=djemEditorialPage_h [accessed September 21, 2011].
7. "US National Debt & Interest Expense by Presidential Term, Percentage of GDP." [January 2, 2012] http://www.presidentialdebt.org/ [accessed September, 21 2011].
8. "Debt to the Penny and Who Holds It." *Treasury Direct.* http://www.treasurydirect.gov/NP/BPDLogin?application=np [accessed September 21, 2011].
9. "Interest Expense on the Debt Outstanding." *Treasury Direct.* http://www.treasurydirect.gov/govt/reports/ir/ir_expense.htm [accessed September 21, 2011].
10. Nelson D. Schwartz. "Interest Rates Have Nowhere to Go but Up." *New York Times.* [April 10, 2010] http://www.nytimes.com/2010/04/11/business/economy/11rates.html [accessed September 21, 2011].
11. Michael Pollaro. "Interest on U.S. Government Debt, a Brewing Time Bomb." *True/Slant.* [February 19, 2010]. http://trueslant.com/michaelpollaro/2010/02/19/interest-on-u-s-government-debt-a-brewing-time-bomb/ [accessed September 21, 2011]. For charts, see http://www.lewrockwell.com/orig11/pollaro1.1.1.html.
12. Schwartz. "Interest Rates Have Nowhere to Go but Up."

Chapter 5. The Community Organizer Collapses Housing

1. Nick Timiraos. "Obama: Housing Market Faces 'Tough Decisions.'" *Wall Street Journal.* [September 20, 2010] http://blogs.wsj.com/developments/2010/09/20/obama-housing-market-faces-tough-decisions/ [accessed October 10, 2011].
2. The number of homes completed in the United States between January and December 2006. U.S. Census Bureau and U.S. Department of Housing and Urban Development. "New Residential Construction in December 2006." Table 5. [January 18, 2007] http://www.census.gov/const/newresconst_200612.pdf [accessed September 6, 2011].
3. The number of homes completed in the United States between January and December 2010. U.S. Census Bureau and U.S. Department of Housing and Urban Development. "New Residential Construction in December 2010." Table 5. [January 19, 2011]. http://www.census.gov/const/newresconst_201012.pdf [accessed September 6, 2011].

4. The number of homes completed in the United States between January and July 2011. U.S. Census Bureau and U.S. Department of Housing and Urban Development. "New Residential Construction in December 2010." Table 5. [August 16, 2011]. http://www.census.gov/const/newresconst_201107 .pdf [accessed September 6, 2011]. For the sake of comparison: in 2010, 4,880,000 (or 62 percent) of the 7,866,000 homes completed were built by July; in 2006, 10,274,000 (or 43 percent) of the 23,869,000 homes completed were built by July.

5. Russ Lay. "How Many Jobs Does It Take to Build a House?" *The Outer Banks.* [July 30, 2010]. http://outerbanksvoice.com/2010/07/30/how-many -jobs-does-it-take-to-build-a-house-3/ [accessed September 6, 2011]. The last in a series of four blog posts about the process of building a house in North Carolina and a record of the people and jobs required for its completion.

6. Good introductory resource: Jonathan Jarvis. "Crisis of Credit Visualized." http://jonathanjarvis.com/crisis-of-credit [accessed September 6, 2011].

7. "The number of total foreclosure filings rose from about 885,000 in 2005 to 1,259,118 in 2006. While that is a substantial increase, it is still within the scope of normal historical averages." From "More than 1.2 million foreclosure filings reported in 2006." *RealtyTrac.* [February 8, 2001] http://www .realtytrac.com/content/press-releases/more-than-12-million-foreclosure -filings-reported-in-2006-2234 [accessed September 6, 2011].

8. "US Foreclosures Rise in December; Reach 2.2 Mln in 207, Up 75 Pct from 2006." *Forbes.* [January 29, 2008] http://webcache.googleuser content.com/search?q=cache:YykAaqq3i4IJ:www.forbes.com/feeds/ afx/2008/01/29/afx4584956.html+&cd=1&hl=en&ct=clnk&gl=us&client= firefox-a [accessed February 6, 2012].

9. Stephanie Armour. "2008 Foreclosure Filings Set Record." *USA Today.* [February 3, 2009] http://www.usatoday.com/money/economy/housing/2009-01-14 -foreclosure-record-filings_N.htm [accessed September 6, 2011]. This set a new annual record.

10. Venessa Wong. "Foreclosures: An Increase of 21% in 2009 and Climbing." *Businessweek.* [January 14, 2010] http://www.businessweek.com/lifestyle/ content/jan2010/bw20100113_985068.htm [accessed September 7, 2011]; and Jon Prior. "Foreclosure Filings Hit New Record in 2009: RealtyTrac." *HousingWire.* http://www.housingwire.com/2010/01/14/foreclosure-filings -climb-another-21-in-2009-realtytrac [accessed September 7, 2011]. CNNMoney reports the number to be 2,824,674. Les Christie. "Record 3 Million Households Hit with Foreclosure in 2009." *CNNMoney.* [January 14, 2010] http://money.cnn.com/2010/01/14/real_estate/record_foreclosure_year/ [accessed September 6, 2011].

11. Jon Prior. "Foreclosures in 2011 to Break Last Year's Record: RealtyTrac." *HousingWire.* [January 12, 2011] http://www.housingwire.com/2011/01/12/ foreclosures-reach-record-high-in-2010-realtytrac [accessed September 7, 2011]; Corbett B. Daly. "Home Foreclosures in 2010 Top 1 Million for First Time." *Reuters.* [January 13, 2011] http://www.reuters.com/article/ 2011/01/13/us-usa-housing-foreclosures-idUSTRE70C0YD20110113 [accessed September 7, 2011]. This cites 2.9 million foreclosure filings in

2010. I used the former number because its original source is the same as the original source of the other numbers I've cited—RealtyTrac.

12. Jon Prior. "Foreclosures in 2011 to break last year's record: RealtyTrac"; Janna Herron. "Banks Repossessed 1 Million Homes Last Year—and 2011 Will Be Worse." *MSNBC.* [January 13, 2011] http://www.msnbc.msn.com/id/41051419/ns/business-real_estate/t/banks-repossessed-million-homes-last-year-will-be-worse/ [accessed September 7, 2011]; and "Bernanke Predicts High Level of Foreclosure Starts in 2011." *Fox.* [April 4, 2011] http://www.myfoxny.com/dpps/your_money/bernanke-predicts-high-level-of-foreclosure-starts-in-2011-dpgonc-20110404-bb_12624879 [accessed September 7, 2011].

13. These prices include the price of the land. U.S. Census Bureau. "Median and Average Sales Prices of New Homes Sold in United States." http://www.census.gov/const/uspricemon.pdf [accessed September 7, 2011].

14. "National Real Estate Trends." *RealtyTrac.* http://www.realtytrac.com/trendcenter/trend.html [accessed February 6, 2012].

15. Austin Kilgore. "Shadow Inventory Could Reach 5.5m by 2011: Report." *HousingWire.* [May 21, 2010], http://www.housingwire.com/2010/05/21/shadow-inventory-could-reach-5-5m-by-2011-report [accessed September 7, 2011].

16. Bureau of Labor Statistics. "Real Estate Brokers and Sales Agents." In *Occupational Outlook Handbook, 2010–11 Edition.* [May 17, 2010] http://www.bls.gov/oco/ocos120.htm [accessed September 7, 2011].

17. "Q1 2011 Negative Equity Report." *CoreLogic.* [June 7, 2011] http://www.corelogic.com/about-us/researchtrends/negative-equity-report.aspx# [accessed September 7, 2011]; "Q2 Negative Equity Declines in Hardest Hit Markets." *CoreLogic.* [September 13, 2011] http://www.corelogic.com/about-us/researchtrends/asset_upload_file591_13850.pdf [accessed February 6, 2012].

18. CNNMoney published a helpful guide to "Obama's housing scorecard" on August 31, 2011, written by Les Christie, which lists the various government-sponsored initiatives intended to help home owners, participation in the program, and what measurable effects the programs have had; it's available at http://money.cnn.com/2011/08/31/real_estate/obama_housing_scorecard/index.htm [accessed September 7, 2011].

Chapter 6. Swelling the Rolls of the Unemployed

1. George Will. "Will: Obama Said Stimulus Would Cap Unemployment at 8 Percent." *Politifact.com.* [July 11, 2010] http://www.politifact.com/truth-o-meter/statements/2010/jul/13/george-will/will-obama-said-stimulus-would-cap-unemployment-8-/ [accessed September 15, 2011].

2. Alex Wagner. "Biden Lays Out Plans for 'Recovery Summer.'" *Politics Daily.* [June 18, 2010] http://www.politicsdaily.com/2010/06/18/biden-lays-out-plans-for-recovery-summer/ [accessed September 15, 2011].

3. Bureau of Labor Statistics. Labor Force Statistics from the Current Popula-

tion Survey." [September 2, 2011] http://www.bls.gov/web/empsit/cpseea01 .htm [accessed September 15, 2011].

4. Bureau of Labor Statistics. "Labor Force Statistics from the Current Population Survey." Databases, Tables & Calculators by Subject. [September 15, 2011] http://data.bls.gov/timeseries/LNS14000000 [accessed February 7, 2012].

5. U.S. Department of Commerce. Bureau of Economic Analysis. http://www .bea.gov/newsreleases/national/gdp/gdpnewsrelease.htm [accessed September 15, 2011].

6. Bureau of Economic Analysis. National Economic Accounts. "Percent Change from Preceding Period." [August 26, 2011] http://www.bea.gov/ national/index.htm#gdp [accessed September 15, 2011].

7. Ibid.

8. Jillian Berman. "Consumer Sentiment in U.S. Plunges to a Three-Decade Low." *Bloomberg Businessweek*. [August 12, 2011] http://www.businessweek .com/news/2011-08-12/consumer-sentiment-in-u-s-plunges-to-a-three -decade-low.html [accessed September 15, 2011].

9. Michael J. Boskin. "The Obama Presidency by the Numbers." *Wall Street Journal*. [September 8, 2011] http://online.wsj.com/article/SB10001424053 111904583204576544712358583844.html [accessed September 15, 2011].

10. Richard W. Stevenson. "Early Economic Projections Could Haunt Obama in 2012." *New York Times*. [November 4, 2011] http://thecaucus.blogs .nytimes.com/2011/11/04/early-economic-projections-could-haunt -obama-in-2012/?scp=1&sq=unemployment_and_obama_and _predictions&st=cse [accessed November 8, 2011].

Chapter 7. Soaring Gas Prices and Green Energy Scams

1. The White House. Office of the Press Secretary. "Weekly Address: Instead of Subsidizing Yesterday's Energy Sources, We Need to Invest in Tomorrow's." [April 23, 2011] http://www.whitehouse.gov/the-press-office/2011/ 04/23/weekly-address-instead-subsidizing-yesterdays-energy-sources -we-need-inv [accessed October 8, 2011].

2. The White House. Office of the Press Secretary. "Remaks by the President on State of the Union Address." [January 25, 2011] http://www.whitehouse .gov/the-press-office/2011/01/25/remarks-president-state-union-address [accessed March 24, 2012].

3. U.S. Energy Information Administration (hereinafter USEIA). "Weekly U.S All Grades All Formulations Retail Gasoline Prices (Dollars per Gallon)." U.S. Retail Gasoline Historical Prices. [October 3, 2011] http://www.eia .gov/petroleum/gasdiesel/xls/pswrgvwall.xls [accessed February 7, 2012].

4. Ibid.

5. USEIA. "Weekly U.S All Grades All Formulations Retail Gasoline Prices (Dollars per Gallon)"; and Rory Cooper. "In Pictures: Bush vs. Obama on Gas Prices." *The Foundry*. [March 4, 2011] http://blog.heritage .org/2011/03/04/ in-pictures-bush-vs-obama-on-gas-prices/ [accessed October 7, 2011].

6. USEIA. "Weekly U.S All Grades All Formulations Retail Gasoline Prices (Dollars per Gallon)."

7. Ibid.

8. The White House. Office of the Press Secretary. "Weekly Address: Instead of Subsidizing Yesterday's Energy Sources, We Need to Invest in Tomorrow's." [April 23, 2011] http://www.whitehouse.gov/the-press -office/2011/04/23/weekly-address-instead-subsidizing-yesterdays-energy -sources-we-need-inv [accessed October 8, 2011].

9. Jake Tapper and Huma Khan. "Drill, Baby, Drill: Obama Opens Up Off- shore Drilling and Exploration." *ABC News*. [March 31, 2010] http:// abcnews.go.com/WN/Politics/obama-opens-offshore-drilling-oil-gas -exploration/story?id=10249811 [accessed October 8, 2011].

10. "Timeline—Gulf of Mexico Oil Spill." *Reuters*. [June 3, 2010] http://www .reuters.com/article/2010/06/03/oil-spill-events-idUSN0322326220100603 [accessed October 8, 2011].

11. "Gulf of Mexico Oil Spill: Timeline and Q&A." *GOP.gov*. [June 16, 2010] http://www.gop.gov/policy-news/10/06/16/gulf-of-mexico-oil-spill [accessed October 8, 2011].

12. Huma Khan. "White House Says No New Offshore Drilling Until Investi- gation is Complete." *ABC News*. [April 30, 2010] http://abcnews.go.com/ GMA/Politics/gulf-mexico-oil-spill-jeopardize-obamas-offshore-drilling/ story?id=10512504 [accessed October 8, 2011].

13. "Gulf of Mexico Oil Spill: Timeline and Q&A."

14. "Gulf of Mexico Oil Spill: Timeline and Q&A"; 33 U.S.C. 26 §1321(c)(1) (a-b). http://www.gpo.gov/fdsys/pkg/USCODE-2009-title33/pdf/USCODE -2009-title33-chap26-subchapIII.pdf [accessed February 8, 2012].

15. The White House. Office of the Press Secretary. "Remarks by the President to the Nation on the BP Oil Spill." [June 15, 2010] http://www.whitehouse.gov/ the-press-office/remarks-president-nation-bp-oil-spill [accessed October 8, 2011].

16. Campbell Robertson. "Efforts to Repel Oil Spill Are Described as Chaotic." *New York Times*. [June 14, 2010] http://www.nytimes.com/2010/06/15/ science/earth/15cleanup.html?pagewanted=all [accessed October 8, 2011].

17. Daniel Kaniewski and James Carafano. "Flooded with Help—But Still Flail- ing." *Homeland Security Policy Institute Commentary* 13. [June 24, 2010] http://www.gwumc.edu/hspi/policy/commentary13_OilSpill.cfm [accessed October 8, 2011].

18. Juliet Eilperin and Glenn Kessler. "After Delays, U.S. Begins to Tap Foreign Aid for Gulf Oil Spill." *Washington Post*. [June 14 2010] http://www.wash ingtonpost.com/wp-dyn/content/article/2010/06/13/AR2010061304232. html?sid=ST2010061305087 [accessed October 8, 2011].

19. "Obama Extends Moratorium on Offshore Drilling." *CBS News*. [May 27, 2010] http://www.cbsnews.com/stories/2010/05/27/politics/main6523412 .shtml [accessed October 8, 2011].

20. "Drilling Bits of Fiction." *Wall Street Journal*. [June 10, 2010] http:// online.wsj.com/article/SB10001424052748704575304575290678267562

5258.html?KEYWORDS=Drilling+Bits+of+Fiction [accessed October 8, 2011].

21. Ibid.

22. Jan Crawford. "Judge Slams Administration, Lifts Drilling Moratorium." *CBS News.* [June 22, 2010] http://www.cbsnews.com/8301-504564_162 -20008490-504564.html [accessed October 8, 2011]; and "Judge Blocks Offshore Drilling Moratorium." *CBS News.* [June 23, 2010] http://www .cbsnews.com/stories/2010/06/22/national/main6607071.shtml?tag=conte ntMain;contentBody [accessed October 8, 2011].

23. Brian Montopoli. "White House Will Appeal Decision Blocking Oil Drilling Moratorium." *CBS News.* [June 22, 2010] http://www.cbsnews.com/ 8301-503544_162-20008463-503544.html?tag=contentMain;content Body [accessed October 8, 2011].

24. Ashby Jones. "Fifth Circuit Rejects Obama's Request on Drilling Moratorium." *Wall Street Journal.* [July 9, 2010] http://blogs.wsj.com/law/ 2010/07/09/fifth-circuit-rejects-obamas-appeal-on-drilling-moratorium/ [accessed October 8, 2011].

25. "Obama Offshore Drilling Moratorium: Administration Issues New Rule." *Huffington Post.* [July 12, 2010] http://www.huffingtonpost .com/2010/07/12/obama-offshore-drilling-m_n_643568.html [accessed October 8, 2011]; and Bryan Walsh. "Obama Issues New Offshore Drilling Moratorium." *Time.* [July 12, 2010] http://ecocentric.blogs.time .com/2010/07/12/obama-issues-new-offshore-drilling-moratorium/ [accessed October 8, 2011].

26. John R. Parkinson. "Obama Administration Lifts Off-Shore Drilling Moratorium." *ABC News.* [October 12, 2010] http://abcnews.go.com/ blogs/politics/2010/10/obama-administration-lifts-off-shore-drilling -moratorium/ [accessed October 8, 2011].

27. Juliet Eilperin. "Obama Administration Reimposes Offshore Oil Drilling Ban." *Washington Post.* [December 1, 2010] http://voices.washington post.com/post-carbon/2010/12/obama_administration_will_ban.html [accessed October 8, 2011].

28. John M. Broder and Clifford Krauss. "U.S. Halts Plan to Drill in Eastern Gulf." *New York Times.* [December 1, 2010] http://www.nytimes.com/ 2010/12/02/us/02drill.html?_r=1&nl=todaysheadlines&emc=a2 [accessed October 8, 2011].

29. Ryan Dezember. "Salazar Cautious on Drilling." *Wall Street Journal.* [February 26, 2011] http://online.wsj.com/article/SB10001424052748704150604576166781536820162.html [accessed October 9, 2011].

30. Amanda Carey. "Louisiana Sen. Mary Landrieu Grills Salazar on Offshore Drilling." *The Daily Caller.* [March 2, 2011] http://dailycaller.com/ 2011/03/02/louisiana-sen-mary-landrieu-grills-salazar-on-offshore -drilling/ [accessed October 9, 2011].

31. USEIA. "Weekly U.S All Grades All Formulations Retail Gasoline Prices (Dollars per Gallon)."

32. Carey. "Louisiana Sen. Mary Landrieu Grills Salazar on Offshore Drilling."

33. Curry W. Smith. "GPI—Gulf Permit Index—as of February 1." *Greater New Orleans Inc.* [February 3, 2011] http://gnoinc.org/press-releases/gpi-gulf-permit-index-as-of-february-1 [accessed October 9, 2011]; and Rob Bluey. "Permitorium: 103 Gulf of Mexico Drilling Plans Await Government Approval." *The Foundry.* http://blog.heritage.org/2011/02/04/permitorium-103-gulf-of-mexico-drilling-plans-await-government-approval/ [accessed October 9, 2011].

34. Steve Hargreaves. "Court Orders Obama to Act on Drilling Permits." *CNNMoney.* [February 21, 2011] http://money.cnn.com/2011/02/18/news/economy/oil_drilling_permits/ [accessed October 9, 2011]; and Carey. "Louisiana Sen. Mary Landrieu Grills Salazar on Offshore Drilling."

35. Amanda Carey. "Interior Secretary Salazar Cracks under Pressure and Begins Issuing Gulf of Mexico Drilling Permits." *The Daily Caller.* [March 1, 2011] http://dailycaller.com/2011/03/01/interior-secretary-salazar-cracks-under-pressure-and-begins-issuing-gulf-of-mexico-drilling-permits/ [accessed October 9, 2011].

36. Dan Berman. "Judge Holds Interior Department in Contempt." *Politico.* [February 2, 2011] http://www.politico.com/news/stories/0211/48745.html [accessed October 9, 2011].

37. Mark Tapscott. "Federal Judge to Salazar: Stop Stalling Drilling Permits." *Washington Examiner.* [February 17, 2011] http://washingtonexaminer.com/blogs/beltway-confidential/2011/02/federal-judge-orders-salazar-act-drilling-permits-within-month [accessed October 9, 2011]; and Hargreaves. "Court Orders Obama to Act on Drilling Permits."

38. "Update 1—Factbox—Deepwater Rigs Moved Out of the Gulf of Mexico." *Reuters.* [January 27, 2011] http://af.reuters.com/article/congoNews/idAFN2726555420110127 [accessed October 9, 2011].

39. Curry W. Smith. "GPI—Gulf Permit Index—As of September 20." *Greater New Orleans Inc.* [September 21, 2011] http://gnoinc.org/press-releases/gpi-gulf-permit-index-as-of-september-20 [accessed October 9, 2011].

40. Rob Bluey. "Rob Bluey: Off-Shore Drilling Bans, Delays Cost Government Revenue." *Washington Examiner.* [January 14, 2011] http://washingtonexaminer.com/opinion/op-eds/2011/01/rob-bluey-shore-drilling-bans-delays-cost-government-revenue [accessed October 9, 2011].

41. Ibid.

42. Ibid.

43. Juliet Eilperin. "White House Presses for New Climate, Wilderness Protections." *Washington Post.* [December 24, 2010] http://www.washingtonpost.com/wp-dyn/content/article/2010/12/23/AR2010122305643.html [accessed October 9, 2011].

44. U.S. Department of State. "Keystone XL Pipeline Project." http://www.keystonepipeline-xl.state.gov/clientsite/keystonexl.nsf?Open [accessed October 9, 2011].

45. David Sassoon. "EPA slows approval for Canada-Texas oil pipeline." *Guardian* (London). [July 27, 2010] http://www.guardian.co.uk/environment/2010/jul/27/epa-approval-canada-texas-oil-pipleine [accessed October 9, 2011]; and Juliet Eilperin. "Keystone XL Pipeline Becomes a Political Headache for White

House." *Washington Post.* http://www.washingtonpost.com/national/health-science/keystone-pipeline-issue-becomes-a-headache-for-the-white-house/2011/10/07/gIQAJJZ8TL_story.html [accessed October 9, 2011].

46. "House Natural Resources Chairman Doc Hastings on Why Gas Is So High Now." *The Hugh Hewitt Show.* [March 16, 2011] http://www.hughhewitt.com/transcripts.aspx?id=0fd39025-0369-4055-a897-d5a42307079d [accessed October 9, 2011].

47. U.S. Department of the Interior. "Salazar Launches 'Smart from the Start' Initiative to Speed Offshore Wind Energy Development off the Atlantic Coast." Press release. [November 23, 2010] http://www.doi.gov/news/pressreleases/Salazar-Launches-Smart-from-the-Start-Initiative-to-Speed-Offshore-Wind-Energy-Development-off-the-Atlantic-Coast.cfm [accessed October 9, 2011].

48. USEIA. "Weekly U.S All Grades All Formulations Retail Gasoline Prices (Dollars per Gallon)."

49. Ben Geman. "Obama Taps Strategic Oil to Help Supply, Economy." *The Hill.* [June 23, 2011] http://thehill.com/blogs/e2-wire/677-e2-wire/168049-obama-to-release-oil-from-strategic-reserve [accessed October 9, 2011].

50. USEIA. "Weekly U.S All Grades All Formulations Retail Gasoline Prices (Dollars per Gallon)."

51. The White House. Office of the Press Secretary. "President Bush Discusses Outer Continental Shelf Exploration." [July 14, 2008] http://georgewbush-whitehouse.archives.gov/news/releases/2008/07/20080714-4.html [accessed October 9, 2011].

52. USEIA. "Weekly U.S All Grades All Formulations Retail Gasoline Prices (Dollars per Gallon)"; and Rory Cooper. "In Pictures: Bush Vs. Obama On Gas Prices."

53. The White House. Office of the Press Secretary. "Weekly Address: Instead of Subsidizing Yesterday's Energy Sources, We Need to Invest in Tomorrow's." April 23, 2011.

54. Ibid.

55. Chart included in Martin LaMonic. "Once Booming, Green-Tech Investing Shifts Down." *CNET.* [July 20, 2011] http://news.cnet.com/8301-11128_3-20081107-54/once-booming-green-tech-investing-shifts-down/ [accessed October 10, 2011].

56. AIM Environmental Technology Program. "Environmental Investment Initiatives." *CalPERS.* http://www.calpers.ca.gov/index.jsp?bc=/investments/environ-invest/home.xml [accessed October 10, 2011].

57. "CalSTRS' Clean Technology Advisory Board Convenes First Meeting." *CalSTRS.* [October 21, 2004] http://www.calstrs.com/newsroom/2004/news102104.aspx [accessed October 10, 2011].

58. Chris DeArmond. "Google Invests Big In The Green Energy Revolution." *Green Conduct News.* [October 4, 2011] http://www.greenconduct.com/news/2011/10/04/google-invests-big-in-the-green-energy-revolution/ [accessed October 10, 2011].

59. Ucilia Wang. "Chevron Is Really Bearish on Cleantech Investing." *Gigaom.* [October 7, 2011]. http://gigaom.com/cleantech/chevron-is-really-bearish-on-cleantech-investing/ [accessed October 10, 2011].

60. Annys Shin. "Internet Visionaries Betting on Green Technology Boom." *Washington Post*. [April 18, 2006] http://www.washingtonpost.com/wp-dyn/content/article/2006/04/17/AR2006041701563.html [accessed October 10, 2011].

61. Elisabeth Rosenthal. "Gulf Oil States Seeking a Lead in Clean Energy." *New York Times*. [January 12, 2009] http://www.nytimes.com/2009/01/13/world/middleeast/13greengulf.html?pagewanted=all [accessed October 10, 2011].

62. Aaron Glantz. "Number of Green Jobs Fails to Live Up to Promises." *New York Times*. [August 18, 2011] http://www.nytimes.com/2011/08/19/us/19bcgreen.html?pagewanted=all [accessed October 7, 2011].

63. "Green Supply Chain News: Clean Energy Jobs Continue to Disappoint, New Reports Say." *TheGreenSupplyChain.com*. [August 24, 2011] http://www.thegreensupplychain.com/news/11-08-24-1.php?cid=4879 [accessed February 8, 2012].

64. Jeff St. John. "Mixed Signals for Q1 Greentech." *Gigaom*. [April 20, 2011] http://gigaom.com/cleantech/mixed-signals-for-q1-greentech-investment/ [accessed October 10, 2011]; Jeff St. John. "Funding for Clean Energy Projects Took a Dive in Q1." *Gigacom*. [April 15, 2011] http://gigaom.com/cleantech/funding-for-clean-energy-projects-took-a-dive-in-q1/ [accessed October 10, 2011]; "Venture Capital Investments Rise 19% In Q2 2011 to $7.5 Billion in 966 Deals." *PRWeb*. [July 20, 2011] http://www.prweb.com/releases/2011/7/prweb8656117.htm [accessed October 10, 2011]; and Martin LaMonica. "Once Booming, green-tech investing shifts down." *CNET*. [July 20, 2011] http://news.cnet.com/8301-11128_3-20081107-54/once-booming-green-tech-investing-shifts-down/ [accessed October 10, 2011].

65. Todd Woody. "Green-Tech Investment Plummets." *New York Times*. [October 1, 2010] http://green.blogs.nytimes.com/2010/10/01/green-tech-investment-plummets/ [accessed October 10, 2011].

66. Jeff St. John. "Global Greentech Stimulus Half Spent, Now What?" *Gigaom*. [March 8, 2011] http://gigaom.com/cleantech/global-greentech-stimulus-half-spent-now-what/ [accessed October 10, 2011].

67. "Green Supply Chain News: Clean Energy Jobs Continue to Disappoint, New Reports Say." [August 24, 2011] http://www.thegreensupplychain.com/news/11-08-24-1-php?cid=4847 [accessed February 8, 2012].

68. Ibid.

69. Alexis Madrigal. "Green Tech Could Get Economy High, with a Little Help from the Feds." *Wired*. [January 13, 2009] http://www.wired.com/wiredscience/2009/01/greenmoney/ [accessed October 10, 2011].

70. Ucilia Wang. "Vinod Khosla: Greentech Has Generated Huge Profits." *Gigaom*. [September 27, 2011] http://gigaom.com/cleantech/vinod-khosla-greentech-has-generated-huge-profits/ [accessed October 10, 2011].

71. Ibid.

72. Wang. "Chevron Is Really Bearish on Cleantech Investing."

73. Mark Muro et al. "Sizing the Clean Economy: A National and Regional Green Jobs Assessment." *Brookings*. [July 13, 2011] http://www.brookings

.edu/reports/2011/0713_clean_economy.aspx [accessed October 7, 2011], especially see video, 2:17–2:57; Matthew Lynley. "Peter Thiel: Clean Technology Is a 'Disaster.'" *GreenBeat*. [September 12, 2011] http://venturebeat. com/2011/09/12/thiel-cleantech-disaster-disrupt/ [accessed October 10, 2011].

74. Lynley. "Peter Thiel: Clean Technology Is a 'Disaster.'"
75. National Economic Council. "A Strategy for American Innovation: Driving Towards Sustainable Growth and Quality Jobs." [September 21, 2009] http://www.whitehouse.gov/administration/eop/nec/StrategyforAmerican Innovation/ [accessed October 7, 2011].
76. Diana Farrell and Thomas Kalil. "United States: A Strategy for Innovation." *Issues Online*. [Spring 2010] http://www.issues.org/26.3/farrell.html [accessed October 7, 2011].
77. Ibid.
78. Dan Primack. "Obama: I Don't Regret Solyndra." *CNNMoney*. [October 4, 2011] http://finance.fortune.cnn.com/2011/10/04/obama-i-dont-regret -solyndra/ [accessed October 6, 2011].
79. Steven F. Hayward. "President Solyndra." *Weekly Standard*. [October 3, 2011]. http://www.weeklystandard.com/articles/president-solyndra_594151 .html?page=1 [accessed October 5, 2011].
80. U.S. Department of Energy. Loan Programs Office. https://lpo.energy.gov/ ?page_id=39 [accessed October 5, 2011].
81. Hayward. "President Solyndra."
82. Ibid.
83. Bill Allison. "Solyndra Investor Had Three White House Meetings on Energy Policy." *The Sunlight Foundation* (blog), *Huffington Post*. [October 4, 2011] http://www.huffingtonpost.com/the-sunlight-foundation/solyndra -investor-had-thr_b_994187.html [accessed October 6, 2011].
84. Ashley Kindergan. "Shedding Light on Solyndra." *The Daily*. [September 18, 2011] http://www.thedaily.com/page/2011/09/18/091811-news-solyndra -2-2/ [accessed October 6, 2011].
85. Ibid.
86. Ibid.
87. Ibid.
88. Ibid.
89. Hayward. "President Solyndra." *The Weekly Standard*.
90. The White House. Office of the Vice President. "Vice President Biden Announces Finalized $525 Million Loan Guarantee for Solyndra." [September 4, 2009] http://www.whitehouse.gov/the-press-office/vice-president -biden-announces-finalized-535-million-loan-guarantee-solyndra [accessed October 6, 2011].
91. "Flashback: White House Video of Sec. Chu and VP Biden at Solyndra Groundbreaking." Video, 2:37–3:06. *Verum Serum*. [September 8, 2011] http://www.verumserum.com/?p=29012 [accessed October 6, 2011].
92. Ibid., 3:07–3:30.
93. Ibid., 4:41–5:03.
94. Hayward. "President Solyndra."

95. Carol D. Leonning and Joe Stephens. "Obama Was Advised against Visiting Solyndra after Financial Warnings." *Washington Post.* [October 3, 2011] http://www.washingtonpost.com/politics/donor-officials-warned-obama-not-to-visit-solyndra-due-to-financial-warnings/2011/10/03/gIQA5M2 MIL_story.html [accessed October 6, 2011].
96. Hayward. "President Solyndra."
97. Leonning and Stephens. "Obama Was Advised against Visiting Solyndra after Financial Warnings"; and Deborah Solomon. "White House Brushed Off Solyndra Alarms." *Wall Street Journal.* [October 4, 2011] http://online.wsj.com/article/SB10001424052970204524604576608952821321690.html?mod=googlenews_wsj [accessed October 7, 2011].
98. Fred Lucas. "WH Denies Involvement in Solyndra Loan, Despite E-Mails Indicating Otherwise." *CNS News.* [September 16, 2011] http://cnsnews.com/news/article/wh-denies-involvement-solyndra-loan-despite-e-mails-indicating-otherwise [accessed October 6, 2011]. Also see http://www.solyndra.com/technology-products/videos/#200series [accessed October 6, 2011] and http://www.whitehouse.gov/the-press-office/remarks-president-economy-0 [accessed October 6, 2011].
99. Kindergan. "Shedding Light on Solyndra."
100. Matthew L. Wald and Charlie Savage. "Furor over Loans to Failed Solar Firm." *New York Times.* [September 14, 2011] http://www.nytimes.com/2011/09/15/us/politics/in-solyndra-loan-guarantees-white-house-intervention-is-questioned.html?_r=2 [accessed October 7, 2011].
101. Deborah Solomon. "White House Brushed Off Solyndra Alarms." *Wall Street Journal.* [October 4, 2011] http://online.wsj.com/article/SB10001424052970204524604576608952821321690.html?mod=googlenews_wsj [accessed October 7, 2011].
102. Hayward. "President Solyndra"; MJ Lee. "Cliff Stearns Has Questions for Steven Chu." *Politico.* [October 28, 2011] http://www.politico.com/news/stories/1011/67075.html [accessed February 8, 2012].
103. Ibid.
104. Scott McGrew. "Solyndra to Declare Bankruptcy." *NBC.* [September 2, 2011] http://www.nbcbayarea.com/news/local/Solyndra-Shutting-Down-128802718.html [accessed October 7, 2011]; Tom Hals. "U.S. Solar Firm Solyndra Files for Bankruptcy." *Reuters.* [September 6, 2011] http://www.reuters.com/article/2011/09/06/us-solyndra-idUSTRE77u5k420110906 [accessed March 14, 2012].
105. "Solyndra Execs Will Decline to Testify at Hearing." *Reuters.* [September 20, 2011] http://af.reuters.com/article/commoditiesNews/idAFS1E78J1KE20110920 [accessed October 7, 2011].
106. Matthew Mosk and Ronnie Greene. "U.S. Officials Say Solyndra Execs Stonewall On Financial Info." *ABC News.* [September 30, 2011] http://abcnews.go.com/Blotter/feds-solyndra-execs-provide-financial-info/story?id=14642995 [accessed October 7, 2011].
107. Justin Sink. "Issa to Launch Probe of Obama Actions on Solyndra, LightSquared." *The Hill.* [September 30, 2011] http://thehill.com/blogs/blog

-briefing-room/news/182553-issa-to-investigate-government-loan
-programs?page=2#comments [accessed October 7, 2011].

108. Matthew L. Wald. "Solyndra Officials Take Fifth at House Hearing." *New York Times.* [September 23, 2011] http://www.nytimes.com/2011/09/24/us/politics/solyndra-executives-take-fifth-at-house-hearing.html [accessed October 7, 2011].

109. Mosk and Greene. "U.S. Officials Say Solyndra Execs Stonewall On Financial Info."

110. Darius Dixon. "DOE Loan Program Official Jonathan Silver Steps Down." *Politico.* [October 6, 2011] http://www.politico.com/news/stories/1011/65370.html [accessed October 7, 2011].

111. Kindergan. "Shedding Light on Solyndra."

112. Tim Worstall. "Solyndra: Yes, It Was Possible to See This Failure Coming." *Forbes.* [September 17, 2011] http://www.forbes.com/sites/timworstall/2011/09/17/solyndra-yes-it-was-possible-to-see-this-failure-coming/ [accessed October 7, 2011].

113. Hayward. "President Solyndra"; Wald and Savage. "Furor over Loans to Failed Solar Firm"; and Jerry Taylor and Peter Van Doren. "A Teachable Moment Courtesy of Solyndra." *Forbes.* [September 13, 2011] http://www.forbes.com/sites/powerlunch/2011/09/13/a-teachable-moment-courtesy-of-solyndra/ [accessed October 7, 2011].

114. Leonning and Stephens. "Obama Was Advised against Visiting Solyndra after Financial Warnings."

115. Hayward. "President Solyndra."

116. Dan Primack. "Obama: I Don't Regret Solyndra."

117. Joe Stephens and Carol D. Leonnig. "During Solyndra Probe, Energy Dept. Has to Move Billions in Loans." *Washington Post.* [September 16, 2011] http://www.washingtonpost.com/politics/during-solyndra-probe-energy-dept-has-to-move-billions-in-loans/2011/09/16/gIQARIxXYK_story.html [accessed October 7, 2011].

Chapter 8. The "Dodd Frank" Head-Fake: Inmates Keep the Asylum

1. Council on Foreign Relations. "Obama's Remarks at Signing of Dodd-Frank Wall Street Reform and Consumer Protection Act." [July 21, 2010] http://www.cfr.org/united-states/obamas-remarks-signing-dodd-frank-wall-street-reform-consumer-protection-act/p22682 [accessed October 10, 2011].

2. Matthew G. Lamoreau. "Financial Regulatory Reform: What You Need To Know." *Journal of Accountancy.* [September 2010] http://www.journalofaccountancy.com/Issues/2010/Sep/20103108.htm [accessed November 2, 2011].

3. "A Decent Start." *Economist.* [July 1, 2010] http://www.economist.com/node/16481494 [accessed November 2, 2011].

4. "Dodd and Countrywide." *Wall Street Journal.* [October 10, 2008] http://online.wsj.com/article/SB122360116724221681.html [accessed November 2, 2011].

5. "Dodd's Peek-A-Boo Disclosure." *Wall Street Journal.* [February 3, 2009] http://online.wsj.com/article/SB123362399705441875.html [accessed November 2, 2011].

6. The White House. Office of the Press Secretary. "Setting the Record Straight: Six Years of Unheeded Warnings for GSE Reform." [October 8, 2008] http://georgewbush-whitehouse.archives.gov/news/releases/2008/10/20081009-10.html [accessed November 2, 2011]; Karl Rove. "President Bush Tried to Rein in Fan and Fred." *Wall Street Journal.* [January 8, 2009] http://online.wsj.com/article/SB123137220550562585.html   [accessed November 2, 2011].

7. John Berlau and Matthew Melchiorre. "Dodd-Frank's Fannie Trap." *National Review Online.* [July 21, 2011] http://www.nationalreview.com/articles/272368/dodd-frank-s-fannie-trap-john-berlau?pg=1 [accessed November 2, 2011].

8. Newt Gingrich. "To Create Jobs, Repeal the Dodd-Frank Law Immediately." *Human Events.* [July 20, 2011] http://www.humanevents.com/article.php?id=44957 [accessed November 2, 2011].

9. Alexander Burns. "New Hampshire Debate: Newt Gingrich Slams Chris Dodd, Barney Frank and—Wait for It—the Media." *Politico.* [October 11, 2011] http://www.politico.com/news/stories/1011/65696.html#ixzz1cSck5g1h [accessed November 2, 2011]; CHeinze2012. "GOP12.com: Gingrich: Put Dodd, Frank in Jail." Video. *YouTube.* [October 12, 2011] http://www.youtube.com/watch?v=4rJdXZhZUBE [accessed November 2, 2011].

10. Sarah N. Lynch and Christopher Doering. "Republicans Continue Efforts to Delay, Weaken Dodd-Frank Rules." *Huffington Post.* [May 5, 2011] http://www.huffingtonpost.com/2011/05/05/dodd-frank-republican-financial-regulation_n_857917.html [accessed November 2, 2011].

11. The White House. Office of the Press Secretary. "Remarks by the President at Signing of Dodd-Frank Wall Street Reform and Consumer Protection Act." [July 21, 2010] http://www.whitehouse.gov/the-press-office/remarks-president-signing-dodd-frank-wall-street-reform-and-consumer-protection-act [accessed November 2, 2011].

12. Ibid.; Jake Tapper. "President Obama Threatens to Veto Bill to Change Dodd-Frank Financial Regulation Bill." *ABC News.* [July 20, 2011] http://abcnews.go.com/blogs/politics/2011/07/obama-threatens-veto-bill-change-dodd-frank-financial-regulation-bill/ [accessed November 2, 2011].

13. The White House. Office of the Press Secretary. "Remarks by the President in Nominating Richard Cordray as Director of the Consumer Financial Protection Bureau." [July 18, 2011] http://www.whitehouse.gov/the-press-office/2011/07/18/remarks-president-nominating-richard-cordray-director-consumer-financial [accessed November 2, 2011]; Edward Wyatt. "Dodd-Frank under Fire a Year Later." *New York Times.* [July 18, 2011] http://www.nytimes.com/2011/07/19/business/dodd-frank-under-fire-a-year-later.html [accessed November 2, 2011].

14. John B. Taylor. "The End of the Growth Consensus." *Wall Street Journal.* [July 21, 2011] http://online.wsj.com/article/SB10001424053111903554904576457752586269450.html [accessed November 2, 2011].

Chapter 9. The *"Fast and Furious" Debacle and Cover-Up*

1. "Obama on 'Gunwalking'—'Serious Mistakes' May Have Been Made." *CBS News.* Video. [March 23, 2011] http://www.cbsnews.com/video/watch/?id=7360542n&tag=mncol;lst;8 [accessed October 3, 2011].
2. The White House. Office of the Press Secretary. "President Obama News Conference." [June 29, 2011] http://www.whitehouse.gov/photos-and-video/video/2011/06/29/president-obama-news-conference#transcript [accessed October 25, 2011].
3. Fred Lucas. "Gun-Running Timeline: How DOJ's 'Operation Fast and Furious' Unfolded." *CNS News.* [July 7, 2011] http://www.cnsnews.com/news/article/gun-running-timeline-how-doj-s-operation-fast-and-furious-unfolded [accessed October 1, 2011].
4. House Committee on Oversight and Government Reform. "Briefing Paper. Phoenix Field Division. Phoenix Group VII (Gunrunner/Strike Force)." [January 8, 2010]. http://oversight.house.gov/images/stories/Other_Documents/4-7.pdf [accessed October 1, 2011].
5. Lucas. "Gun-Running Timeline: How DOJ's 'Operation Fast and Furious' Unfolded."
6. Ibid.
7. Fred Lucas. "Gun-Running Timeline: How DOJ's unfolded." *CNS News.* (July 7, 2011) http://www.cnsnews.com/news/article/gun-running-timeline-how-doj's-operation-fast-and-furious-unfolded [accessed October 1, 2011].
8. Sharyl Attkisson. "Agent: I Was Ordered to Let U.S. Guns into Mexico." *CBS News.* [March 3, 2011] http://www.cbsnews.com/stories/2011/03/03/eveningnews/main20039031.shtml [accessed October 4, 2011]; Lucas. "Gun-Running Timeline: How DOJ's 'Operation Fast and Furious' Unfolded."
9. Terry Wallace. "ATF: Gun in US Agent's Death Traced to Texas Man." *Brownsville Herald.* [February 28, 2011] http://www.brownsvilleherald.com/articles/atf-123352-dallas-death.html [accessed October 3, 2011].
10. State of Arizona. Office of the Governor. Statement by Governor Jan Brewer. [June 15, 2011] http://azgovernor.gov/dms/upload/PR_061511_FastAndFurious.pdf [accessed October 4, 2011].
11. Darrell Issa and Charles E. Grassley. "Letter to Eric H. Holder, Jr." [July 5, 2011] http://grassley.senate.gov/judiciary/upload/ATF-07-05-11-CEG-Issa-letter-to-Holder-Melson-interview.pdf [accessed October 3, 2011].
12. Ibid.
13. Geneva Sands-Sadowitz. "Issa: Fast and Furious Probe 'Stonewalled' by DOJ." Video. *The Hill.* [September 22, 2011] http://thehill.com/video/house/183167-issa-fast-and-furious-probe-stonewalled-by-doj [accessed October 3, 2011].
14. Jim Kouri. "Holder, DOJ Stonewalling of Fast & Furious Probe Creating Anger." *National Examiner.* [September 29, 2011] http://www.examiner.com/law-enforcement-in-national/holder-doj-stonewalling-of-fast-furious-probe-creating-anger [accessed October 3, 2011].
15. "House Gov't Oversight & Investigations Chairman Darrell Issa on the Growing Fast and Furious Scandal." *HughHewitt.com.*[August 30, 2011]

http://www.hughhewitt.com/transcripts.aspx?id=131ae193-fde4-4946
-9051-16d819ecb55b [accessed October 6, 2011].

16. Martin Gould. "Issa, Grassley: DOJ Prepped Fast and Furious Witnesses."
    Newsmas.com. [July 12, 2011] http://www.newsmax.com/InsideCover/
    Issa-Grassley-FastandFurious/2011/07/12/id/403373 [accessed October 4,
    2011]; and Sands-Sadowitz. "Issa: Fast and Furious Probe 'Stonewalled' by
    DOJ." Video, 4:40–6:00.

17. Sands-Sadowitz. "Issa: Fast and Furious Probe 'Stonewalled' by DOJ."
    Video, 3:55–4:30.

18. Geneva Sands-Sadowitz. "Issa: Fast and furious probe 'stonewalled' by DOJ."
    The Hill. [September 22, 2011] http://thehill.com/video/house/183167-issa
    -fast-and-furious-probe-stonewalled-by-doj [accessed October 4, 2011],
    video: 1:27–1:50.

19. Sharyl Attkisson. "'Gunwalker's Allegation: ATF Target Was FBI Infor-
    mant." Video. *CBS News.* [September 28, 2011] http://www.cbsnews.com/
    8301-31727_162-20112834-10391695.html [accessed October 4, 2011].

20. Ibid., 6:00–6:57.

21. "The documents show extensive communications between then-ATF Spe-
    cial Agent in Charge of the Phoenix office Bill Newell—who led Fast and
    Furious—and then-White House National Security Staffer Kevin O'Reilly.
    Emails indicate the two also spoke on the phone." Sharyl Attkisson. "New
    Fast and Furious Docs Released by White House." *CBS News.* [September
    30, 2011] http://www.cbsnews.com/8301-31727_162-20114184-10391695
    .html [accessed October 4, 2011]. Also, see Katie Pavlich. "Document Dump:
    White House in Heavy Communication about Operation Fast and Furious."
    Townhall.com. [October 1, 2011] http://townhall.com/tipsheet/katiepavlich/
    2011/10/01/document_dump_white_house_in_heavy_communication
    _about_operation_fast_and_furious [accessed October 6, 2011].

22. Lucas. "Gun-Running Timeline: How DOJ's 'Operation Fast and Furious'
    Unfolded."

23. Fred Lucas. "Issa Says He Doesn't Believe Holder's Testimony Was Accu-
    rate." *CNS News.* [July 7, 2011] http://www.cnsnews.com/news/article/issa
    -says-he-doesn-t-believe-holder-s-testimony-was-accurate [accessed Octo-
    ber 3, 2011]; "Memorandum to the Attorney General. Department of Jus-
    tice. From Michael F. Walther, Director, National Drug Intelligence Center."
    CBS News. [July 5, 2010]. http://www.cbsnews.com/htdocs/pdf/pdf_40_43
    .pdf?tag=contentMain;contentBody [accessed October 5, 2011]; and "Mem-
    orandum to Attorney General and Acting Deputy Attorney General. Depart-
    ment of Justice. Criminal Division. From Lanny A. Breuer, Assistant Attorney
    General." *CBS News.* [November 1, 2010] http://www.cbsnews.com/htdocs/
    pdf/pdf_65_67.pdf [accessed October 5, 2011].

24. It is worth noting that the U.S. attorney in Arizona, Dennis Burke, who was
    directly involved in Operation Fast and Furious and resigned over the fallout
    (see note 37), has close ties to Janet Napolitano. See "House Gov't Oversight &
    Investigations Chairman Darrell Issa on the Growing Fast and Furious
    Scandal." *HughHewitt.com.* [August 30, 2011] http://www.hughhewitt
    .com/transcripts.aspx?id=131ae193-fde4-4946-9051-16d819ecb55b

[accessed October 6, 2011]; and Hugh Hewitt. "The Fast and Furious Melt-down." *HughHewitt.com.*[August 30, 2011] http://www.hughhewitt.com/ blog/g/de06af12-3731-485c-85fb-5f5bd5dc1216 [accessed October 6, 2011].

25. Katie Pavlich. "Napolitano, FBI Give Non-Answers to Questions Surrounding Operation Fast and Furious." *HughHewitt.com.* [September 13, 2011] http:// www.hughhewitt.com/blog/g/8247e7f0-f6d2-45df-b9f7-31f7fd985a0c [accessed October 6, 2011].

26. Sands-Sadowitz. "Issa: Fast and Furious Probe 'Stonewalled' by DOJ." Video,1:27–1:50.

27. "Obama on 'Gunwalking'—'Serious Mistakes' May Have Been Made."

28. The White House. Office of the Press Secretary. "President Obama News Conference." [June 29, 2011] http://www.whitehouse.gov/photos-and-video/ video/2011/06/29/president-obama-news-conference#transcript [accessed October 25, 2011].

29. House Committee on Oversight & Government Reform. "Issa Statement on President's Operation Fast and Furious Remarks." http://oversight.house .gov/index.php?option=com_content&task=view&id=1362&Itemid=29 [accessed October 6, 2011].

30. House Committee on Oversight and Government Reform. "Statement of John Dodson." [June 15, 2011]. Cited in Hugh Holub. "Statement of John Dodson about ATF Gunwalker Scandal: 'The Very Idea of Letting Guns Walk Is Unthinkable to Most Law Enforcement.'" *TucsonCitizen.com.* [June 15, 2011]. http://tucsoncitizen.com/view-from-baja-arizona/2011/06/15/statement-of -john-dodson-about-atf-gunwalker-scandal-the-very-idea-of-letting-guns -walk-is-unthinkable-to-most-law-enforcement/ [accessed October 4, 2011].

31. House of Representatives. "Statement of Senator Charles E. Grassley Before the United States House of Representatives. Fast and Furious." [June 15, 2011] http://democrats.oversight.house.gov/images/stories/FULLCOM/615%20 fast%20and%20furious/2011-06-15%20ATF%20House%20Testi mony%20(footnoted)%20Final.pdf [accessed October 4, 2011].

32. Evan Perez. "Agents Resisted Weapons Tracking." *Wall Street Journal.* [June 15, 2011] http://online.wsj.com/article/SB100014240527023046659045763 85993445351016.html [accessed October 3, 2011].

33. U.S. Congress. *The Department of Justice's Operation Fast and Furious: Accounts of ATF Agents.* Joint Staff Report. [June 14, 2011] Available at http://dailycaller.com/wp-content/uploads/2011/06/ATF_Report-1.pdf [accessed February 10, 2012].

34. U.S. Senate. Letter from Sen. Charles E. Grassley to Ho. Eric H. Holder, Jr, and Kenneth E. Nelson. [March 3, 2011] http://www.cbsnews.com/htdocs/ pdf/Grassley_2011_03.pdf?tag=contentmain;contentbody [accessed October 4, 2011], p. 2.

35. Attkisson. "Agent: I Was Ordered to Let U.S. Guns into Mexico." Video: 2:35–2:52.

36. Sands-Sadowitz. "Issa: Fast and Furious Probe 'Stonewalled' by DOJ." Video, 1:20–1:27.

37. U.S. Congress. Joint Staff Report. *The Department of Justice's Operation Fast and Furious: Accounts of ATF Agents.* 112th Cong., June 14, 2011.

http://dailycaller.com/wp-content/uploads/2011/06/ATF_Report-1.pdf [accessed February 10, 2012], p. 34.

38. Mary Anastasia O'Grady. "O'Grady: ATF Plan Goes Awry." *Richmond Times-Dispatch*. [June 24, 2011] http://www2.timesdispatch.com/news/oped/2011/jun/24/tdopin02-ogrady-atf-plan-goes-awry-ar-1129464/ [accessed October 3, 2011].

39. Ibid.

40. Sharyl Attkisson. "Gunwalker Scandal: ATF Director out of Top Job." *CBS News*. [August 30, 2011] http://www.cbsnews.com/8301-31727_162-20099228-10391695.html [accessed October 4, 2011].

41. Ibid.

42. Ibid; William Lajeunesse. "ATF Director Reassigned; U.S. Attorney Out Amid 'Fast and Furious' Uproar." *FoxNews.com*. [August 30, 2011] http://www.foxnews.com/politics/2011/08/30/sources-atf-director-to-be-reassigned-amid-fast-and-furious-uproar/ [accessed March 14, 2012].

43. "Rick Santorum and Darryl Issa." *HughHewitt.com*. [February 1, 2012] http://www.hughhewitt.com/blog/print.aspx?guid=f8dc6adb-3471-4882-a15d-fb371ff1f50a [accessed February 11, 2012].

Chapter 10. The President's Attacks on Catholics, Congress, and the Constitution

1. Elise Foley. "Obama: Defense of Marriage Issue Will Be Settled Soon." *Huffington Post*. [September 29, 2011] http://www.huffingtonpost.com/2011/09/28/obama-defense-of-marriage-act_n_985283.html [accessed October 10, 2011].

2. "Civil Forum on the Presidency." Video, 21:00–22:50. *Saddleback Civil Forum*. http://saddlebackcivilforum.com/thepresidency/.

3. "2008 Presidential Questionnaire—Senator Barack Obama." *Human Rights Campaign*. http://www.lgbtforobama.com/pdf/Obama_HRC_questionaire.pdf [accessed November 9, 2011].

4. "Barack Obama on the Issues: Equality." *eQualityGiving.org*. [December 10, 2009] http://www.equalitygiving.org/Barack-Obama-on-the-issues-Equality-Quotes-Gay-Rights [accessed November 9, 2011].

5. Defense of Marriage Act. Public Law 104-199. 110 Stat. 2419. 104th Congress (1996). http://frwebgate.access.gpo.gov/cgi-bin/getdoc.cgi?dbname=104_cong_public_laws&docid=f:publ199.104.pdf [accessed November 10, 2011].

6. Department of Justice. Office of Public Affairs. "Letter from the Attorney General to Congress on Litigation Involving the Defense of Marriage Act." [February 23, 2011]. http://www.justice.gov/opa/pr/2011/February/11-ag-223.html [accessed November 10, 2011].

7. *Gill v. Office of Personnel Management* and *Massachusetts v. United States Department of Health and Human Services*. There are several cases currently in progress where rulings on DOMA are expected. For more information, see http://www.domawatch.org.

8. Hans von Spakovsky. "Obama Drops Pretense, Administration Will Not Defend DOMA." *The Foundry*. [February 23, 2011] http://blog.heritage.org/2011/02/23/obama-drops-pretense-administration-will-not-defend-doma/ [accessed November 10, 2011].

9. Seth P. Waxman. "Defending Congress." *Scholarly Commons*. Georgetown University Law Center. 79 N. C. L. Rev. 1073–1088 (2001). http://www.law.stanford.edu/display/images/dynamic/events_media/Defending%20Congress.pdf [accessed November 10, 2011].

10. Frank James and Liz Halloran. "Boehner: House Will Defend DOMA; Courts, Not Obama, Should Decide." *NPR*. [March 4, 2011] http://www.npr.org/blogs/itsallpolitics/2011/03/04/134268656/boehner-house-will-defend-doma-courts-not-obama-should-decide [accessed November 4, 2011].

Chapter 11. *Standing By As Iranians Die: Or, Learning to Love the Mullahs and Their Bomb*

1. The White House. Office of the Press Secretary. "Statement from the President on Iran." [June 20, 2009] http://www.whitehouse.gov/blog/The-Presidents-Statement-on-Iran/ [accessed September 23, 2011].

2. Iran's Shaha-3 missile is thought to have a maximum range of approximately 2,000 kilometers, or 1,250 miles. Most of the Middle East (including Israel) and some countries in eastern Europe are within this range ("Q&A: US Missile Defence." *BBC News*. [September 20, 2009] http://news.bbc.co.uk/2/hi/europe/6720153.stm [accessed August 31, 2011]). In 2009 the National Air and Space Intelligence Center estimated that "with sufficient foreign assistance, Iran could develop and test an ICBM capable of reaching the United States by 2015" (cited in Trey Obering and Eric Edelman. "Iran Missile Defense in Europe Should Proceed." *Washington Post*. [July 6, 2009] http://www.washingtonpost.com/wp-dyn/content/article/2009/07/05/AR2009070501744.html [accessed September 6, 2011]). Iran is aggressively seeking such aid (Ibid.). Furthermore, according to reports by German intelligence, Iran has enough uranium for testing nuclear weapons, and is close to developing the technology for deploying nuclear warheads ("Iran Could Have a Nuclear Bomb in Six Months." *bild.de*. [July 16, 2009] http://www.bild.de/news/bild-english/news/german-intelligence-sources-give-chilling-six-months-weapons-warning-9031264.bild.html [accessed September 6, 2011]). Reports released in September 2009 indicate that "Iran has created enough nuclear fuel to make a rapid, if risky, sprint for a nuclear weapon." Israeli intelligence estimates Iran could have its first nuclear weapon ready by 2014 (David E. Sanger. "U.S. Says Iran Could Expedite Nuclear Bomb." *New York Times*. [September 9, 2009] http://www.iranfocus.com/en/index.php?option=com_content&view=article&id=22953:obama-voices-stronger-support-for-iranian-opposition&catid=4:iran-general&Itemid=26 [accessed September 23, 2011]).

3. "Ahmadinejad Victory Confirmed in Iran." *BBC News*. [June 29, 2009] http://news.bbc.co.uk/2/hi/middle_east/8125619.stm [accessed September 23, 2011];

and Michael Slackman. "Iran Council Certifies Ahmadinejad Victory." *New York Times*. [June 29, 2009] http://www.nytimes.com/2009/06/30/world/middleeast/30iran.html [accessed September 23, 2011].

4. Juan Cole. "StealingtheIranianElection." *InformedComment*. [June 13, 2009] http://www.juancole.com/2009/06/stealing-iranian-election.html [accessed September 24, 2011].

5. Casey L. Addis. "Iran's 2009 Presidential Elections." Congressional Research Service. 7-5700 R40653. [June 22, 2009] http://fpc.state.gov/documents/organization/125709.pdf [accessed September 23, 2011].

6. Ibid.

7. Ibid.

8. Ian Black and Saeed Kamali Dehghan. "Iran Protesters Hijack 30th Anniversary of US Embassy Seizure." *Guardian* (London). [November 4, 2009] http://www.guardian.co.uk/world/2009/nov/04/iran-protests-embassy-30th-anniversary [accessed September 23, 2011]; Iason Athanasiadis. "Iran Green Movement promising big February protests." *Christian Science Monitor*. [January 27, 2010] http://www.csmonitor.com/World/Middle-East/2010/0127/Iran-Green-Movement-promising-big-February-protests [accessed September 23, 2011]; and "Protests Wash over Iran, Bahrain and Yemen, Inspired by Arab World Unrest." *Haaretz*. [February 14, 2011] http://www.haaretz.com/news/international/protests-wash-over-iran-bahrain-and-yemen-inspired-by-arab-world-unrest-1.343352 [accessed September 23, 2011].

9. "Instant View: Iran's Election Result Staggers Analysts." *Reuters*. [June 13, 2009] http://www.reuters.com/article/2009/06/13/us-iran-election-sb-idUSTRE55C0W620090613?sp=true [accessed September 24, 2011].

10. Ibid.

11. Ibid.

12. Ibid.

13. "Sarkozy Denounces 'Fraud' in Iran Elections." *France24*. [June 16, 2009] Available at http://www.google.com/hostednews/afp/article/ALeqM5gGWaYHT1MAWSjDJaCrPmLR-dCw0Q [accessed February 8, 2012].

14. "UKs Brown Steps Up Criticism of Iran." *Reuters*. [June 19, 2009] http://www.reuters.com/article/2009/06/19/us-iran-election-britain-sb-idUSTRE55I2H920090619 [accessed September 24, 2011].

15. Jacques Martin. "Franco Frattini Wants the EU to Accept 'Wounded Asylum Refugees Due to Voting Crisis in Iran." *European Union Times*. [June 24, 2009] http://www.eutimes.net/2009/06/franco-frattini-wants-the-eu-to-accept-wounded-asylum-refugees-due-to-voting-crisis-in-iran/ [accessed September 24, 2011].

16. Ariel Farrar-Wellman. "Germany-Iran Foreign Relations." *AEI Iran Tracker*. [July 27, 2010] http://www.irantracker.org/foreign-relations/germany-iran-foreign-relations#_ftn1 [accessed September 24, 2011].

17. "Obama's Iran Abdication." *Wall Street Journal*. [June 18, 2009] http://online.wsj.com/article/SB124520170103721579.html [accessed September 23, 2011].

18. The White House. Office of the Press Secretary. "Remarks by President Obama and Prime Minister Berlusconi of Italy." [June 15, 2009] http://www.whitehouse.gov/the_press_office/Remarks-by-President-Obama-and-Prime-Minister-Berlusconi-in-press-availability-6-15-09/ [accessed September 23, 2011].

19. Jeff Zeleny and Helene Cooper. "Obama Warns Against Direct Involvement by U.S. in Iran." *New York Times.* [June 16, 2009] http://www.nytimes.com/2009/06/17/us/politics/17prexy.html [accessed September 23, 2011].

20. The White House, Office of the Press Secretary. "Statement from the President on Iran." [June 20, 2009] http://www.whitehouse.gov/blog/The-Presidents-Statement-on-Iran/ [accessed September 23, 2011].

21. Jesse Lee. "The President's Opening Remarks on Iran, with Persian Translation." *The White House Blog.* [June 23, 2009] http://www.whitehouse.gov/blog/The-Presidents-Opening-Remarks-on-Iran-with-Persian-Translation/ [accessed September 23, 2011].

22. Jordan Michael Smith. "Inside Obama's Iran Policy Shop." *World Politics Review.* [October 28, 2009] http://www.worldpoliticsreview.com/articles/4505/inside-obamas-iran-policy-shop [accessed September 23, 2011].

23. Tsuneo Wantanabe. "Obama's Iran Policy: Engage or Isolate?" *The Tokyo Foundation.* [December 24, 2010] http://www.tokyofoundation.org/en/articles/2010/obama2019s-iran-policy-engage-or-isolate [accessed September 23, 2011].

24. Roger Cohen. "The Making of an Iran Policy." *New York Times.* [July 30, 2009] http://www.nytimes.com/2009/08/02/magazine/02Iran-t.html?pagewanted=all [accessed September 23, 2011].

25. "U.S., Iran: Wielding the Sanctions Threat." *Stratfor.* [May 18, 2010] http://www.stratfor.com/memberships/162689/analysis/20100518_us_iran_wielding_sanctions_threat [accessed September 23, 2011].

26. Paul Richter. "U.S. Changing Focus of Iran Policy." *Los Angeles Times.* [March 9, 2010] http://articles.latimes.com/2010/mar/09/world/la-fg-obama-iran10-2010mar10 [accessed September 23, 2011]; Howard LaFrachi. "New US Stance on Iranian Protests: Stress Human Rights Violations." *Christian Science Monitor.* [December 23, 2009] http://www.csmonitor.com/USA/Foreign-Policy/2009/1223/New-US-stance-on-Iranian-protests-stress-human-rights-violations [accessed September 23, 2011]; and Jay Solomon. "Obama Voices Stronger Support for Iranian Opposition." *Wall Street Journal.* [March 22, 2011] http://www.iranfocus.com/en/index.php?option=com_content&view=article&id=22953:obama-voices-stronger-support-for-iranian-opposition&catid=4:iran-general&Itemid=26 [accessed September 23, 2011].

27. Jonathan Weisman. "Obama's Response Has Its Critics, Defenders." *Wall Street Journal.* [June 22, 2009] http://online.wsj.com/article/SB12455986 4396134983.html [accessed September 23, 2011].

28. Charles Krauthammer. "Obama Misses the Point with Iran Response." *Washington Post.* [June 19, 2009] http://www.washingtonpost.com/wp-dyn/content/article/2009/06/18/AR2009061803495.html [accessed February 8, 2012].

29. Paul Wolfowitz. "Obama Needs to Change Stance on Iran." *Washington Post.* [June 19, 2011] http://www.washingtonpost.com/wp-dyn/content/article/2009/06/18/AR2009061803496.html [accessed September 23, 2011].

30. Glenn Kessler. "U.S. Struggling for Right Response to Iran." *Washington Post.* [June 18, 2009] http://www.washingtonpost.com/wp-dyn/content/article/2009/06/17/AR2009061703850.html [accessed September 23, 2011].

31. Obama clearly stated his concerns about perceptions of U.S. involvement in Iran's domestic affairs. In an interview on June 19, 2009, he said, "The last thing that I want to do is to have the United States be a foil for those forces inside Iran who would love nothing better than to make this an argument about the United States. That's what they do. That's what we've already seen. We shouldn't be playing into that. There should be no distractions from the fact that the Iranian people are seeking to let their voices be heard" ("Obama: Iran Protestors 'Seeking Justice.'" *CBS News.* [June 19, 2009] http://www.cbsnews.com/stories/2009/06/19/eveningnews/main5099083.shtml [accessed September 23, 2011]).

32. David Feith and Bari Weiss. "Denying the Green Revolution." *Wall Street Journal.* [October 23, 2009] http://online.wsj.com/article/SB100014240527487042240045744897728745644430.html [accessed September 23, 2011].

33. The White House, Office of the Press Secretary. "Videotaped Remarks by the President in Celebration of Nowruz." Transcript. [March 20, 2009] http://www.whitehouse.gov/the_press_office/Videotaped-Remarks-by-The-President-in-Celebration-of-Nowruz/. Video available at http://www.whitehouse.gov/Nowruz [accessed September 23, 2011].

34. The White House, Office of the Press Secretary. "Remarks by President Obama to the Turkish Parliament." [April 6, 2009] http://www.whitehouse.gov/the_press_office/Remarks-By-President-Obama-To-The-Turkish-Parliament/ [accessed September 23, 2011].

35. Philip Elliott. "Iranian Response To Obama: 'Minor Changes Will Not End the Differences.'" *Huffington Post.* [March 20, 2009] http://www.huffingtonpost.com/2009/03/20/iranian-response-to-obama_n_177320.html [accessed September 23, 2011].

36. "Text—Iranian Official's Response to Obama Appeal." *Reuters.* [March 20, 2009] http://uk.reuters.com/article/2009/03/20/iran-usa-obama-idUKDAH03878820090320 [accessed September 23, 2011].

37. "Iranian Leader: Obama's Rhetoric Not Enough." *CNN.* [March 21, 2009] http://articles.cnn.com/2009-03-21/world/iran.us.obama_1_iaea-official-islamic-republic-news-agency-ayatollah-ali-khamenei?_s=PM:WORLD [accessed September 23, 2011]; and Peter Eisner. "Reading between the Lines of Iran's Response to Obama." *World Focus.* [March 23, 2009] http://worldfocus.org/blog/2009/03/23/reading-between-the-lines-of-irans-response-to-obama/4585/ [accessed September 23, 2011].

38. Juan Cole. "Khamenei Adopts a Wait and See Attitude to Obama; 'If You Change Your Attitude, We Will Change Ours.'" *Informed Comment.* [March 22, 2009] http://www.juancole.com/2009/03/khamenei-adopts-wait-and-see-attitude.html [accessed September 23, 2011].

39. Borzou Daragahi. "Obama Overture Elicits Cautious Response from Iran." *Los Angeles Times.* [March 21, 2009] http://articles.latimes.com/2009/mar/21/world/fg-obama-iran21 [accessed September 23, 2011].

40. In response to some of Obama's rhetoric during the week after the election, Mahmoud Ahmadinejad released a statement: "To take such a rude tone with a great nation is inexcusable. We understand that you are still gaining experience and you are still trying to work out what's hot and what's cold. And I want to give you a bit of friendly advice: We don't want to see a repetition of the mess that was created during the Bush era" (Antoine Blua. "G8 Calls For Halt to Iran Violence." *Radio Free Europe Radio Liberty.* [June 26, 2009] http://www.rferl.org/content/G8_Calls_For_Halt_To_Iran_Violence_/1763430.html [accessed September 24, 2011]).

41. Daniel Brumberg has written a post in the *Washington Post*'s On Faith column that suggests diplomatic failures may also be due to a fundamental misunderstanding about the process and methods of diplomatic negotiations themselves ("Obama's Overtures to Iran." *Washington Post.* [March 20, 2009] http://newsweek.washingtonpost.com/onfaith/georgetown/2009/03/obamas_overtures_to_iran.html#more [accessed September 23, 2011]). This does not change the fact that on every relevant issue besides, perhaps, Afghanistan, the national interests of the United States and Iran are diametrically opposed.

Chapter 12. Abandoning Israel to Its Fate

1. Mark Memott. "Obama Urges Israel, Palestinians To 'Stand In Each Other's Shoes.'" *NPR.* [September 21, 2011] http://www.npr.org/blogs/thetwo-way/2011/09/21/140663207/live-blog-obama-addresses-un-general-assembly [accessed October 10, 2011].

2. Adrian Blomfield. "Obama Snubbed Netanyahu for Dinner with Michelle and the Girls, Israelis Claim." *Telegraph* (London). [March 25, 2010] http://www.telegraph.co.uk/news/worldnews/barackobama/7521220/Obama-snubbed-Netanyahu-for-dinner-with-Michelle-and-the-girls-Israelis-claim.html [accessed October 26, 2011].

3. Ibid.

4. "President Obama Press Conference Sept 10, 2010 pt.4." Video, 00:40–4:48. *YouTube.* [September 11, 2010] http://www.youtube.com/watch?v=fu8EnrRMLts&NR=1 [accessed October 26, 2011].

5. "President Obama Press Conference Sept 10, 2010 pt.5." Video, 10:45–12:40. *YouTube.* [September 11, 2010] http://www.youtube.com/watch?v=Hv6p06yJT5U&NR=1 [accessed October 26, 2011].

6. Jacqueline Klingebiel. "Axelrod: Israel Settlement Approval an 'Affront'; 'Insult.'" *ABC News.* [March 14, 2010] http://abcnews.go.com/blogs/politics/2010/03/axelrod-israel-settlement-approval-an-affront-insult/ [accessed October 26, 2011].

7. The White House. Office of the Press Secretary. "Remarks by the President at the AIPAC Policy Conference 2011." [May 22, 2011] http://www.whitehouse.gov/the-press-office/2011/05/22/remarks-president-aipac-policy-conference-2011 [accessed October 26, 2011].

8. Helene Cooper. "Obama Presses Israel to Make 'Hard Choices.'" *New York Times*. [May 22, 2011] http://www.nytimes.com/2011/05/23/world/middleeast/23aipac.html?pagewanted=all [accessed October 26, 2011]; and Chris Mitchell and Julie Stahl. "Return to Israel's 1967 Borders National Suicide?" *CBN News*. [May 23, 2011] http://www.cbn.com/cbnnews/insideisrael/2011/May/Return-to-Israels-1967-Borders-National-Suicide/ [accessed October 26, 2011].
9. "AJC Annual Survey Reveals Declining Jewish Support for President Obama." *AJC*. [September 26, 2011] http://www.ajc.org/site/apps/nlnet/content2.aspx?c=ijITI2PHKoG&b=849241&ct=11233023 [accessed October 26, 2011].
10. Peter Wallsten. "Allies of Palestinians See a Friend in Obama." *Los Angeles Times*. [April 10, 2008] http://articles.latimes.com/2008/apr/10/nation/na-obamamideast10 [accessed October 26, 2011].

Chapter 13. Hollowing Out the American Military

1. The White House. Office of the Press Secretary. "Remarks by the President at the Signing of the National Defense Authorization Act for Fiscal Year 2010." [October 28, 2009] http://www.whitehouse.gov/the-press-office/remarks-president-signing-national-defense-authorization-act-fiscal-year-2010 [accessed October 11, 2011].
2. "30 Years of Spending Priorities." *Washington Post*. [February 14, 2011] http://www.washingtonpost.com/wp-srv/special/politics/30-years-spending-priorities-federal-budget-2012/ [accessed February 8, 2012].
3. "Update 1—Obama Seeks Record $708 Bln in 2001 Defense Budget." *Reuters*. [February 1, 2010] http://www.reuters.com/article/2010/02/01/obama-budget-pentagon-idUSN0120383520100201 [accessed February 8, 2012].
4. The White House. Office of the Press Secretary. "Remarks by the President on Fiscal Policy." [April 13, 2011] http://www.whitehouse.gov/the-press-office/2011/04/13/remarks-president-fiscal-policy [accessed November 9, 2011].
5. David S. Cloud and Christi Parsons. "President Obama calls for leaner military." *Los Angeles Times*. [January 5, 2012] http://articles.latimes.com/2012/jan/05/nation/la-na-pentagon-spending-20120106 [accessed March 24, 2012]; Christopher Drew. "Obama Wins Crucial Senate Vote on F-22." *New York Times*. [July 21, 2009] http://www.nytimes.com/2009/07/22/business/22defense.html [accessed March 24, 2012].
6. Baker Spring. "President Obama's Disconnect on the Defense Budget." *The Heritage Foundation*. [April 15, 2011] http://www.heritage.org/research/reports/2011/04/president-obamas-disconnect-on-the-defense-budget [accessed November 9, 2011].
7. Mackenzie Eaglen. "Slashing Defense Makes America Less Safe While Allowing Politicians to Kick the Can Down the Road on Entitlement Reform." *The Heritage Foundation*. [July 21, 2011] http://www.heritage.org/Research/Reports/2011/07/Slashing-Defense-Makes-America-Less-Safe [accessed November 9, 2011].

Chapter 14. *"Resetting" Russia Back to Great Power Status*

1. The White House. Office of the Press Secretary. "Remarks by President Obama and President Medvedev of Russia at Joint Press Conference." [June 24, 2010] http://www.whitehouse.gov/the-press-office/remarks-president -obama-and-president-medvedev-russia-joint-press-conference [accessed October 11, 2011].
2. "Video: Wrong Red Button." *Politico.* [March 6, 2009] http://www.politico .com/news/stories/0309/19719.html [accessed October 26, 2011].
3. Suzanne Malveaux and Per Nyberg. "U.S. Scraps Missile Defense Shield Plans." *CNN.* [September 17, 2009] http://edition.cnn.com/2009/WORLD/ americas/09/17/united.states.missile.shield/index.html [accessed October 26, 2011].
4. Ibid.
5. Richard Rousseau. "UN Security Council Sanctions on Iran—Russia Making the Best of Both Worlds." *Europe's World.* [January 6, 2010] http://www.europesworld.org/NewEnglish/Home_old/CommunityPosts/ tabid/809/PostID/1460/language/en-US/Default.aspx [accessed October 26, 2011].
6. "IAEA Pressed to Publish Less Iran Nuclear Data, Diplomats Say." *National Journal Group.* Global Security Newswire. [October 26, 2011] http://www .globalsecuritynewswire.org/gsn/nw_20111026_4701.php[accessedOctober 26, 2011].
7. Fredrik Dahl. "U.N. Report Seen Worsening Fear over Iran Nuclear Plans." *Reuters.* [October 24, 2011] http://www.reuters.com/article/2011/10/24/us -nuclear-iran-iaea-idUSTRE79N3NW20111024 [accessed October 26, 2011].
8. The White House. Office of the Press Secretary. "Remarks by President Obama and President Medvedev of Russia after Bilateral Meeting in Deauville, France." [May 26, 2011] http://www.whitehouse.gov/the -press-office/2011/05/26/remarks-president-obama-and-president -medvedev-russia-after-bilateral-me [accessed October 11, 2011].
9. "Envoys: Russia Blocks UN Report on Iran Arms." *Reuters.* [May 12, 2011] http://www.msnbc.msn.com/id/42995447/ns/world_news-mideast_n_africa/ t/envoys-russia-blocks-un-report-iran-arms/ [accessed October 26, 2011].
10. Michael Stott. "Demise of U.S. Shield May Embolden Russia Hawks." *Reuters.* [September 17, 2009] http://www.reuters.com/article/2009/09/17/ us-usa-europe-shield-analysis-sb-idUSTRE58G1YX20090917?sp=true [accessed October 26, 2011].

Chapter 15. *Abandoning Iraq and Afghanistan*

1. "Obama's Speech to the United Nations General Assembly." *New York Times.* [September 23, 2009] http://www.nytimes.com/2009/09/24/us/ politics/24prexy.text.html?pagewanted=all [accessed February 9, 2012].
2. "Text of President Obama's Speech on Afghanistan." *New York Times.* [June 22, 2011] http://www.nytimes.com/2011/06/23/world/asia/23obama -afghanistan-speech-text.html?pagewanted=all [accessed February 9, 2012].

3. The White House. Office of the Press Secretary. "Remarks by the President
on Ending the War in Iraq." [October 21, 2011] http://www.whitehouse
.gov/the-press-office/2011/10/21/remarks-president-ending-war-iraq
[accessed November 1, 2011].
4. Barbara Starr. "US Mulling Option for 3000 Troops to Remain in Iraq." *CNN.*
[September 6, 2011] http://security.blogs.cnn.com/2011/09/06/us-mulling
-option-for-3000-troops-to-remain-in-iraq/ [accessed November 1, 2011].
5. Tim Arango and Michael S. Schmidt. "U.S. Scales Back Diplomacy
in Iraq amid Fiscal and Security Concerns." *New York Times.* [Octo-
ber 22, 2011] http://www.nytimes.com/2011/10/23/world/middleeast/
us-scales-back-diplomacy-in-iraq-amid-fiscal-and-security-concerns
.html?pagewanted=1&ref=timarango [accessed November 1, 2011].
6. "Romney on President Obama's Decision to Withdraw Troops from
Iraq." Press release. *MittRomney.com.* [October 21, 2011] http://www
.mittromney.com/news/press/2011/10/romney-president-obamas-decision
-withdraw-troops-iraq [accessed November 1, 2011].
7. Ibid.
8. Arlette Saenz. "Rick Perry Talks Iraq and His 'Love Affair' With Guns." *ABC
News.* [October 22, 2011] http://abcnews.go.com/blogs/politics/2011/10/
rick-perry-talks-iraq-and-his-love-affair-with-guns/ [accessed November 1,
2011].
9. Eli Clifton. "Iraq by The Numbers: The World's Costliest Cakewalk."
ThinkProgress. [October 21, 2011] http://thinkprogress.org/security/2011/
10/21/350368/iraq-by-the-numbers-the-worlds-costliest-cakewalk/
[accessed February 9, 2012].
10. Jay Solomon and Farnaz Fassihi. "For Iran Watchers, Cause for Concern."
Wall Street Journal. [October 22, 2011] http://online.wsj.com/article/SB10
001424052970203752604576645512455449144.html [accessed November
1, 2011].
11. "Leaving Iraq Behind." *Wall Street Journal.* [October 24, 2011] http://
online.wsj.com/article/SB10001424052970204485304576645373150817 5
48.html [accessed November 1, 2011].
12. Ibid.
13. Ibid.

Chapter 16. Ignoring the Border

1. "State Of The Union Quotes: Best Lines From Obama's 2011 Address."
Huffington Post. [January 25, 2011] http://www.huffingtonpost
.com/2011/01/25/quotes-obama-2011-state-of-the-union_n_814044
.html#s229984&title=Illegal_Immigration [accessed October 10, 2011].
2. "Barack Obama on Immigration." *Glassbooth.* http://glassbooth.org/
explore/index/barack-obama/11/immigration/10/ [accessed November 24,
2011].
3. "Encore Presentation: Interview with Barack Obama." *CNN Larry King
Live.* Transcript. [March 24, 2007] http://transcripts.cnn.com/TRAN
SCRIPTS/0703/24/lkl.01.html [accessed November 24, 2011].

4. "The CNN Democratic Presidential Debate in Texas." *CNN*. Transcript. [February 21, 2008] http://www.cnn.com/2008/POLITICS/02/21/debate .transcript/index.html [accessed November 24, 2011].

5. U.S. Government Accountability Office. "DHS Progress and Challenges in Securing the U.S. Southwest and Northern Borders. Statement of Richard M. Stana, Director Homeland Security and Justice Issues." Testimony before the Senate Committee on Homeland Security and Governmental Affairs. [March 30, 2011] http://www.gao.gov/new.items/d11508t.pdf#page=11 [accessed November 24, 2011].

6. Tracy Wilkinson and Ken Ellingwood. "Mexico Drug Cartels Thrive Despite Calderon's Offensive." *Los Angeles Times*. [August 7, 2010] http:// articles.latimes.com/2010/aug/07/world/la-fg-mexico-cartels-20100808 [accessed November 24, 2011].

7. "Border Threat May Pose Biggest U.S. Terror Risk." *CBS Los Angeles*. [October 29, 2010] http://losangeles.cbslocal.com/2010/10/29/border -threat-may-pose-biggest-us-terror-risk/ [accessed November 24, 2011].

8. "Me Thinks Thee Doth Protest Too Much—US DHS says, 'No Hezbollah in Mexico' Ver.2.0." *American Sentry* (blog), *Townhall.com*. [July 12, 2010] http://americansentry.blogtownhall.com/2011/02/22/me_thinks_thee _doth_protest_too_much-us_dhs_says,_no_hezbollah_in_mexico_ver20 .html [accessed November 24, 2011].

9. Adam Housley. "Hezbollah Working with Cartels." *Fox News*. [February 21, 2011] http://liveshots.blogs.foxnews.com/2011/02/21/hezbollah -working-with-cartels/ [accessed November 24, 2011].

10. Katie Pavlich. "A Growing Terror Threat: Hezbollah in Latin America." *Townhall.com*. [July 8, 2011] http://townhall.com/columnists/katiepavlich/ 2011/07/08/a_growing_terror_threat_hezbollah_in_latin_america/page/ full/ [accessed November 24, 2011].

11. Nedra Pickler. "Plot to Kill Ambassador Unraveled on SW Border." Associated Press, *Tulsa World*. [October 12, 2011] http://www.tulsa world.com/news/article.aspx?subjectid=13&articleid=20111012_13_0 _WASHIN77822 [accessed November 24, 2011].

12. The White House. Office of the Press Secretary. "Remarks by the President on Comprehensive Immigration Reform in El Paso, Texas." [May 10, 2011] http://www.whitehouse.gov/the-press-office/2011/05/10/remarks-president -comprehensive-immigration-reform-el-paso-texas [accessed November 24, 2011].

13. Glenn Kessler. "Obama Administration Boasting about Border Security." *Washington Post*. [May 11, 2011] http://www.washingtonpost.com/ blogs/fact-checker/post/obama-administration-boasting-about-border -security/2011/05/10/AFj71ZkG_blog.html [accessed November 24, 2011].

14. Clark S. Judge. "Arizona and the Southern Border." *HughHewitt.com*. [May 3, 2010] http://www.hughhewitt.com/blog/g/367fcaad-38f2-4450 -9744-f98380c5697c [accessed November 24, 2011].

15. Ibid.

16. "Arizona Governor Jan Brewer on SB1070, her drive to impeach the redistricting commission, and her book, *Scorpions for Breakfast*." *HughHewitt*

.com. [November 3, 2011] http://www.hughhewitt.com/transcripts.aspx?id=
24b278bb-23d3-410c-a691-7be65d001c1c [accessed November 24, 2011].

Chapter 17. Bowing to China

1. The White House. Office of the Vice President. "Op-ed by Vice President
   Biden in the *New York Times*: China's Rise Isn't Our Demise." [Septem-
   ber 8, 2011] http://www.whitehouse.gov/the-press-office/2011/09/08/
   op-ed-vice-president-biden-new-york-times-china-s-rise-isn-t-our-demise
   [accessed October 11, 2011].
2. The White House. Office of the Press Secretary. "Joint Press Statement by
   President Obama and President Hu of China." [November 17, 2009] http://
   www.whitehouse.gov/the-press-office/joint-press-statement-president
   -obama-and-president-hu-china [accessed October 10, 2011].
3. "Drudge: Obama Bows to Chinese Communist Leader." *Freerepublic.com.*
   [April 12, 2010] http://www.freerepublic.com/focus/f-news/2491718/posts
   [accessed November 20, 2011].
4. "Conservative Media Continue Tired Obsession with Obama's Supposed
   'Bowing.'" *Media Matters.* [April 13, 2010] http://mediamatters.org/
   research/201004130016 [accessed November 20, 2011].
5. "Henry Kissinger on the 40th Anniversary of His Secret Trip to China."
   HughHewitt.com. [July 7, 2011] http://www.hughhewitt.com/blog/g/
   80bd2dc3-5bce-4190-a180-b5dc155aa3f7 [accessed November 20, 2011].
6. "Jon Huntsman Endorses (Sort Of) the Toomey-Hensarling Tax Hikes."
   HughHewitt.com. [November 17, 2011] http://www.hughhewitt.com/blog/
   g/80634506-483d-48a8-92d6-53fba68e74c8 [accessed November 20, 2011].
7. "Mitt Romney on the Supercommittee, the President's Rhetoric about America, China and Afghanistan." *HughHewitt.com.* [November 18, 2011] http://
   www.hughhewitt.com/blog/g/d450a898-c4d7-4171-ac9b-e5cb405c76df
   [accessed November 20, 2011].

Chapter 18. Ignoring North Korea

1. The White House. Office of the Press Secretary. "Remarks by President
   Barack Obama and President Lee Myung-Bak of Republic of Korea in Joint
   Press Conference." [November 19, 2009] http://www.whitehouse.gov/the
   -press-office/remarks-president-barack-obama-and-president-lee-myung
   -bak-republic-korea-joint-pre [accessed October 10, 2011].
2. "Newt on Israel, Sarkozy and Obama." *HughHewitt.com.* [November 9, 2011]
   http://www.hughhewitt.com/blog/g/f0c62cc6-cab2-4c5a-a069-949961da9183
   [accessed November 21, 2011].
3. *Meet the Press.* "MTP Transcript for Oct. 22." *MSNBC.* [October 22,
   2006] http://www.msnbc.msn.com/id/15304689/#.Tsqu4650shg [accessed
   November 21, 2011].
4. Ibid.
5. Jayshree Bajoira and Carin Zissis. "The Six-Party Talks on North Korea's
   Nuclear Program." Backgrounder, *Council on Foreign Relations.* [July 1,

2009] http://www.cfr.org/proliferation/six-party-talks-north-koreas-nuclear -program/p13593 [accessed November 21, 2011].

6. Ibid.

7. "North Korea's Missile Programme." *BBC.* [May 27, 2009] http://news.bbc .co.uk/2/hi/2564241.stm [accessed November 21, 2011]

8. The White House. Office of the Press Secretary. "Statement by the President from Prague, Czech Republic." [April 5, 2009] http://www.whitehouse .gov/the_press_office/Statement-by-the-President-North-Korea-launch/ [accessed November 21, 2011].

9. The White House. Office of the Press Secretary. "Statement by the President." [May 25, 2009] http://www.whitehouse.gov/the-press-office/statement -president-regarding-north-korea [accessed November 21, 2011].

10. "The Cheonan (Ship)." Times Topics, *New York Times.* [May 20, 2010] http://topics.nytimes.com/top/reference/timestopics/subjects/c/cheonan _ship/index.html?inline=nyt-classifier [accessed November 21, 2011].

11. The White House. Office of the Press Secretary. "Remarks by President Obama and President Lee Myung-Bak of the Republic of Korea after Bilateral Meeting." [June 26, 2010] http://www.whitehouse.gov/the-press-office/ remarks-president-obama-and-president-lee-myung-bak-republic-korea-after -bilateral [accessed November 21, 2011].

12. United Nations Security Council. Department of Public Information. News and Media Division. "Security Council, Acting Unanimously, Condemns in Strongest Terms Democratic People's Republic of Korea Nuclear Test, Toughens Sanctions." [June 12, 2009] http://www.un.org/News/Press/ docs/2009/sc9679.doc.htm [accessed November 21, 2011].

13. The White House. Office of the Press Secretary. "Letter from the President— Prohibiting Certain Transactions with Respect to North Korea." [April 18, 2011] http://www.whitehouse.gov/the-press-office/2011/04/18/letter-president -prohibiting-certain-transactions-respect-north-korea [accessed November 21, 2011].

14. Mark McDonald. "'Crisis Status' in South Korea after North Shells Island." *New York Times.* [November 23, 2010] http://www.nytimes .com/2010/11/24/world/asia/24korea.html?hp=&pagewanted=1 [accessed November 21, 2011].

15. The White House. Office of the Press Secretary. "Statement by the Press Secretary on North Korean Shelling of South Korean Island." [November 23, 2010] http://www.whitehouse.gov/the-press-office/2010/11/23/statement-press -secretary-north-korean-shelling-south-korean-island [accessed November 21, 2011].

16. "Mitt Romney Assesses the Pratfalls of Barack Obama Foreign Policy." Transcript. *HughHewitt.com.* [April 22, 2009] http://www.hughhewitt .com/transcripts.aspx?id=9868c393-6cfb-44d1-9661-8c621865225d [accessed November 21, 2011].

17. "Victor Davis Hanson on Obama's schoolchildren address next week, and where we are in Afghanistan." Transcript. *HughHewitt.com.* [September 2, 2009] http://www.hughhewitt.com/transcripts.aspx?id=33282bab-cd76 -4d03-af2c-6e049027597f [accessed November 21, 2011].

Chapter 19. Naivete and the Arab Spring

1. The White House. Office of the Press Secretary. "Remarks by the President on the Way Forward in Afghanistan." [June 22, 2011] http://www.white house.gov/the-press-office/2011/06/22/remarks-president-way-forward -afghanistan [accessed October 10, 2011].

2. The *Guardian* has created an excellent resource for visualizing and digging deeper into the events of the Arab Spring: Gary Blight, Shelia Pulham, and Paul Torpey. "Arab Spring: An Interactive Timeline of Middle East Protests." *Guardian* (London). [October 20, 2011] http://www.guardian.co.uk/ world/interactive/2011/mar/22/middle-east-protest-interactive-timeline [accessed October 27, 2011].

3. "Witnesses Report Rioting in Tunisian Town." *Reuters.* [December 19, 2010] http://af.reuters.com/article/topNews/idAFJOE6BI06U20101219 [accessed October 27, 2011].

4. "Algerian Riots Resume over Food Prices." *Guardian* (London). [January 7, 2011] http://www.guardian.co.uk/world/2011/jan/07/algeria-riots-food -prices [accessed October 27, 2011].

5. Ian Black. "Tunisia's Protests Spark Suicide in Algeria and Fears through Arab World." *Guardian* (London). [January 16, 2011] http://www.guardian .co.uk/world/2011/jan/16/tunisia-protests-suicide-algeria-arab [accessed October 27, 2011].

6. Angelique Chrisafis and Ian Black. "Zine al-Abidine Ben Ali Forced to Flee Tunisia as Protesters Claim Victory." *Guardian* (London). [January 14, 2011] http://www.guardian.co.uk/world/2011/jan/14/tunisian-president-flees -country-protests [accessed October 27, 2011].

7. The White House. Office of the Press Secretary. "Statement by the President on Events in Tunisia." [January 14, 2011] http://www.whitehouse.gov/the -press-office/2011/01/14/statement-president-events-tunisia [accessed October 27, 2011].

8. Matthew Weaver. "Muammer Gaddafi Condemns Tunisia Uprising." *Guardian* (London). [January 16, 2011] http://www.guardian.co.uk/world/2011/ jan/16/muammar-gaddafi-condemns-tunisia-uprising [accessed October 27, 2011].

9. Sam Jones. "Man Sets Himself on Fire near Egyptian Parliament." *Guardian* (London). [January 17, 2011] http://www.guardian.co.uk/world/2011/ jan/17/man-sets-himself-on-fire-egypt-protest [accessed October 27, 2011].

10. Jack Shenker. "Mohamed ElBaradei Warns of 'Tunisia-Style Explosion' in Egypt." *Guardian* (London). [January 18, 2011] http://www.guardian .co.uk/world/2011/jan/18/mohamed-elbaradei-tunisia-egypt [accessed October 27, 2011].

11. Tom Finn. "Yemen Arrests Anti-Government Activist." *Guardian* (London). [January 23, 2011] http://www.guardian.co.uk/world/2011/jan/23/ yemen-arrests-protest-leader [accessed October 27, 2011].

12. "The Path of Protest." *Guardian* (London). [October 2011] http://www .guardian.co.uk/world/interactive/2011/mar/22/middle-east-protest -interactive-timeline [accessed October 27, 2011]; and "Egypt: Thousands

Protest against President Hosni Mubarak." *Guardian* (London). [January 25, 2011] http://www.guardian.co.uk/world/video/2011/jan/25/egypt -protest-president-murabak-video [accessed October 27, 2011].

13. "Lebanon's 'Day of Rage'—in Pictures." *Guardian* (London). [January 25, 2011] http://www.guardian.co.uk/world/gallery/2011/jan/25/lebanon -protests-rage-pictures#/?picture=371004958&index=4 [accessed October 27, 2011].

14. Peter Beaumont. "Egypt Protesters Defy Tanks and Teargas to Make the Streets Their Own." *Guardian* (London). [January 28, 2011] http://www .guardian.co.uk/world/2011/jan/28/egypt-protests-latest-cairo-curfew [accessed October 27, 2011].

15. Ewen MacAskill. "US and World Wrongfooted by Mubarak as White House Tries to Keep Up." *Guardian* (London). [February 10, 2011] http://www .guardian.co.uk/world/2011/feb/10/obama-wrongfooted-mubarak-egypt [accessed October 27, 2011].

16. Ibid.

17. Jason Ryan. "President Obama Got Egypt Warning in 2010, CIA Official Says." *ABC News.* [February 3, 2011] http://abcnews.go.com/News/egypt -unrest-president-obama-warning-2010-cia-official/story?id=12835550 [accessed October 27, 2011].

18. Chris McGreal and Jack Shenker. "Hosni Mubarak Resigns—and Egypt Celebrates a New Dawn." *Guardian* (London). [February 11, 2011] http:// www.guardian.co.uk/world/2011/feb/11/hosni-mubarak-resigns-egypt -cairo [accessed October 27, 2011].

19. Ian Black. "Arrests and Deaths as Egypt Protest Spreads across Middle East." *Guardian* (London). [February 14, 2011] http://www.guardian .co.uk/world/2011/feb/14/middle-east-iran-bahrain-yemen [accessed October 27, 2011].

20. Ibid.

21. Ibid.

22. "Libyan Protesters Clash with Police in Benghazi." *Guardian* (London). [February 16, 2011] http://www.guardian.co.uk/world/2011/feb/16/libyan -protesters-clash-with-police [accessed October 27, 2011].

23. "Violence in Bahrain and Libya—Friday 18 February." *Guardian* (London). [February 18, 2011] http://www.guardian.co.uk/world/blog/2011/feb/18/ middle-east-protests-live-updates [accessed October 27, 2011].

24. Ibid.

25. Jesse Lee. "President Obama Speaks on the Turmoil in Libya: 'This Violence Must Stop.'" *The White House Blog.* [February 23, 2011] http://www .whitehouse.gov/blog/2011/02/23/president-obama-speaks-turmoil-libya -violence-must-stop [accessed October 27, 2011].

26. "Syrian Police Seal Off City of Daraa after Security Forces Kill Five Protesters." *Guardian* (London). [March 19, 2011] http://www.guardian.co.uk/ world/2011/mar/19/syria-police-seal-off-daraa-after-five-protesters-killed [accessed October 27, 2011]; "Syrian Forces Kill At Least Six in Midnight Mosque Attack, Say Deraa Residents." *Guardian* (London). [March 23, 2011] http://www.guardian.co.uk/world/2011/mar/23/syria-kills-six-mosque

-attack-deraa [accessed October 27, 2011]; "Shots Fired as Syrians Defy Crackdown to March at Funerals of Slain Protesters." *Guardian* (London). [March 24, 2011] http://www.guardian.co.uk/world/2011/mar/24/syria-funeral-marchers-defy-government-crackdown [accessed October 27, 2011]; "Syrian Protesters Come under Fire from Security Forces." *Guardian* (London). [March 28, 2011] http://www.guardian.co.uk/world/2011/mar/28/syrian-protesters-come-under-fire [accessed October 27, 2011]; The White House. Office of the Press Secretary. "Statement by the Press Secretary on Violence in Syria." [March 24, 2011] http://www.whitehouse.gov/the-press-office/2011/03/24/statement-press-secretary-violence-syria [accessed October 27, 2011]; and Kori Schulman. "A Statement by President Obama on Syria." *The White House Blog.* [April 22, 2011] http://www.whitehouse.gov/blog/2011/04/22/statement-president-obama-syria [accessed October 27, 2011].

27. Tom Finn. "45 Protesters Killed in Yemen." *Guardian* (London). [March 18, 2011] http://www.guardian.co.uk/world/2011/mar/18/yemen-police-massacre-45-protesters [accessed October 27, 2011]; The White House. Office of the Press Secretary. "Statement by the President on violence in Yemen." [March 18, 2011] http://www.whitehouse.gov/the-press-office/2011/03/18/statement-president-violence-yemen [accessed October 27, 2011]; The White House. Office of the Press Secretary. "Statement by the Press Secretary on Violence in Yemen." [April 5, 2011] http://www.whitehouse.gov/the-press-office/2011/04/05/statement-press-secretary-violence-yemen [accessed October 27, 2011]; and The White House. Office of the Press Secretary. "Statement by the Press Secretary on Developments in Yemen." [April 23, 2011] http://www.whitehouse.gov/the-press-office/2011/04/23/statement-press-secretary-developments-yemen [accessed October 27, 2011].

28. Simon Tisdall. "Bahrain Royal Family Welcomes Saudi Troops to Face Down Violent Protests." *Guardian* (London). [March 14, 2011] http://www.guardian.co.uk/world/2011/mar/14/bahrain-saudi-troops-violent-protests [accessed October 27, 2011]; Martin Chulov. "Bahrain Destroys Pearl Roundabout." *Guardian* (London). [March 18, 2011] http://www.guardian.co.uk/world/2011/mar/18/bahrain-destroys-pearl-roundabout [accessed October 27, 2011]; "Bahrain Accused of Systematic Attacks on Doctors." *Guardian* (London). [April 22, 2011] http://www.guardian.co.uk/world/2011/apr/22/bahrain-accused-attacks-doctors [accessed October 27, 2011]; Robert Booth. "Bahrain: Four Protesters Sentenced to Death by Firing Squad." *Guardian* (London). [April 28, 2011] http://www.guardian.co.uk/world/2011/apr/28/bahrain-four-protesters-sentenced-death [accessed October 27, 2011]; "Bahrain Oil Company Fires Almost 300 over Anti-Government Protests." *Guardian* (London). [May 11, 2011] http://www.guardian.co.uk/world/2011/may/11/bahrain-oil-company-fires-300-protests [accessed October 27, 2011]; The White House. Office of the Press Secretary. "Statement by the President on Bahrain." [February 27, 2011] http://www.whitehouse.gov/the-press-office/2011/02/27/statement-president-bahrain [accessed October 27, 2011]; The White House. Office

of the Press Secretary. "Statement from the Press Secretary on Violence in Yemen and Bahrain." [March 13, 2011] http://www.whitehouse.gov/the-press-office/2011/03/13/statement-press-secretary-violence-yemen-and-bahrain [accessed October 27, 2011]; The White House. Office of the Vice President. "Readout of the Vice President's Call with Bahraini Crown Prince Salman bin Hamad al-Khalifa." [March 27, 2011] http://www.whitehouse.gov/the-press-office/2011/03/27/readout-vice-presidents-call-bahraini-crown-prince-salman-bin-hamad-al-k [accessed October 27, 2011]; and The White House. Office of the Press Secretary. "Readout of President Obama's Call with the King of Bahrain." [April 30, 2011] http://www.whitehouse.gov/the-press-office/2011/04/30/readout-president-obama-s-call-king-bahrain [accessed October 27, 2011].

29. Patricia Campion. "So Obama Is Ready to Roll Up His Sleeves—Again?" *Yahoo News*. [July 12, 2011] http://news.yahoo.com/obama-ready-roll-sleeves-again-212700261.html [accessed October 27, 2011].

30. The White House. The Office of the Press Secretary. "Remarks by the President on the Way Forward in Afghanistan." [June 22, 2011] http://www.whitehouse.gov/photos-and-video/video/2011/06/22/president-obama-addresses-nation#transcript [accessed October 27, 2011].

31. Ryan Lizza. "The Consequentialist." *New Yorker*. [May 2, 2011] http://www.newyorker.com/reporting/2011/05/02/110502fa_fact_lizza?currentPage=all [accessed October 27, 2011].

32. "*New Yorker*'s Ryan Lizza on Barack Obama Foreign Policy, the Consequentialist." Transcript. *HughHewitt.com*. [April 26, 2011] http://www.hughhewitt.com/transcripts.aspx?id=daf95729-9b04-484a-acb3-6c834217a155 [accessed October 27, 2011].

33. Paul Kengor. "The Jimmy Carter Chronicles." *American Spectator*. [February 18, 2011] http://spectator.org/archives/2011/02/18/the-jimmy-carter-chronicles/print [accessed October 27, 2011].

Chapter 20. Gitmo and the Trials of Terrorists

1. The White House. Office of the Press Secretary. "Remarks by the President to the United Nations General Assembly." [September 23, 2009] http://www.whitehouse.gov/the-press-office/remarks-president-united-nations-general-assembly [accessed October 10, 2011].

2. Sash Issenberg and Farah Stockman. "McCain Blasts Ruling on Guantanamo." *Boston Globe*. [June 14, 2008] http://www.boston.com/news/nation/articles/2008/06/14/mccain_blasts_ruling_on_guantanamo/ [accessed November 26, 2011].

3. Elizabeth White. "Obama Says Gitmo Facility Should Close." *Washington Post*. [June 24, 2007] http://www.washingtonpost.com/wp-dyn/content/article/2007/06/24/AR2007062401046.html [accessed November 26, 2011].

4. "Khalid Shaikh Mohammed." *New York Times*. [April 4, 2011] http://topics.nytimes.com/top/reference/timestopics/people/m/khalid_shaikh_mohammed/index.html [accessed November 26, 2011].

5. "Obama Signs Order to Close Guantanamo Bay Facility." *CNN.* [January 22, 2009] http://articles.cnn.com/2009-01-22/politics/guantanamo.order_1_detention-guantanamo-bay-torture?_s=PM:POLITICS [accessed November 26, 2011]; and Jonathan Masters. "Closing Guantanamo?" Backgrounder, *Council on Foreign Relations.* [November 9, 2011] http://www.cfr.org/terrorism-and-the-law/closing-guantanamo/p18525 [accessed November 27, 2011].
6. David Espo. "Senate Votes to Block Funds for Guantanamo Closure." *Huffington Post.* [May 20, 2009] http://www.huffingtonpost.com/2009/05/20/senate-votes-to-block-fun_n_205797.html [accessed November 26, 2011].
7. "Ill. Town Welcomes Plan to House Detainees." Associated Press, *MSNBC.* [December 12, 2009] http://www.msnbc.msn.com/id/34424834/ns/us_news-security/#.TtKMZ67XJUg [accessed November 27, 2011].
8. Jake Sherman. "Illinois GOP Seeks to Block Gitmo Detainees." *Politico.* [November 16, 2009] http://www.politico.com/news/stories/1109/29574.html [accessed November 27, 2011].
9. Stephen Dinan. "House Acts to Block Closing of Gitmo." *Washington Times.* [December 8, 2010] http://www.washingtontimes.com/news/2010/dec/8/congress-deals-death-blow-gitmo-closure/ [accessed November 27, 2011].
10. Scott Shane and Mark Landler. "Obama Clears Way for Guantanamo Trials." *New York Times.* [March 7, 2011] http://www.nytimes.com/2011/03/08/world/americas/08guantanamo.html [accessed November 27, 2011].
11. "Obama Signs Order to Close Guantanamo Bay Facility."
12. Susan Gardner. "President Obama's Inaugural Address." *Daily Kos.* [January 20, 2009] http://www.dailykos.com/story/2009/01/20/686506/-President-Obamas-Inaugural-Address [accessed November 27, 2011].
13. "Victor Davis Hanson's Sober Assessment of Barack Obama's First Year." Transcript. *HughHewitt.com.* [January 6, 2010] http://www.hughhewitt.com/transcripts.aspx?id=2fd8a022-33e5-4dae-a2e7-9ff78fe246de [accessed November 27, 2011].

Chapter 21. The Hyperpartisanship of a Chicago Ward Heeler: Obama Is the Most Destructively Partisan President of the Past 40 Years

1. Huma Khan. "'I Won': President Obama Works to Be Bipartisan but Shows There Are Clear Limits." *ABC News.* [January 23, 2009] http://abcnews.go.com/blogs/politics/2009/01/i-won-president/ [accessed November 3, 2011].
2. "Text of Obama Speech on the Deficit." *Wall Street Journal.* [April 13, 2011] http://blogs.wsj.com/washwire/2011/04/13/text-of-obama-speech-on-the-deficit/ [accessed November 3, 2011].
3. The White House. Office of the Press Secretary. "Address by the President to a Joint Session of Congress." [September 8, 2011] http://www.whitehouse.gov/the-press-office/2011/09/08/address-president-joint-session-congress [accessed November 3, 2011].

4. Fred Lucas. "Obama: Republicans Want 'Dirtier Air, Dirtier Water.'" *CNS News*. [October 17, 2011] http://www.cnsnews.com/news/article/obama-republicans-want-dirtier-air-dirtier-water-0 [accessed November 3, 2011].
5. Robert Blake, *Disraeli* (New York: St. Martin's, 1967), p. 389.
6. David Jackson and Ray Long. "Obama Knows His Way around a Ballot." *Chicago Tribune*. [April 3, 2007] http://www.chicagotribune.com/news/politics/obama/chi-070403obama-ballot-archive,0,5297304,full.story [accessed November 3, 2011].
7. "A 40-Year Wish List." *Wall Street Journal*. [January 28, 2009] http://online.wsj.com/article/SB123310466514522309.html [accessed November 3, 2011].
8. The White House. Office of the Press Secretary. "Remarks by the President in State of the Union Address." [January 27, 2010] http://www.whitehouse.gov/the-press-office/remarks-president-state-union-address [accessed November 3, 2011].
9. "Justice Alito Mouths 'Not True.'" *Politico*. [January 27, 2010] http://www.politico.com/blogs/politicolive/0110/Justice_Alitos_You_lie_moment.html [accessed February 9, 2012].
10. "Text of Obama Speech on the Deficit." *Wall Street Journal*. [April 13, 2011 http://blogs.wsj.com/washwire/2011/04/13/text-of-obama-speech-on-the-deficit/ [accessed November 3, 2011].
11. Lucas. "Obama: Republicans Want 'Dirtier Air, Dirtier Water.'"

Chapter 22. *The Unilateralism of an Anti-Constitutional President*

1. "Obama At House Republican Retreat In Baltimore: Full Video, Text." Transcript. *Huffington Post*. [March 31, 2010] http://www.huffingtonpost.com/2010/01/29/transcript-of-president-o_n_442423.html [accessed October 10, 2011].
2. Peter Baker. "Obama Making Plans to Use Executive Power." *New York Times*. [February 12, 2010] http://www.nytimes.com/2010/02/13/us/politics/13obama.html [accessed November 17, 2011].
3. Ibid.
4. Jordy Yager. "Obama Flexes Executive Powers, Bypassing Congressional Opposition." *The Hill*. [July 12, 2011] http://thehill.com/homenews/administration/170837-president-is-flexing-his-exec-powers [accessed November 18, 2011].
5. Tom Hamburger and Christi Parsons. "President Obama's Czar System Concerns Some." *Los Angeles Times*. [March 5, 2009] http://articles.latimes.com/2009/mar/05/nation/na-obama-czars5 [accessed November 18, 2011].
6. "List of Obama's Czars." *GlennBeck.com*. [August 21, 2009] http://www.glennbeck.com/content/articles/article/198/29391/ [accessed November 18, 2011].
7. Ibid.
8. Yossi Gestetner. "By the Numbers: Obama's Alliances vs. Bush's Unilateralism." *American Thinker*. [March 21, 2011] http://www.americanthinker.com/blog/2011/03/by_the_numbers_obamas_alliance.html [accessed November 18, 2011].

Chapter 23. *The Smartest President Ever? The Fumbler-in-Chief and His Lazy, Soft Countrymen*

1. "Jim Payne Interviews President Obama: Part 2." Video, 1:20–1:42. *WESH* *.com*. [September 29, 2011] http://www.wesh.com/video/29341330/detail .html [accessed November 18, 2011].
2. "Obama: 'We Have Lost Our Ambition, Our Imagination.'" *Real Clear Politics*. [October 25, 2011] http://www.realclearpolitics.com/ video/2011/10/25/obama_we_have_lost_our_ambition_our_imagination .html [accessed November 18, 2011].
3. Jon Garcia. "President Obama to CEOs: 'We've Been a Bit Lazy.'" *ABC News*. [November 12, 2011] http://abcnews.go.com/blogs/politics/2011/ 11/president-obama-to-ceos-weve-been-a-bit-lazy/ [accessed November 18, 2011].
4. "President Barack Obama Talks to Bret Baier About Health Care Reform Bill." *Fox News*. [March 17, 2010] http://www.foxnews.com/ story/0,2933,589589,00.html [accessed November 18, 2011]; CBSNews Online. "Obama's Contentious Fox News Interview." Video. *YouTube*. [March 17, 2010] http://www.youtube.com/watch?v=URJUSlfTgGU [accessed November 18, 2011]. Also see Johnnydollar01. "Bret Baier on his Obama Interview and Why the Interruptions!" Video. *YouTube*. [March 18, 2010] http://www.youtube.com/watch?v=3bP3SiCYQ_w&feature=related [accessed November 18, 2011].
5. "Obama, O'Reilly Interview: Super Bowl Sit-Down between President & Fox News Host (Video)." Video. *Huffington Post*. [February 6, 2011] http://www.huffingtonpost.com/2011/02/06/obama-oreilly-interview -s_n_819315.html [accessed November 18, 2011].
6. "Top 10 Obama Gaffes." *Human Events*. [July 10, 2011] http://www .humanevents.com/article.php?id=44749 [accessed November 18, 2011].

Chapter 24. *Avoiding the Fecklessness Argument: Martha's Vineyard, Presidential Bracketology, and Commander-in-Chief Golf*

1. "Obama's Bracket for 2011 NCAA Tournament: President Picks Kansas to Win March Madness (Video)." Video, 0:15–1:25. *Huffington Post*. [March 16, 2011] http://www.huffingtonpost.com/2011/03/16/obama-bracket -2011-ncaa-tournament_n_836595.html [accessed October 11, 2011].
2. Keith Koffler. "Obama Golfs Twice This Weekend—75th Time as President." *WhiteHouseDossier.com*. [June 26, 2011] http://www.whitehouse dossier.com/2011/06/26/obama-golfs-time-weekend/ [accessed November 18, 2011].
3. Dan Eggen. "Bush Says He's Not a Golfer in Wartime." *Washington Post*. [May 14, 2008] http://www.washingtonpost.com/wp-dyn/content/arti cle/2008/05/13/AR2008051302783.html [accessed November 18, 2011].
4. "Obama Bracketology—He Picks Kansas, Again!" *Reuters*. [March 16, 2011] http://blogs.reuters.com/talesfromthetrail/2011/03/16/obama -bracketology-he-picks-kansas-again/ [accessed November 18, 2011].

5. Massmurdermedia. "Obama and Bracketology." *The Activity Pit.* [March 17, 2011] http://activitypit.ning.com/forum/topics/obama-and-bracketology [accessed November 18, 2011].

6. Jonathan Alter. *The Defining Moment: FDR's Hundred Days and the Triumph of Hope.* (New York: Simon & Schuster, 2007), pp. 90–91.

7. Matt Hadro. "Jon Meacham: Bush Would Be 'More Barbecued' Than Obama for Touting NCAA Bracket During Crises." *NewsBuster.* [March 17, 2011] http://newsbusters.org/blogs/matt-hadro/2011/03/17/jon-meacham-bush -would-be-more-barbecued-obama-touting-ncaa-bracket-duri#ixzz1e4c1l1JZ [accessed November 18, 2011].

Chapter 25. The "Decline and Despair" President

1. "Jim Payne Interviews President Obama: Part 2." Video, 1:20–1:42. *WESH .com.* [September 29, 2011] http://www.wesh.com/video/29341330/detail .html [accessed November 18, 2011].

2. "Obama: 'We Have Lost Our Ambition, Our Imagination...'" *Fox News.* [October 27, 2011] http://nation.foxnews.com/president-obama/2011/10/26/ obama-we-have-lost-our-ambition-our-imagination [accessed November 4, 2011].

3. Jon Garcia. "President Obama to CEOs: 'We've Been a Bit Lazy.'" *ABC News.* [November 12, 2011] http://abcnews.go.com/blogs/politics/2011/11/ president-obama-to-ceos-weve-been-a-bit-lazy/ [accessed November 18, 2011].

4. "Obama Acknowledges Decline of US Dominance." *Times of India.* [November 8, 2010] http://articles.timesofindia.indiatimes.com/2010-11-08/india/ 28228910_1_largest-economy-globalisation-unemployment-rate [accessed November 4, 2011].

5. Nile Gardiner. "Why Barack Obama Is the Decline and Despair President." *Telegraph* (London). [October 27, 2011] http://blogs.telegraph.co.uk/news/ nilegardiner/100113190/why-barack-obama-is-the-decline-and-despair -president/ [accessed November 4, 2011].

6. Sabrina Tavernise. "Soaring Poverty Casts Spotlight on 'Lost Decade.'" *New York Times.* [September 13, 2011]. http://www.nytimes.com/2011/09/14/ us/14census.html?_r=2&pagewanted=all [accessed November 4, 2011]; Lydia Saad. "Americans Express Historic Negativity toward U.S. Government." *Gallup.* [September 26, 2011] http://www.gallup.com/poll/149678/Americans -Express-Historic-Negativity-Toward-Government.aspx?version=print [accessed November 4, 2011]; Mike Lillis. "The Hill Poll: Voters Say US Is in Decline." *The Hill.* [October 24, 2011] http://thehill.com/polls/189273-the -hill-poll-most-voters-say-the-us-is-in-decline [accessed November 4, 2011]; and Richard Wike. "From Hyperpower to Declining Power." *Pew Research Center.* [September 7, 2011] http://www.pewglobal.org/2011/09/07/from -hyperpower-to-declining-power/ [accessed November 4, 2011].

7. Ibid.

8. The White House. Office of the Press Secretary. "News Conference by President Obama." [April 4, 2009] http://www.whitehouse.gov/the-press

-office/news-conference-president-obama-4042009 [accessed November 4, 2011].

9. Andrew Sullivan. "The Big Lie." *Atlantic*. [November 9, 2010] http://www.theatlantic.com/daily-dish/archive/2010/11/the-big-lie/180117/ [accessed November 4, 2011].

10. Ibid.

11. Karl Rove. "The President's Apology Tour." *Wall Street Journal*. [April 23, 2009] http://online.wsj.com/article/SB124044156269345357.html [accessed November 4, 2011].

12. Ibid.

13. The White House. Office of the Press Secretary. "Remarks by the President on the Way Forward in Afghanistan." [June 22, 2011] http://www.whitehouse.gov/the-press-office/2011/06/22/remarks-president-way-forward-afghanistan [accessed November 4, 2011].

14. Ibid.

15. Margaret Thatcher. "Speech at Hoover Institution Lunch." *Margaret Thatcher Foundation*. [March 8, 1991] http://www.margaretthatcher.org/document/108264 [accessed November 4, 2011].

16. "Remarks by the President on the Way Forward in Afghanistan."

17. The White House. Office of the Press Secretary. "News Conference by the President, 2/9/10." [February 9, 2010] http://www.whitehouse.gov/photos-and-video/video/president-obama-holds-news-conference#transcript [accessed November 4, 2011].

18. The White House. Office of the Press Secretary. "President Obama's Oval Office Address on BP Oil Spill & Energy." [June 15, 2010] http://www.whitehouse.gov/photos-and-video/video/president-obama-s-oval-office-address-bp-oil-spill-energy#transcript [accessed November 4, 2011].

19. The White House. Office of the Press Secretary. "Weekly Address: The New Year." [January 1, 2011] http://www.whitehouse.gov/photos-and-video/video/2011/01/01/weekly-address-new-year#transcript [accessed November 4, 2011].

20. The White House. Office of the Press Secretary. "The Country We Believe In: Improving America's Fiscal Future." Video. [April 13, 2011] http://www.whitehouse.gov/photos-and-video/video/2011/04/13/country-we-believe-improving-america-s-fiscal-future#transcript [accessed November 4, 2011].

21. Ibid.

22. "Pence: Obama Sees His Job as 'Managing American Decline,' But the 'Job of the Prez Is to Reverse It.'" Video. *YouTube*. [February 19, 2010] http://www.youtube.com/watch?v=NXeB9VGILbA [accessed November 4, 2011].

23. "Mitt Romney on the Supercommittee, the President's Rhetoric about America, China, and Afghanistan." *HughHewitt.com*. [November 18, 2011] http://www.hughhewitt.com/blog/g/d450a898-c4d7-4171-ac9b-e5cb405c76df [accessed November 21, 2011].

24. The Country We Believe In: Improving America's Fiscal Future.

25. "Obama: 'We Have Lost Our Ambition, Our Imagination...'"

Conclusion. *Back to the Future of 1980 and 1981*

1. BarackObamadotcom. "Barack Obama: Yes We Can." Video. *YouTube .com*. [January 9, 2008] http://www.youtube.com/watch?v=Fe751kMBwms [accessed February 9, 2012].
2. Hugh Hewitt. "Optimistic or Pessimistic About America: Hugh Hewitt." *Commentary*. [November 3, 2011] http://www.commentarymagazine .com/2011/11/03/optimistic-or-pessimistic-about-america-hugh-hewitt/ [accessed February 9, 2012].
3. David Bernstein. "Brandeis Brief Myths." *Green Bag* 15, no. 1. [Autumn 2011] http://www.greenbag.org/v15n1/v15n1_articles_bernstein.pdf [accessed February 9, 2012].
4. Hugh Hewitt. "U.S. Supreme Court Associate Justice Stephen Breyer on Making our Democracy Work." Transcript. *HughHewitt.com*. [September 15, 2011] http://www.hughhewitt.com/transcripts.aspx?id=d0c4a956 -c0ce-47ba-b4cc-6e6544871276 [accessed February 9, 2012].

Index

tax cuts
  Bush tax rates extension, 40, 188
  steps for long-term growth,
    54–55
Tea Party, 19, 39
  Alaska Senate contest (2008)
    and, 3
  Obamacare and, 19, 193
  website, 19
terrorism, 174–80
  attempts in 2009, 179
  Bush and, 176, 177–78
  intelligence gathering for finding
    bin Laden, 179
  Obama on returning America to
    the "moral high ground," 176
  Obama's Terrorism Czar, 199
  trials for Gitmo detainees,
    175, 197
  underwear bomber, 177–78
  Victor Davis Hanson on Obama's
    rhetoric and consequences,
    177–79
  Wahhabism and, 178
Terry, Brian, 79, 146
Thatcher, Margaret, 127, 217–18
Tonight Show, The (TV show),
    38–39
Towers Watson, 23
Townhall.com, 203
Truman, Harry S., 185, 200
Tunisia, 166–67

unemployment, 5–6, 50–55
  annual rate, 2000–2011, 51
  housing starts and jobs, 47
  Jobs Bill, 184
  Obama's Green Jobs Czar, 199
  Obama's under 8% promise,
    4, 50
  prediction for 2013, 31
  rising numbers, 27, 31
  the Stimulus and, 27, 53–54,
    239n 9
unilateralism, 195–201
  Obama on the "loyal opposition,"
    (2010), 195

Obama's disregard of War Powers
    Act and, 200–201
Obama's policy czars,
    197–200
Obama's use of executive
    authority, 195–97
Obama's use of signing
    statements, 196
Yager's review of Obama's,
    196–97
United Kingdom, 102, 129–30, 133
  Middle East withdrawal (1967),
    127, 136
  Obama's return of Churchill
    bust, 7
  Thatcher on America, 217–18
Univision network, 84
U.S. Bureau of Alcohol, Tobacco,
    Firearms and Explosives,
    78–86
U.S. Constitution, 221
  Hewitt on, 227, 228–29
  Justice Breyer on Hewitt show
    and, 226–27
  Obama's attacks on, 8, 18, 20, 89,
    90, 94, 96, 187
  originalism, 226
U.S. Consumer Products Safety
    Commission, 9
U.S. Department of Defense
  appropriations (2011),
    116–17
  appropriations (2012), 117
  Obama's military spending cuts,
    117–20
  spending (2001), 116
U.S. Department of Energy
  Energy Policy Act of 2005
    and, 65
  resignation of Silver, 70
  Solyndra and, 65–66, 69, 70, 71
U.S. Department of Health and
    Human Services
  "The CLASS Act," 21–22
  insurance coverage and Catholic
    Church, 8–9, 16, 23–24, 88,
    89–90